GREAT SOURCE

Vocabulary for Achievement

Introductory Course

Margaret Ann Richek
Arlin T. McRae
Susan K. Weiler

Great Source Education Group
A Houghton Mifflin Company
Boston, Massachusetts

Authors

Margaret Ann Richek
Professor of Education, Northeastern Illinois University; consultant in reading and vocabulary study; author of *The World of Words*

Arlin T. McRae
Supervisor of English, Evansville-Vanderburgh School Corporation, Evansville, Indiana; Adjunct Instructor in English, University of Evansville

Susan K. Weiler
Teacher of Latin, Beaumont School for Girls, Cleveland Heights, Ohio

Classroom Consultants

Jack Pelletier
Teacher of English, Mira Loma High School, Sacramento, California

Valerie M. Webster
Teacher of English, Walnut Hill School, Natick, Massachusetts

Acknowledgments
Definitions for the three hundred words taught in this textbook are based on Houghton Mifflin dictionaries—in particular, the *Houghton Mifflin Student Dictionary*—but have been abbreviated and adapted for instructional purposes. The dictionary entries in the skill lessons on pages 19–20 and 39–40 are from the *Houghton Mifflin Student Dictionary,* copyright © 1986. The pronunciation key on the inside cover is adapted from *The American Heritage Dictionary of the English Language, Third Edition,* copyright © 1992.

Credits
Design and art production: Design Office, San Francisco

Illustration
Anthony Accardo: pages 17, 65, 97, 105; Alex Bloch: pages 71, 91, 125, 157; Simon Galkin: pages 37, 171, 197; Norman Nicholson: page 191; Charles Scogins: pages 25, 45, 57, 151

Copyright © 1994, 1988 by Houghton Mifflin Company. All rights reserved.
No part of this work may be reproduced or transmitted in any form or by any means, electronic or mechanical, including photocopying and recording, or by any information storage or retrieval system without prior written permission of Houghton Mifflin Company unless such copying is expressly permitted by federal copyright law. Address inquiries to School Permissions, Houghton Mifflin Company, 222 Berkeley Street, Boston, MA 02116.

Printed in the U.S.A.

ISBN: 0-395-67504-9

789-SM-97 96

Contents

Lesson 1 Building Your Vocabulary **1**
Lesson 2 Words from Animals **7**
Lesson 3 Liking and Disliking **13**
Dictionary Skills The Parts of a Dictionary Entry **19**

Lesson 4 Honesty and Pretense **21**
Lesson 5 Health and Illness **27**
Lesson 6 The Roots *-vid-* and *-vis-* **33**
Dictionary Skills Finding the Right Definition **39**

Lesson 7 Movement **41**
Lesson 8 Appearance and Texture **47**
Lesson 9 Words from Spanish **53**
Test-Taking Skills Synonym Tests **59**

Lesson 10 Friends and Foes **61**
Lesson 11 The Law **67**
Lesson 12 The Root *-meter-* **73**
Test-Taking Skills Antonym Tests **79**

Lesson 13 Anger and Forgiveness **81**
Lesson 14 Stops and Delays **87**
Lesson 15 Music and Sound **93**
Reading Skills Context Clues **99**

Lesson 16 Activity and Inactivity **101**
Lesson 17 Agreement and Disagreement **107**
Lesson 18 The Roots *-man-* and *-ped-* **113**
Reading Skills Dividing Words into Parts **119**

Lesson 19 Amount **121**
Lesson 20 Usualness and Unusualness **127**
Lesson 21 Government **133**
Reading Skills The Prefixes *non-* and *un-* **139**

Lesson 22 Limiting and Releasing **141**
Lesson 23 Necessities and Extras **147**
Lesson 24 *-sta-* and Related Roots **153**
Reading Skills The Prefix *trans-* **159**

Lesson 25 Attack and Defense **161**
Lesson 26 Certainty and Uncertainty **167**
Lesson 27 The Suffix *-logy* **173**
Reading Skills The Prefix *de-* **179**

Lesson 28 The Family **181**
Lesson 29 The Roots *-mit-* and *-mis-* **187**
Lesson 30 Literature **193**
Reading Skills The Suffixes *-ity* and *-hood* **199**

Flash cards **201**

Complete Word List

___ absurd, 127
___ accessory, 147
___ accumulate, 121
___ acute, 27
___ adequate, 121
___ adjourn, 87
___ admit, 187
___ allergic, 27
___ alleviate, 27
___ aloof, 61
___ altimeter, 73
___ amiable, 61
___ ample, 121
___ ancestor, 181
___ anthropology, 173
___ antisocial, 61
___ antonym, 1
___ apparent, 21
___ appease, 81
___ appropriate, 147
___ approximate, 167
___ archaeology, 173
___ assuage, 81
___ assumption, 167
___ attentive, 167
___ authentic, 127
___ autobiography, 193
___ auxiliary, 147
___ awe, 13

___ badger, 7
___ ballad, 93
___ bankrupt, 67
___ barometer, 73
___ battalion, 161
___ beastly, 7
___ belligerent, 81
___ betray, 61
___ biography, 193
___ biology, 173
___ bizarre, 127
___ bluff, 21
___ blunt, 47
___ bolero, 53
___ brisk, 41

___ camouflage, 161
___ casualty, 161
___ cease, 87
___ certify, 167
___ choral, 93
___ circumstance, 153
___ clan, 181
___ clinic, 27
___ coarse, 47
___ colossal, 121
___ compatible, 181
___ compress, 141
___ compromise, 187
___ concept, 1
___ concise, 141
___ condone, 81
___ conflict, 107
___ Congress, 133
___ consent, 107
___ consistent, 153
___ constitution, 153
___ contagious, 27
___ context, 1
___ contrary, 107
___ convalescence, 27
___ cooperative, 107
___ corps, 161
___ corroborate, 107
___ crave, 13

___ decisive, 87
___ defendant, 67
___ define, 1
___ democratic, 133
___ dense, 47
___ destination, 153
___ destiny, 153
___ destitute, 153
___ detain, 87
___ detestable, 13
___ diameter, 73
___ dingy, 47
___ distinguish, 167
___ domestic, 181
___ dormant, 101

___ economy, 133
___ effective, 1
___ eject, 141
___ emancipate, 113
___ emit, 187
___ emphasize, 167
___ encampment, 161
___ enchanting, 13
___ endorse, 133
___ endurance, 27
___ energetic, 101
___ enmity, 61
___ entail, 147
___ escapade, 53
___ essence, 147
___ essential, 167
___ ethical, 21
___ evident, 67
___ exception, 127
___ excess, 147
___ exclusion, 141
___ exotic, 127
___ expulsion, 141
___ extensive, 121

___ fabricate, 21
___ fascinate, 13
___ fiesta, 53
___ filial, 181
___ fleet, 41
___ folklore, 193
___ fondness, 13
___ forum, 133
___ frank, 21
___ friction, 107
___ frivolous, 147
___ fugitive, 67

___ garrison, 161
___ genuine, 21
___ geology, 173
___ geometry, 73
___ guerrilla, 53

___ habitual, 127
___ hereditary, 181
___ hinder, 87
___ horseplay, 7
___ hound, 7

___ illusion, 167
___ impartial, 21
___ impede, 113
___ imperative, 147
___ improvise, 33
___ indignant, 81
___ industrious, 101
___ infiltrate, 161
___ infuriate, 81
___ institution, 153
___ integrity, 21
___ iridescent, 47
___ irk, 13

___ judicial, 133
___ just, 67

___ kilometer, 73
___ kin, 181

___ larceny, 67
___ lariat, 53
___ legislation, 133
___ lenient, 67
___ liberate, 141
___ linger, 41
___ lionize, 7
___ loathe, 13
___ loiter, 101
___ lull, 101
___ lyric, 93

___ mammoth, 7
___ manacle, 113
___ maneuver, 113
___ manipulate, 113
___ manual, 113
___ manuscript, 113
___ matrimony, 181
___ meager, 121
___ mesa, 53
___ metaphor, 193
___ metric, 73
___ metronome, 73
___ micrometer, 73
___ mingle, 41
___ mission, 187
___ monarchy, 133
___ municipal, 133
___ mustang, 53
___ mythology, 173

___ narrate, 193
___ negotiate, 107
___ nimble, 41
___ norm, 127
___ novel, 127

___ obvious, 21
___ odometer, 73
___ omit, 187
___ opaque, 47
___ opera, 93

___ pact, 107
___ paralysis, 27
___ parrot, 7
___ parry, 161
___ partial, 121
___ pedestal, 113
___ pedestrian, 113
___ pedigree, 113
___ perimeter, 73
___ permissible, 187
___ perpetual, 41
___ pertinent, 147
___ physiology, 173
___ pigheaded, 7
___ poncho, 53
___ premise, 187
___ probable, 167
___ prolong, 87
___ propel, 141
___ prose, 193
___ proverb, 193
___ provoke, 161
___ psychology, 173

___ radiant, 47
___ rapport, 107
___ rave, 13
___ recluse, 61
___ recoil, 13
___ reconcile, 81
___ regulate, 141
___ reliable, 21
___ remit, 187
___ repetition, 1
___ repress, 87
___ resent, 81
___ resonant, 93
___ responsive, 61
___ restless, 101
___ restrain, 141
___ restriction, 141
___ retain, 1
___ retaliate, 81
___ revision, 33
___ rhythm, 93
___ rift, 107
___ rival, 61

___ saunter, 41
___ scapegoat, 7
___ scurry, 41
___ serenade, 93
___ shackle, 87
___ sheen, 47
___ sheepish, 7
___ shrill, 93
___ siege, 161
___ siesta, 53
___ significant, 147
___ sluggish, 101
___ sociology, 173
___ solitary, 61
___ soothe, 27
___ sparse, 121
___ specialize, 1
___ spouse, 181
___ spry, 101
___ stampede, 53
___ stanza, 193
___ stately, 153
___ stationary, 153
___ statistic, 153
___ strenuous, 101
___ stride, 41
___ submit, 187
___ superlative, 127
___ surpass, 121
___ symbol, 193
___ symphony, 93
___ synonym, 1

___ tarry, 87
___ technology, 173
___ tenor, 93
___ terminology, 1
___ testimony, 67
___ theme, 193
___ theology, 173
___ thrive, 27
___ tinge, 47
___ totter, 41
___ tradition, 181
___ transmit, 187
___ transparent, 47
___ treacherous, 61
___ trifle, 121

___ undermine, 87
___ universal, 127

___ vague, 167
___ verdict, 67
___ veto, 133
___ video, 33
___ viewpoint, 33
___ vigor, 101
___ visible, 33
___ visionary, 33
___ visor, 33
___ vista, 33
___ visual, 33
___ visualize, 33

___ witness, 67
___ wrath, 81

Lesson 1

Building Your Vocabulary

All your life you will be exploring new areas of learning. Each year you will start new school subjects. Sometimes you will explore a topic of your own simply because it fascinates you. From time to time, too, you will begin a new sport or learn a new skill. In each of these subjects or activities, you will learn a new set of words.

Every time you learn a new group of words, you will find that you need to use a basic set of vocabulary words when you study and discuss the new terms. What you need, you see, are *words about words*. Ten such words are presented in this lesson. Learning these words will give you an approach to any new topic.

As you work your way through this book, you will learn more than three hundred words. You will learn additional words about words. And as you enlarge your vocabulary, you will enlarge the sum of what you know.

WORD LIST
antonym
concept
context
define
effective
repetition
retain
specialize
synonym
terminology

DEFINITIONS

After you have studied the definitions and example for each vocabulary word, write the word on the line to the right.

1. **antonym** (ăn′tə-nĭm′) *noun* A word that means the opposite of another word. 1. ______________

   EXAMPLE *Light* and *dark* are *antonyms.*

2. **concept** (kŏn′sĕpt′) *noun* **a.** A general idea or understanding: *a person with no concept of fairness.* **b.** A thought or notion: *a concept worth trying.* 2. ______________

   RELATED WORD **conceive** *verb*

   EXAMPLE The *concept* of democracy as explained in our Constitution owes a great deal to the ideas of Thomas Jefferson and John Adams.

3. **context** (kŏn′tĕkst′) *noun* **a.** The words or ideas surrounding a particular word or idea. **b.** A general setting or situation: *in the context of city life.* 3. ______________

   EXAMPLE In one *context* the word *mad* means "insane"; in another, it means "angry."

Copyright © 1988 Houghton Mifflin Company. All rights reserved.

4. **define** (dĭ-fīn′) *verb* **a.** To state the meaning of: *define a word.* **b.** To explain: *define one's duties.* **c.** To make exact or specific: *a treaty defining the borders between countries.*

RELATED WORDS **definite** *adjective;* **definitely** *adverb;* **definition** *noun*

EXAMPLE Try to *define* a word yourself before looking it up in a dictionary or glossary.

4. ______________

5. **effective** (ĭ-fĕk′tĭv) *adjective* **a.** Producing a desired impression or result: *an effective speech.* **b.** In operation: *a law becoming effective at once.*

RELATED WORDS **effect** *noun;* **effect** *verb;* **effectively** *adverb;* **effectiveness** *noun*

EXAMPLE Learning a word a day is one *effective* way to build vocabulary.

5. ______________

USAGE NOTE As a noun *effect* means a result or influence: "Advice has no *effect* on him." As a verb it means to bring about or make: "Will the new principal *effect* any changes?"

6. **repetition** (rĕp′ĭ-tĭsh′ən) *noun* **a.** The act or process of repeating. **b.** Something repeated or produced by repeating.

RELATED WORDS **repeat** *verb;* **repetitive** *adjective*

EXAMPLE The older we get, the more we prefer learning by example over learning by *repetition.*

6. ______________

7. **retain** (rĭ-tān′) *verb* To keep or hold in possession, use, or memory: *retain a job.*

EXAMPLE Do you *retain* facts better if you hear them talked about or if you read about them?

7. ______________

8. **specialize** (spĕsh′ə-līz′) *verb* **a.** To train or work in one special area: *specialize in eye surgery.* **b.** To deal or trade in one thing: *The shop specialized in wide shoes.* **c.** To adapt to a particular environment: *claws specialized for tunneling.*

RELATED WORDS **special** *adjective;* **specialist** *noun;* **specially** *adverb;* **specialty** *noun*

EXAMPLE Law dictionaries *specialize* in legal words and phrases.

8. ______________

USAGE NOTE A *specialist* is a person. A *specialty* is a special activity, job, service, or product.

9. **synonym** (sĭn′ə-nĭm′) *noun* A word with a meaning very close to that of another word.

RELATED WORD **synonymous** *adjective*

EXAMPLE *Flag* and *banner* are *synonyms.*

9. ______________

10. **terminology** (tûr′mə-nŏl′ə-jē) *noun* The special vocabulary of a particular trade, science, or art; technical terms.

RELATED WORDS **term** *noun;* **term** *verb*

EXAMPLE *Debug* is an example of computer *terminology* that has become an everyday word.

10. ______________

Copyright © 1988 Houghton Mifflin Company. All rights reserved.

Name ______________________________ Date ____________

Exercise 1 Matching Words and Definitions

Match the definition in Column B with the word in Column A. Write the letter of the correct definition on the answer line.

1. ______
2. ______
3. ______
4. ______
5. ______
6. ______
7. ______
8. ______
9. ______
10. ______

Column A	*Column B*
1. specialize	a. the act or process of repeating
2. define	b. a particular group of technical terms
3. repetition	c. a word meaning the opposite of another word
4. antonym	d. a general idea or understanding; a thought
5. context	e. producing a desired impression or result
6. concept	f. the setting of a word or idea
7. effective	g. to state the meaning of; explain
8. synonym	h. to keep in possession, use, or memory
9. terminology	i. a word with a meaning very close to that of another word
10. retain	j. to train or work in a particular area

Exercise 2 Using Words Correctly

Decide whether the italicized vocabulary word has been used correctly in the sentence. On the answer line, write *Correct* for correct use and *Incorrect* for incorrect use.

1. Cliff's joke was so *effective* that we all yawned. 1. ______
2. Songs like "Row, Row, Row Your Boat" make use of *repetition.* 2. ______
3. *Terminology* is the study of insects. 3. ______
4. Mom spiced the applesauce with nutmeg and a little *synonym.* 4. ______
5. "Without knowing the *context,* I can't figure out this note," said Beth. 5. ______
6. Words have been *defined* as "pegs to hang ideas on." 6. ______
7. The garage *specialized* in rebuilding engines. 7. ______
8. China accepted the *concept* of a round earth before Europe did. 8. ______
9. "Please *retain* from chewing gum in class," said Mr. Kawada. 9. ______
10. The words *reply* and *answer* are *antonyms.* 10. ______

Exercise 3 Choosing the Best Word

Decide which vocabulary word or related form best expresses the meaning of the italicized word or phrase in the sentence. On the answer line, write the letter of the correct choice.

1. What is the most *result-producing* way of learning a new word? 1. ______
   a. effective **b.** synonymous **c.** repetitive **d.** special

Copyright © 1988 Houghton Mifflin Company. All rights reserved.

2. It is a good idea to learn related *technical terms* together. 2. ______
a. synonyms **b.** concepts **c.** terminology **d.** definitions

3. When possible, try to get meaning from *surrounding material.* 3. ______
a. terminology **b.** effect **c.** definitions **d.** context

4. If you have a hobby, *work in one area;* choose one aspect of the hobby and study words about it. 4. ______
a. specialize **b.** retain **c.** repeat **d.** define

5. Ask family members to suggest *words close in meaning.* 5. ______
a. contexts **b.** synonyms **c.** antonyms **d.** repetitions

6. Search your memory for some *words that are opposites.* 6. ______
a. synonyms **b.** concepts **c.** specialties **d.** antonyms

7. Review new words weekly and you will *hold onto* them. 7. ______
a. repeat **b.** retain **c.** effect **d.** define

8. For hard *ideas* find definitions with example sentences. 8. ______
a. terminology **b.** synonyms **c.** contexts **d.** concepts

9. If a word has several *meanings,* study each one. 9. ______
a. terms **b.** contexts **c.** repetitions **d.** definitions

10. If all else fails, try *repeating* again and again. 10. ______
a. terminology **c.** antonyms
b. effectiveness **d.** repetition

Exercise 4 Using Different Forms of Words

Decide which form of the vocabulary word in parentheses best completes the sentence. The form given may be correct. Write your answer on the answer line.

1. "I cannot __?__ of such an idea," Amy said. *(concept)* 1. ______
2. Larry studied the __?__ of the unfamiliar word. *(context)* 2. ______
3. José consulted a dictionary to find appropriate __?__. *(synonym)* 3. ______
4. Marcy had trouble __?__ any of her weekly allowance. *(retain)* 4. ______
5. *Double play* is a baseball __?__. *(terminology)* 5. ______
6. On the car trip, the children thought up __?__ for a word game. *(antonym)* 6. ______
7. "That line needs sharper __?__," advised the artist. *(define)* 7. ______
8. What kind of __?__ would you like to be? *(specialize)* 8. ______
9. The popular song had a __?__ beat. *(repetition)* 9. ______
10. The new reed helped Arnie to play his clarinet __?__. *(effective)* 10. ______

Copyright © 1988 Houghton Mifflin Company. All rights reserved.

Name ______________________________ Date ______________

Reading Comprehension

Each numbered sentence in the following passage contains an italicized vocabulary word. After you read the passage, you will complete an exercise.

The Power of Words

Anyone who has really thought about the saying "Sticks and stones may break my bones, but words will never hurt me!" knows that it is not always true. (1) Words do have power and can, when thoughtlessly spoken, be an ***effective*** way of hurting someone. Happily, most people choose not to use the destructive power of words. They concentrate instead on the useful power that comes through building a better vocabulary.

Building a large vocabulary can increase your understanding of yourself, the people around you, and the world in general. On the practical side, speaking and writing with a wide variety of words helps you to make a good impression. For example, people with large vocabularies are likely to earn good grades and are looked upon favorably in interview situations. How can you start to gain this important power?

You may not realize it, but you are already working on building a better vocabulary. In school you are required to learn new words quickly. (2) Each subject, such as science or math, has its own ***terminology.*** (3) Along with these new terms come unfamiliar ***concepts*** that must be explained and included in your working vocabulary. (4) You may also find yourself ***specializing*** in a hobby, such as astronomy or tropical fish, that introduces you to a new set of terms. In addition, you are exposed to many new words whenever you read a novel, thumb through a magazine, or watch television.

(5) Your exposure to new words is great, but how can you ***retain*** all the new words that come your way? The following study hints should help you to remember and use a large part of your new vocabulary.

(6) First, when you come across an unfamiliar word in your reading, try to guess the meaning of that new word from the ***context*** in which it appears. (7) Next, consult the dictionary to make sure that you are ***defining*** the word correctly. Remember that words often have more than one meaning.

If you are afraid that you might not remember a new term, consider using flash cards. You might even make your own. Follow the example of the flash cards that begin on page 201 of this book. Start by recording on an index card the new word that you want to learn. (8) Then fill in the pronunciation and the definition, including one or two ***synonyms*** if the word has any. (9) If possible, you might also list an ***antonym.***

Now say the new word aloud several times. (10) This ***repetition*** should help you to remember it. Finally, look through your flash cards on a regular basis. Review old words as you add new ones.

Do not be afraid to incorporate new words into your speaking and writing vocabulary. The more you actually use these words, the less chance you will have of forgetting them. Be sure to take advantage of an important power that is only as far away as your dictionary.

Please turn to the next page.

Copyright © 1988 Houghton Mifflin Company. All rights reserved.

Reading Comprehension Exercise

Each of the following statements corresponds to a numbered sentence in the passage. Each statement contains a blank and is followed by four answer choices. Decide which choice fits best in the blank. The word or phrase that you choose must express roughly the same meaning as the italicized word in the passage. Write the letter of your choice on the answer line.

1. Speaking thoughtlessly can be a __?__ way to hurt someone. 1. ______
   a. childish b. sure-fire c. foolish d. cruel

2. Every subject in school has its own __?__. 2. ______
   a. time period c. special vocabulary
   b. difficult ideas d. end-of-year tests

3. New __?__ need explaining. 3. ______
   a. ideas b. subjects c. textbooks d. vocabulary words

4. __?__ a hobby introduces you to new vocabulary words. 4. ______
   a. Having fun with c. Spending time with
   b. Carefully choosing d. Training in one special area through

5. How can you __?__ new words? 5. ______
   a. get rid of b. add to c. remember d. find

6. The __?__ a new word are important. 6. ______
   a. definitions of c. earlier forms of
   b. words or ideas surrounding d. endings and beginnings of

7. Check to see whether you are __?__ the word correctly. 7. ______
   a. stating the meaning of c. pronouncing
   b. using d. writing and spelling

8. Try to include __?__ on your flash cards. 8. ______
   a. word histories c. words with opposite meanings
   b. related words d. words with similar meanings

9. Mention __?__ if they are available. 9. ______
   a. words with similar meanings c. related words
   b. words with opposite meanings d. word histories

10. You can remember vocabulary words by __?__ them. 10. ______
    a. rhyming b. writing about c. repeating d. picturing

Writing Assignment

Select a word with which you are unfamiliar. You may have come across this word in your reading, or you may have heard someone use it in conversation. With the dictionary as your reference, write an explanation of the word. The explanation should be one that you could present to the class. In your explanation include any words that are opposite in meaning or close in meaning to the word that you are discussing. Within your explanation use four words from this lesson and underline each one.

Copyright © 1988 Houghton Mifflin Company. All rights reserved.

Lesson 2

Words from Animals

If animals were people, would they be pleased or insulted by how we refer to them? Would they have phrases to match our "act like an animal," "outfox," "weasel out of," "debug," "wolf down," "crow about," or "have a whale of a time"? Just why do we use animal words to describe people?

Animal words add something extra to writing and conversation. For example, which sounds like more fun, to have a *"good* time" or to have a *"whale* of a time"? Which person sounds hungrier, the one who "gulps" or the one who "wolfs down" a meal? Who is more obnoxious, someone who proudly mentions getting 100 on a math test or someone who loudly "crows" about it? (Whom would you be more likely to congratulate?)

A World War II general was called "The Desert Fox" by his enemies because he so often outfoxed them. Did his enemies respect him? Was the nickname an insult or a compliment?

This lesson will introduce you to other animal words. As you study each one, put yourself on the receiving end. Which words might make you uncomfortable? Which would insult you? Which would you take as a compliment?

WORD LIST

badger
beastly
horseplay
hound
lionize
mammoth
parrot
pigheaded
scapegoat
sheepish

DEFINITIONS

After you have studied the definitions and example for each vocabulary word, write the word on the line to the right.

1. **badger** (băj′ər) *verb* To pester, especially with constant questions or protests. 1. ________________

EXAMPLE Marsha *badgered* her parents for a raise in allowance.

2. **beastly** (bēst′lē) *adjective* **a.** Disagreeable; nasty. **b.** Bad; awful. 2. ________________

RELATED WORDS **beastliness** *noun;* **bestial** *adjective*

EXAMPLE *Beastly* treatment of orphans by cruel masters is a common theme in the novels of Charles Dickens.

3. **horseplay** (hôrs′plā′) *noun* Rowdy, rough play. 3. 

EXAMPLE The table tennis game turned into *horseplay,* and before we knew it a light had been broken by flying paddles.

Copyright © Houghton Mifflin Company. All rights reserved.

4. hound (hound) *verb* **a.** To pursue without quitting. **b.** To nag. 4. ___________

EXAMPLE The children *hounded* their parents to take them to the theme park.

5. lionize (lī′ə-nīz′) *verb* To look upon or treat (a person) as a celebrity. 5. ___________

EXAMPLE Movie stars and winning coaches are often *lionized* by their fans.

6. mammoth (măm′əth) *adjective* Of enormous size; gigantic. 6. ___________

EXAMPLE In the *Guinness Book of World Records* are many stories of people with *mammoth* appetites.

USAGE NOTE Similar "size" words are *elephantine* and *mastadonic.*

7. parrot (păr′ət) *verb* To repeat or imitate without meaning or understanding. 7. ___________

EXAMPLE "Give me twenty!" yelled the auctioneer, and the toddler gleefully *parroted,* "Twenty!" as her dismayed parents looked on.

8. pigheaded (pĭg′hĕd′ĭd) *adjective* Stubborn, sometimes stupidly so. 8. ___________

RELATED WORDS **pigheadedly** *adverb;* **pigheadedness** *noun*

EXAMPLE If you hadn't been so *pigheaded* about doing things your way, the picnic committee wouldn't have walked out on us!

9. scapegoat (skāp′gōt′) *noun* A person, group, or thing bearing blame for others. 9. ___________

EXAMPLE It's no fun being made the *scapegoat* for a friend's pranks.

10. sheepish (shē′pĭsh) *adjective* **a.** Embarrassed, often in an apologetic way. **b.** Meek, like a sheep. 10. ___________

RELATED WORDS **sheepishly** *adverb;* **sheepishness** *noun*

EXAMPLE Caught nibbling on the hot bread, I gave a *sheepish* grin and admitted guilt.

Copyright © Houghton Mifflin Company. All rights reserved.

Name ______________________________ Date ______________

Exercise 1 Completing Definitions

On the answer line, write the word from the vocabulary list that best completes each definition.

1. To pursue someone without quitting is to __?__ that person. 1. ________
2. Something of enormous size may be described as __?__. 2. ________
3. If you blame a person unfairly, you are making him or her a __?__. 3. ________
4. A person who is stubborn may be said to be __?__. 4. ________
5. Behavior that is disagreeable or nasty may be __?__. 5. ________
6. A certain kind of embarrassed look is a __?__ look. 6. ________
7. To repeat or imitate without meaning or understanding is to __?__. 7. ________
8. If you pester someone with questions, you __?__ that person. 8. ________
9. When people treat someone as a celebrity, they __?__ that person. 9. ________
10. A person taking part in rowdy play is engaged in __?__. 10. ________

Exercise 2 Using Words Correctly

Each of the following questions contains an italicized vocabulary word. Choose the correct answer to the question, and write *Yes* or *No* on the answer line.

1. Would a *sheepish* person be likely to win a leadership award? 1. ________
2. Do most people enjoy being *badgered?* 2. ________
3. Should *horseplay* be avoided in stores selling dishes? 3. ________
4. When you *hound* someone, do you leave that person alone? 4. ________
5. Would a diamond the size of a basketball be considered *mammoth?* 5. ________
6. Would sleet and hail be good examples of *beastly* weather? 6. ________
7. If you blame your clock for your tardiness, is it your *scapegoat?* 7. ________
8. Would you be *lionizing* someone if you growled at her or him? 8. ________
9. Might a man accuse you of *parroting* if you imitate his walk? 9. ________
10. Is someone who always gives in *pigheaded?* 10. ________

Exercise 3 Choosing the Best Word

Decide which vocabulary word or related form best completes the sentence, and write the letter of your choice on the answer line.

1. Fans __?__ members of the hockey team after their victory. 1. ________
   a. parroted **b.** lionized **c.** pigheaded **d.** badgered

Copyright © 1988 Houghton Mifflin Company. All rights reserved.

2. Without realizing it, the child __?__ the man's accent. 2. ________
a. badgered b. hounded c. lionized d. parroted

3. Julie looked __?__ when her sisters found her taking oatmeal cookies out of the jar in the kitchen. 3. ________
a. mammoth b. beastly c. sheepish d. pigheaded

4. After the game there was a lot of friendly __?__ in the locker room. 4. ________
a. horseplay b. scapegoat c. pigheadedness d. sheepishness

5. Ashley __?__ the country-music star for her autograph. 5. ________
a. lionized b. parroted c. hounded d. pigheaded

6. One officer of the company was made a __?__ for the declining profits of the firm. 6. ________
a. beastliness b. sheepishness c. horseplay d. scapegoat

7. The gymnasium at the new Thomas Jefferson Middle School is __?__. 7. ________
a. mammoth b. beastly c. sheepish d. pigheaded

8. People sometimes call my uncle __?__ because once he starts something, he never gives up. 8. ________
a. sheepish b. pigheaded c. mammoth d. beastly

9. People like Lee even though he has a __?__ temper. 9. ________
a. beastly b. parroted c. lionized d. sheepish

10. The whole class __?__ the teacher with questions about the test. 10. ________
a. parroted b. pigheaded c. lionized d. badgered

Exercise 4 Using Different Forms of Words

Decide which form of the vocabulary word in parentheses best completes the sentence. The form given may be correct. Write your answer on the answer line.

1. "No __?__ around the pool" is the first rule of water safety. *(horseplay)* 1. ________

2. Arthur's __?__ about doing our class project his way ruined the experience for everyone else. *(pigheaded)* 2. ________

3. Stacey __?__ admitted that she still took her teddy bear to bed with her. *(sheepish)* 3. ________

4. Three chapters a night is a __?__ English assignment! *(mammoth)* 4. ________

5. Jill is always __?__ her father for a twelve-speed bicycle. *(badger)* 5. ________

6. The audiences are __?__ the stars of the new musical. *(lionize)* 6. ________

7. My twin is always __?__ me to keep my part of the bedroom clean. *(hound)* 7. ________

8. Beth went to bed with a __?__ toothache. *(beastly)* 8. ________

9. Gregory learned how to dance by __?__ breakdancers on television. *(parrot)* 9. ________

10. Sandy didn't like being a __?__ for the group's horseplay. *(scapegoat)* 10. ________

Copyright © 1988 Houghton Mifflin Company. All rights reserved.

Name ______________________ Date ______________

Reading Comprehension

Each numbered sentence in the following passage contains an italicized vocabulary word. After you read the passage, you will complete an exercise.

The New Kid

Looking back, the new kid who came to our small school was just plain different. (1) Compared with the other kids, he was of ***mammoth*** height — well over six feet tall but very thin. Besides being too tall and too thin, he was too soft-spoken. He didn't fight back.

(2) Soon the new kid became the school ***scapegoat.*** (3) Daily the other kids ***hounded*** him about his size, the way he spoke, and his clothes. Then they capped off their insults by nicknaming him Beanpole.

(4) Teachers tried to stop this ill treatment, but a few ***pigheaded*** boys and girls kept pestering him. (5) Their treatment of the new kid was ***beastly.*** (6) Beanpole's only response was an occasional ***sheepish*** grin.

(7) Not wanting to be ***badgered,*** Beanpole was walking alone outside at lunchtime one cold winter day. (8) The other older boys, who had also braved the sharp wind, were engaged in ***horseplay*** in a field nearby. All of a sudden, the fire alarm rang.

Only Beanpole noticed. He turned toward the school. There were flames — from both doors! The children were trapped inside! A screaming child poked his head out of the window, too scared to jump.

Beanpole raced over. He reached up with his long arms and helped the child through the window. Working fast, he pulled out the other children one by one. The other boys either stood by, helpless, or followed Beanpole's orders.

After that, there was a change. (9) Now Beanpole was ***lionized*** by the whole town. The small children, many of whom he had saved (my little brother included), idolized him. (10) They ***parroted*** his slow speech and often stumbled as they tried to imitate his stride.

When basketball season opened, Beanpole was playing center — in more ways than one.

Reading Comprehension Exercise

Each of the following statements corresponds to a numbered sentence in the passage. Each statement contains a blank and is followed by four answer choices. Decide which choice fits best in the blank. The word or phrase that you choose must express roughly the same meaning as the italicized word in the passage. Write the letter of your choice on the answer line.

1. To the others the new kid at school appeared __?__. 1. __________
   a. enormous **b.** average **c.** stocky **d.** noticeable

2. Needing a(n) __?__ for their pranks, the older boys soon picked on the outsider. 2. __________
   a. outlet **b.** excuse **c.** reason **d.** victim

3. Since they __?__ him about his build, they called him Beanpole. 3. __________
   a. laughed at **b.** asked **c.** nagged **d.** commented to

Copyright © 1988 Houghton Mifflin Company. All rights reserved.

4. Despite the teachers' warnings, the __?__ boys and girls continued to torment him. 4. ______

a. older b. awkward c. stubborn d. fun-loving

5. These pupils' treatment of Beanpole was __?__. 5. ______

a. constant b. mean c. typical d. planned

6. Occasionally the new kid responded with a(n) __?__ grin. 6. ______

a. timid b. hasty c. wide d. angry

7. During one lunch period, Beanpole took a walk alone in the school yard because he was tired of being __?__. 7. ______

a. pestered b. ignored c. scolded d. admired

8. Elsewhere the other boys were involved in their usual __?__ in the school yard. 8. ______

a. merriment b. competition c. roughhousing d. good deeds

9. Following the fire, Beanpole was __?__ by everyone. 9. ______

a. embarrassed c. severely scolded
b. rewarded d. made much of

10. The admiring children often __?__ his slow speech. 10. ______

a. mocked b. praised c. imitated d. discussed

Writing Assignment

Using five of the words from this lesson, imagine that you are Beanpole and write a letter to a friend in which you tell about your first week at the new school. Underline each vocabulary word that you use.

Vocabulary Enrichment

The term *scapegoat* is almost three thousand years old. It is a translation from a Hebrew term meaning "escape goat."

Goats were common animals of sacrifice in ancient days. At one time it was customary to sacrifice a goat and to set another goat loose in the desert as a symbol of people's confessions of their sins. People would write confessions on pieces of cloth, tie them to the goat, and drive it away. Today, someone who takes the blame for others' misdeeds is called a scapegoat.

ACTIVITY Other words derived from the Bible have made their way into ordinary speech and writing. Look up the following words in a high school dictionary, and write their origins and their definitions.

1. shibboleth 2. Good Samaritan 3. maudlin 4. babel 5. pharisee

Copyright © 1988 Houghton Mifflin Company. All rights reserved.

Lesson 3

Liking and Disliking

Many words measure feelings. They act like degrees on a thermometer or zones on a gauge, recording very clear measurements. Everyday language is full of such words and phrases.

Has a friendship of yours ever been in the "deep freeze"? If so, you knew beforehand that it was in a danger zone, didn't you? Someone's temper was "boiling." Perhaps one of you got "hot under the collar" or gave the other "the cold shoulder." You reacted with strong feelings.

The words in this lesson are used to describe extreme emotional reactions. As you study each word, think where you would place it on an emotional gauge. At the PLUS or the MINUS end? Exactly where? How positive? How negative?

WORD LIST

awe
crave
detestable
enchanting
fascinate
fondness
irk
loathe
rave
recoil

Lesson 3 WORD LIST

DEFINITIONS

After you have studied the definitions and example for each vocabulary word, write the word on the line to the right.

1. **awe** (ô) *noun* A feeling of mixed wonder, fear, and deep respect. *verb* To cause a feeling of awe.

   RELATED WORD **awesome** *adjective*

   EXAMPLE We gazed in *awe* as thousands of monarch butterflies settled among the trees like a golden cloud.

1. ______________

USAGE NOTE The related word *awesome* is used in slang to mean "remarkable" or "outstanding."

2. **crave** (krāv) *verb* **a.** To have a very strong desire or need for. **b.** To beg earnestly for something, as forgiveness or mercy.

   RELATED WORD **craving** *noun*

   EXAMPLE The young star *craved* fame in the way that a lion needs meat or a diver needs air.

2. ______________

3. **detestable** (dĭ-tĕs′tə-bəl) *adjective* Deserving strong dislike, even hatred.

   RELATED WORDS **detest** *verb;* **detestation** *noun*

   EXAMPLE "We find the actions of the terrorists *detestable,*" announced the ambassador.

3. ______________

SEE *loathe.*

Copyright © Houghton Mifflin Company. All rights reserved.

4. **enchanting** (ĕn-chăn′tĭng) *adjective* Very charming, attractive, or delightful. 4. ____________

RELATED WORDS **enchant** *verb;* **enchantment** *noun*

EXAMPLE The paper described the holiday decorations as a delight for young and old, claiming "Even a Scrooge would find them *enchanting.*"

5. **fascinate** (făs′ə-nāt′) *verb* **a.** To capture and hold the interest and attention of. **b.** To hold motionless or spellbound. 5. ____________

RELATED WORD **fascination** *noun*

EXAMPLE Isaac Newton was so *fascinated* by a falling apple that he eventually discovered the laws of gravity.

6. **fondness** (fŏnd′nĭs) *noun* **a.** A loving or affectionate feeling; tenderness. **b.** A strong liking for something. 6. ____________

RELATED WORDS **fond** *adjective;* **fondly** *adverb*

EXAMPLE My brother's *fondness* for drums drove me to earplugs and our neighbors to the telephone.

7. **irk** (ûrk) *verb* To annoy; irritate. 7. ____________

RELATED WORD **irksome** *adjective*

EXAMPLE Nothing *irks* a bus driver more than passengers who push and shove.

8. **loathe** (lō*th*) *verb* To dislike greatly; find repulsive. 8. ____________

RELATED WORDS **loathing** *noun;* **loathsome** *adjective*

EXAMPLE Most people *loathe* the sound of fingernails scratching a chalkboard.

USAGE NOTE *Loathe* and *detest* mean "to hate," but *loathe* suggests an almost physical dislike.

9. **rave** (rāv) *verb* **a.** To speak wildly or senselessly. **b.** To speak with great enthusiasm. 9. ____________

RELATED WORDS **raving** *adjective;* **raving** *noun*

EXAMPLE Everyone *raved* about the delicious fish and low prices at the new seafood restaurant.

10. **recoil** (rĭ-koil′) *verb* **a.** To move or jerk back, as a gun upon firing. **b.** To shrink back in fear or dislike. (rē′koil′) *noun* The act of recoiling. 10. ____________

EXAMPLE The rifle *recoiled* so hard that the soldier's shoulder hurt.

USAGE NOTE Some nouns and verbs that are spelled alike are pronounced differently.

Copyright © 1988 Houghton Mifflin Company. All rights reserved.

Name ______________________________ Date ______________

Exercise 1 Writing Correct Words

On the answer line, write the word from the vocabulary list that fits each definition.

1. A loving or affectionate feeling 1. ______
2. To capture and hold the interest and attention of 2. ______
3. To annoy or irritate 3. ______
4. Very charming, attractive, or delightful 4. ______
5. To shrink back in fear or dislike 5. ______
6. A feeling of mixed wonder, fear, and deep respect 6. ______
7. Deserving strong dislike, even hatred 7. ______
8. To speak wildly or with great enthusiasm 8. ______
9. To dislike greatly or find repulsive 9. ______
10. To have a very strong desire or need for 10. ______

Exercise 2 Using Words Correctly

Decide whether the italicized vocabulary word has been used correctly in the sentence. On the answer line, write *Correct* for correct use and *Incorrect* for incorrect use.

1. Legend says that Narcissus found his own face so *enchanting* that he stared at himself all day. 1. ______
2. When Bonnie won the door prize, she shrieked with *awe* and cartwheeled down the theater aisle. 2. ______
3. Adela was almost *fascinated* by fumes from the faulty heater. 3. ______
4. Max *raved* about the play that he had seen the previous night. 4. ______
5. Some Europeans feed corn only to livestock; they do not share Americans' *fondness* for it. 5. ______
6. While on a diet, I *crave* forbidden foods. 6. ______
7. Wild animals instinctively *recoil* in panic from fire. 7. ______
8. Grandparents are usually *irked* by their grandchildren's thank-you letters. 8. ______
9. Elisabeth finds animals *detestable* and cannot resist giving them a good home. 9. ______
10. People who love skiing *loathe* snow. 10. ______

Copyright © 1988 Houghton Mifflin Company. All rights reserved.

Exercise 3 Choosing the Best Word

Decide which vocabulary word or related form best expresses the meaning of the italicized word or phrase in the sentence. On the answer line, write the letter of the correct choice.

1. When callers *speak senselessly,* a talk-show host cuts them off. 1. ________
   a. rave **b.** fascinate **c.** recoil **d.** enchant
2. Fran *shrank back in disgust* when she saw Lisa's pet tarantula. 2. ________
   a. was enchanted **b.** recoiled **c.** was irked **d.** raved
3. Brussels sprouts are the vegetable that Tony truly *finds repulsive.* 3. ________
   a. enchants **b.** irks **c.** craves **d.** loathes
4. When Edwin *has an intense desire for* pizza, he exercises instead. 4. ________
   a. fascinates **b.** detests **c.** loathes **d.** craves
5. Why do cartoons *capture the interest of* so many youngsters? 5. ________
   a. fascinate **b.** crave **c.** irk **d.** awe
6. Baby Annie's parents find her dimples absolutely *charming.* 6. ________
   a. awesome **b.** detestable **c.** enchanting **d.** irksome
7. Jill was *annoyed* when flu kept her from playing in the soccer game. 7. ________
   a. fascinated **b.** enchanted **c.** irked **d.** awed
8. The low-budget horror film was *deserving of intense dislike.* 8. ________
   a. detestable **b.** enchanting **c.** awesome **d.** raving
9. The twins' governess balanced *tenderness* with strict discipline. 9. ________
   a. fondness **b.** awe **c.** fascination **d.** craving
10. The astronaut felt *a mixture of wonder and respect* as she looked up at the towering spacecraft. 10. ________
    a. fondness **b.** loathing **c.** enchantment **d.** awe

Exercise 4 Using Different Forms of Words

Each sentence contains an italicized vocabulary word in a form that does not fit the sentence. On the answer line, write the form of the word that does fit the sentence.

1. "*Enchant* is my specialty," said Pat, who played the Fairy Godmother. 1. ________
2. Grooms often have the *loathing* chore of cleaning stables. 2. ________
3. "Your *irk* quarreling must stop!" commanded the baby sitter. 3. ________
4. Tourists find the size of the Luray Caverns *awed.* 4. ________
5. The children spent hours *rave* about the movie to their parents. 5. ________
6. The sick child *fondness* stroked the purring kitten. 6. ________
7. Jeremy *recoil* in fear at the sight of a scorpion in his shoe. 7. ________
8. Who hasn't had at least one *crave* to be famous or rich? 8. ________

Copyright © 1988 Houghton Mifflin Company. All rights reserved.

Name ______________________________ Date ______________

9. Early in his life, the composer Mozart showed a *fascinate* with music. 9. ______________

10. Pam disliked the book because she *detestable* the main characters. 10. ______________

Reading Comprehension

Each numbered sentence in the following passage contains an italicized vocabulary word or related form. After you read the passage, you will complete an exercise.

A Race for Life

(1) People who love soap operas might also find much to ***rave*** about in Greek and Roman myths. Both are filled with family intrigue, power struggles, and love matches. Consider the story of Atalanta.

Iasus, a king, dearly wants a son and reacts with horror when a daughter, Atalanta, is born. (2) He ***loathes*** the sight of her. (3) So ***detestable*** does he find her that she is left on a mountainside to die.

Fortunately, the newborn baby is found by a friendly bear. Soon a group of hunters takes over her care, and she grows up to be a fine runner and hunter.

One hunt changes Atalanta's life. Prince Melanger, himself a great hunter, has vowed to catch a vicious boar and to award its pelt and tusks to whoever kills it. Atalanta, the only woman on the hunt, outruns her companions and scores the first hit. Melanger himself strikes the third and fatal blow. By rights, he should get the prize. (4) However, he is so in love with Atalanta and in ***awe*** of her skills that he awards her the pelt.

Atalanta's reputation eventually reaches the palace of Iasus. Curious, the king orders Atalanta home and then demands that she marry. (5) Used to life outdoors, Atalanta is clearly ***irked*** at the change. (6) She ***craves*** the carefree life of a hunter.

Nonetheless, Atalanta obeys her father, but only on one condition. Her would-be husband must defeat her in a footrace or die! (7) Understandably, young men ***recoil*** from the royal offer.

Life passes as usual for the hunter-princess until a prince named Melanion accepts the challenge. The goddess Aphrodite gives Melanion three golden apples, and the life-or-death race is on!

Atalanta, sure of victory, takes her time, teasing Melanion by letting him occasionally catch up. Each time this happens, Melanion drops a golden apple. (8) ***Fascinated*** by their beauty, Atalanta stoops to pick up the apples, thus allowing Melanion to sprint ahead. Melanion wins the race, a wife, and his life.

(9) In another version of the story, Melanion is so ***enchanted*** by Atalanta that he joins her hunting band. She just ignores him, and love limps along rather lopsidedly. Like any good hunter, however, Melanion is patient. In time, Atalanta's heart softens. (10) She begins to feel ***fondness*** for Melanion and, at last, love.

Please turn to the next page.

Copyright © 1988 Houghton Mifflin Company. All rights reserved.

Reading Comprehension Exercise

Each of the following statements corresponds to a numbered sentence in the passage. Each statement contains a blank and is followed by four answer choices. Decide which choice fits best in the blank. The word or phrase that you choose must express roughly the same meaning as the italicized word in the passage. Write the letter of your choice on the answer line.

1. Soap-opera fans might find much to __?__ about in Greek and Roman myths. 1. ________
   a. cry **b.** whistle **c.** cheer **d.** frown

2. Wanting a son, King Iasus __?__ his newborn daughter. 2. ________
   a. charms **b.** greets **c.** holds **d.** despises

3. King Iasus finds the baby Atalanta __?__. 3. ________
   a. hateful **b.** lovely **c.** ill **d.** funny

4. The leader of a hunting band looks on Atalanta with __?__. 4. ________
   a. horror and fear **c.** wonder and respect
   b. fear and terror **d.** hate and disgust

5. An outdoor person, Atalanta is __?__ by palace life. 5. ________
   a. irritated **b.** thrilled **c.** bored **d.** dazzled

6. The newfound daughter __?__ her old life. 6. ________
   a. forgets **b.** desires **c.** misses **d.** loses

7. Young men __?__ from Atalanta's marriage offer. 7. ________
   a. escape **b.** return **c.** shrink **d.** stay away

8. The swift princess slows down because the golden apples __?__ her. 8. ________
   a. trip **b.** thrill **c.** sicken **d.** surprise

9. Melanion is also __?__ by Atalanta. 9. ________
   a. tricked **b.** pestered **c.** loved **d.** charmed

10. Atalanta returns Melanion's __?__ only after a long time. 10. ________
    a. affection **b.** ring **c.** stare **d.** feelings

Writing Assignment

People often have strong reactions to movies. Pick a recent movie that you had a strong reaction to, either positive or negative. In a paragraph or two, explain to a friend why the movie affected you in this way. Give specific examples from the movie to show what you mean. Use at least five words from this lesson and underline each one.

Copyright © 1988 Houghton Mifflin Company. All rights reserved.

Name ______________________ Date __________

A B C D E F

DICTIONARY SKILLS

Dictionary Skills

The Parts of a Dictionary Entry

The entries in most dictionaries can be divided into six parts. Each one provides a different type of information. As you read about each part, find it in the following entry for *dizzy*.

> **diz•zy** (dĭz′ē) *adj.* **diz•zi•er, diz•zi•est.** **1.** Having a sensation of whirling or feeling a tendency to fall; giddy. **2.** Producing or tending to produce giddiness; *a dizzy height.* **3.** *Informal.* Scatter-brained; silly; foolish. —*v.* **diz•zied, diz•zy•ing, diz•zies.** To make dizzy; confuse; bewilder. **—diz′zy•ing** *adj.: a dizzying pace.* **—diz′zi•ly** *adv.* **—diz′zi•ness** *n.*

1. *The word.* The word itself appears in bold type. Dots or extra space show its division into syllables. Be alert for words, like *chow,* that are **homographs**—words that are spelled alike but have entirely different meanings. *Chow,* for example, can mean a type of dog, or it can be the slang word for "food." Homographs appear as separate entries.
2. *The pronunciation.* The pronunciation appears within bars or parentheses. It consists of alphabet letters and other symbols that tell you how to say the word. A complete key to those symbols usually appears at the front of the dictionary, and a shortened form of the key is often found on each dictionary page or pair of pages. The stressed (accented) syllable is either printed in bold type or shown with a bold mark (′), or both. If two syllables are stressed, the one receiving the lesser stress is shown with a lighter mark.
3. *The part of speech.* An abbreviation following the pronunciation tells you the part of speech. Common abbreviations are *n.* (noun), *adj.* (adjective), *v.* (verb), *adv.* (adverb), and *prep.* (preposition). Notice that the word *dizzy* can be used as an adjective or as a verb.
4. *Irregular forms.* Irregular forms of the word (including those that offer possible spelling problems) are shown in bold type. These include plurals of nouns, the *-er* and *-est* forms of adjectives and adverbs, and certain endings of verbs. Knowing these forms of a word will help you to use it correctly. Adjective and verb forms of the word *dizzy* are given in the sample entry as an aid to correct spelling.

Please turn to the next page.

Copyright © 1988 Houghton Mifflin Company. All rights reserved.

5. *Definitions.* Many words have more than one meaning. The entry gives each of these definitions, sometimes illustrating them with a phrase or sentence. Numbered definitions may be further divided into parts by alphabet letters.
6. *Related forms.* A word may have related forms that are different parts of speech. For example, the verb *dizzy* has the related forms *dizzily,* an adverb, and *dizziness,* a noun. Related forms appear in bold type at the end of an entry.

Exercise **Using Dictionary Entries**

Two dictionary entries appear at the bottom of the page. Use them when you write the answers to each of the following questions.

1. Write the part of speech of *protector.*

2. Write the symbols for the stressed syllable of *protector.*

3. Write how many definitions the dictionary entry for *protector* has.

4. Can the word *counterfeit* be used as an adverb? Write yes or no.

5. Write the number of syllables that *counterfeit* contains.

6. Write the related form of *counterfeit* and its part of speech.

7. Does *counterfeit* have any irregular forms? Write yes or no.

pro•tec•tor (prə-tĕk′tər) *n.* **1.** Someone or something that protects; a defender or guardian: *She decided to become the protector of the orphan colt. The catcher wore a cushioned chest protector.* **2.** A person appointed to rule a kingdom during the absence or childhood of the monarch.

coun•ter•feit (koun′tər-fĭt) *v.* **1.** To make in imitation of what is genuine in order to deceive: *He was found guilty of counterfeiting money.* **2.** To pretend: *counterfeit remorse.* —*adj.* **1.** Made in imitation of what is genuine in order to deceive: *a counterfeit dollar bill.* **2.** Pretended; simulated: *counterfeit repentance.* —*n.* Something counterfeited. —**coun′ter•feit′er** *n.*

Copyright © 1988 Houghton Mifflin Company. All rights reserved.

Lesson 4

Honesty and Pretense

In life and in fiction, people and situations are not always what they appear to be. Consider the case of Bob, a new student at Grove Street School. In order to make friends, Bob pretends to be wealthier than he is and treats several boys to snacks in the cafeteria. Soon his new friends come to expect the treats and are annoyed when Bob tells them that he has run out of money. Bob now realizes that he should have been honest with them in the first place. Throughout life you will experience situations in which someone is not what he or she appears to be. The words in this lesson can give you a better understanding of the various aspects of honesty and pretense.

WORD LIST

- apparent
- bluff
- ethical
- fabricate
- frank
- genuine
- impartial
- integrity
- obvious
- reliable

DEFINITIONS

After you have studied the definitions and example for each vocabulary word, write the word on the line to the right.

1. **apparent** (ə-păr′ənt) *adjective* **a.** Easily understood or seen; clear. **b.** Seemingly plain to see, but not necessarily so. 1. ____________

RELATED WORD **apparently** *adverb*

EXAMPLE In professional basketball great height is an *apparent* advantage.

2. **bluff** (blŭf) *verb* To mislead or fool by boasting. *noun* The act of misleading by pretense. 2. ____________

RELATED WORD **bluffer** *noun*

EXAMPLE Posing as a visiting general, the spy *bluffed* his way past the security guard.

3. **ethical** (ĕth′ĭ-kəl) *adjective* **a.** Right and proper; moral. **b.** Following accepted rules of behavior, especially professional standards. 3. ____________

RELATED WORDS **ethically** *adverb;* **ethics** *noun*

EXAMPLE It may be legal to profit from someone's bad luck, but is it *ethical?*

USAGE NOTE Use the word *ethics* with a singular verb: "*Ethics* is the study of right and wrong."

Copyright © 1988 Houghton Mifflin Company. All rights reserved.

4. **fabricate** (făb′rĭ-kāt′) *verb* **a.** To make up in order to deceive. **b.** To make, build, or manufacture. 4. ____________

RELATED WORD **fabrication** *noun*

EXAMPLE I stood by speechless as Bonnie *fabricated* a story about why we were late.

5. **frank** (frăngk) *adjective* Open and sincere; to the point. 5. ____________

RELATED WORDS **frankly** *adverb;* **frankness** *noun*

EXAMPLE Sometimes it is hard for friends to have *frank* discussions without hurting each other's feelings.

6. **genuine** (jĕn′yo͞o-ĭn) *adjective* **a.** Actual; not copied or faked. **b.** Sincere; honest. 6. ____________

RELATED WORDS **genuinely** *adverb;* **genuineness** *noun*

EXAMPLE The jeweler frowned and said, "This diamond is as *genuine* as a three-dollar bill."

7. **impartial** (ĭm-pär′shəl) *adjective* Fair-minded; without prejudice. 7. ____________

RELATED WORDS **impartiality** *noun;* **impartially** *adverb*

EXAMPLE A judge should weigh facts in an *impartial* manner before making a decision.

8. **integrity** (ĭn-tĕg′rĭ-tē) *noun* **a.** Honesty in word and deed. **b.** Completeness; unity. **c.** Soundness. 8. ____________

EXAMPLE Being a bank teller requires accuracy with numbers as well as personal *integrity.*

9. **obvious** (ŏb′vē-əs) *adjective* Plain to see or understand; evident; clear. 9. ____________

RELATED WORDS **obviously** *adverb;* **obviousness** *noun*

EXAMPLE The television commercial announced, "This greasy sweatshirt is an *obvious* candidate for Grime Time, the stain people!"

10. **reliable** (rĭ-lī′ə-bəl) *adjective* Dependable; trustworthy. 10. ____________

RELATED WORDS **reliability** *noun;* **reliably** *adverb;* **rely** *verb*

EXAMPLE A *reliable* car starts in all kinds of weather.

Copyright © Houghton Mifflin Company. All rights reserved.

Name ______________________________ Date ______________

Exercise 1 Writing Correct Words

On the answer line, write the word from the vocabulary list that fits each definition.

1. Open and sincere; to the point 1. ______
2. To make up; lie 2. ______
3. Honesty in word and deed 3. ______
4. Right and proper; moral 4. ______
5. To fool by boasting 5. ______
6. Fair-minded; not prejudiced 6. ______
7. Dependable 7. ______
8. Plain to see or understand; evident 8. ______
9. Real; not copied or faked 9. ______
10. Easily understood; seemingly plain to see 10. ______

Exercise 2 Using Words Correctly

Decide whether the italicized vocabulary word has been used correctly in the sentence. On the answer line, write *Correct* for correct use and *Incorrect* for incorrect use.

1. Someone who is *reliable* can always be trusted. 1. ______
2. To someone of *integrity,* a promise is a contract. 2. ______
3. It's *obvious* that rain can make driving dangerous. 3. ______
4. Mike is always *frank;* he can't bear to talk face to face. 4. ______
5. Lucy's fear of crowds becomes most *apparent* at a parade. 5. ______
6. It is not *ethical* to urge people to buy things that they don't need. 6. ______
7. *Fabricate* the "truth" and everyone will respect you. 7. ______
8. Moving away from friends can cause *genuine* grief. 8. ______
9. May I *bluff* my shoes with this nice soft towel? 9. ______
10. I ate only an *impartial* fish sandwich for lunch. 10. ______

Exercise 3 Choosing the Best Definition

For each italicized vocabulary word in the following sentences, write the letter of the best definition on the answer line.

1. Some *apparent* victories become defeats when votes are recounted. 1. ______
   a. unfortunate **b.** unclear **c.** true **d.** seeming

Copyright © Houghton Mifflin Company. All rights reserved.

2. A *genuine* ruby ring can cost thousands of dollars. 2. ________
   a. real **b.** beautiful **c.** old **d.** fake

3. Tom is not involved in the problem; let's ask him for an *impartial* opinion. 3. ________
   a. secondhand **b.** honest **c.** unprejudiced **d.** early

4. Does Ms. Takata object to the plan for *ethical* reasons? 4. ________
   a. logical **b.** criminal **c.** fair **d.** moral

5. It is foolish to *fabricate* lies to cover up your mistakes. 5. ________
   a. remember **b.** invent **c.** quote **d.** forget

6. Give me your *frank* opinion about how this jacket looks on me. 6. ________
   a. intelligent **b.** honest **c.** second **d.** private

7. The book on space flight was too old to be *reliable.* 7. ________
   a. clear **b.** trustworthy **c.** factual **d.** understood

8. How could we have overlooked such an *obvious* solution to that problem? 8. ________
   a. hidden **b.** difficult **c.** evident **d.** simple

9. Termites destroyed the *integrity* of the structure. 9. ________
   a. soundness **b.** balance **c.** design **d.** basement

10. It's not easy to *bluff* Mr. Valdez; his quizzes always test facts. 10. ________
    a. question **b.** fool **c.** anger **d.** believe

Exercise 4 Using Different Forms of Words

Decide which form of the vocabulary word in parentheses best completes the sentence. The form given may be correct. Write your answer on the answer line.

1. The __?__ of the principal's decision pleased both sides. *(impartial)* 1. ________
2. __?__ is a subject not usually taught until college. *(ethical)* 2. ________
3. Ten dollars is __?__ too much to pay for a movie! *(obvious)* 3. ________
4. Something smells bad; one of the peaches I bought is __?__ rotten. *(apparent)* 4. ________
5. Buy only products with a good record of __?__. *(reliable)* 5. ________
6. The __?__ of the experiment was ruined by dirty test tubes. *(integrity)* 6. ________
7. "Quite __?__, Mrs. Hanson," said Sam, "I feel that I deserve extra pay for baby-sitting so late." *(frank)* 7. ________
8. In the long run, __?__ fool themselves most. *(bluff)* 8. ________
9. The manager seemed __?__ interested in the complaint. *(genuine)* 9. ________
10. Instant __?__ of tall tales is a talent that few have. *(fabricate)* 10. ________

 Copyright © 1988 Houghton Mifflin Company. All rights reserved.

Name ______________________________ Date ____________

Reading Comprehension

Each numbered sentence in the following passage contains an italicized vocabulary word or related form. After you read the passage, you will complete an exercise.

Testing New Cars

A new car is "old" long before it rolls off the assembly line. Automobile makers must test each new line of cars extensively before selling even one. (1) Being able to meet certain standards of quality is not only ***ethical*** but also good business. (2) Products that are safe and ***reliable*** create satisfied, loyal customers.

The first of many tests is done on handmade models in a wind tunnel. By driving the model through the tunnel, testers can observe its stability and gas mileage under bad conditions.

Next, drivers take the car over a test track containing dirt, stones, hills, water, and other hazards. After the car has gone over the test track again and again, testers examine it for signs of stress.

(3) The test results are then discussed ***impartially.*** (4) ***Frankness*** at this stage is very important because most design problems are corrected now. (5) ***Obviously,*** if too many problems turn up, the company should decide not to manufacture the car.

If discussion results in a green light, testing continues. Up to this point, cars tested have been made entirely by hand. (6) However, only in actual assembly-line production do some problems become ***apparent.*** (7) Therefore, a few ***genuine*** assembly-line cars are made and road-tested. These first automatically produced cars may not be sold.

(8) Car manufacturers can also prove the ***integrity*** of their product by crash-testing. In a crash test, cars are deliberately crashed from the sides, back, and front, either by actual drivers or by robots and dummies. The object of this kind of testing is to make sure that the bumpers, grilles, sides, air bags, and seat belts protect the passengers.

When a car is ready for market, its manufacturer likes, of course, to talk only about its good points. (9) However, when promoting their products, car makers must never try ***bluffing*** the public with false information. Manufacturers must by law release certain facts to the public. Many of these facts come from test data. (10) It is against the law to ***fabricate*** such information.

Please turn to the next page.

Copyright © Houghton Mifflin Company. All rights reserved.

Reading Comprehension Exercise

Each of the following statements corresponds to a numbered sentence in the passage. Each statement contains a blank and is followed by four answer choices. Decide which choice fits best in the blank. The word or phrase that you choose must express roughly the same meaning as the italicized word in the passage. Write the letter of your choice on the answer line.

1. It is good business to be ___?___. 1. ________
   a. talented b. interesting c. moral d. hopeful

2. Customers like safe, ___?___ cars. 2. ________
   a. attractive b. dependable c. roomy d. cheap

3. Testers discuss the test results ___?___. 3. ________
   a. in detail c. without being prejudiced
   b. with many statistics d. openly

4. ___?___ about test-car problems is necessary. 4. ________
   a. Evidence b. Thoroughness c. Discussion d. Honesty

5. ___?___, if a car has many problems, it should not be made. 5. ________
   a. Perhaps b. Clearly c. Finally d. Sometimes

6. Certain problems may be ___?___ only later. 6. ________
   a. hidden b. evident c. tested d. discussed

7. Tests are run on ___?___ assembly-line cars. 7. ________
   a. strong b. new c. stripped-down d. actual

8. A car that has been crash-tested successfully has ___?___. 8. ________
   a. soundness b. flaws c. options d. structure

9. ___?___ the public with incorrect data would be wrong. 9. ________
   a. Fooling b. Testing c. Alarming d. Informing

10. It is not legal to ___?___ product information. 10. ________
    a. research b. publish c. file d. invent

Writing Assignment

To increase sales, advertising writers say only good things about their products. It's up to the consumer to discover what is bad about a product. Here is a way to make your own test. First, clip a car advertisement from a magazine or list details from an automobile commercial on radio or television. Then, using your notes, write a paragraph in which you explain why you would or would not buy the car. Use five or more words from this lesson and underline each one.

Copyright © 1988 Houghton Mifflin Company. All rights reserved.

Lesson 5

Health and Illness

People live longer and better than they did in the past. However, illness is still a fact of life. We even use the vocabulary of disease a great deal when not talking about disease. (Do the phrases "I'm sick of . . ." and "What a pain!" sound familiar?)

The words in this lesson concern sickness, recovery from sickness, and health. Learn the words and the way in which they are used to describe states of health as well as nonmedical situations.

WORD LIST

acute
allergic
alleviate
clinic
contagious
convalescence
endurance
paralysis
soothe
thrive

DEFINITIONS

After you have studied the definitions and example for each vocabulary word, write the word on the line to the right.

1. **acute** (ə-kyo͞ot′) *adjective* **a.** Very sharp; severe. **b.** Keen. **c.** Quickly reaching a crisis point: *an acute disease.* **d.** Sensitive; reacting quickly to impressions. **e.** In mathematics, angles less than 90°. 1. ______________

   RELATED WORDS **acutely** *adverb;* **acuteness** *noun*

   EXAMPLE Sue was rushed to the hospital with *acute* stomach pain.

2. **allergic** (ə-lûr′jĭk) *adjective* **a.** Very sensitive to something in the environment, such as pollen, dust, bee stings, or certain foods. **b.** *Informal.* Having strong dislike for something. 2. ______________

   RELATED WORD **allergy** *noun*

   EXAMPLE A person who is severely *allergic* should wear a Medic Alert tag listing the allergy, personal data, and an emergency number.

3. **alleviate** (ə-lē′vē-āt′) *verb* To relieve by making more bearable; lessen. 3. ______________

   RELATED WORD **alleviation** *noun*

   EXAMPLE To Ken's relief, an ice pack *alleviated* the swelling of his sprained ankle.

Copyright © 1988 Houghton Mifflin Company. All rights reserved.

4. **clinic** (klĭn′ĭk) *noun* **a.** A specialized medical institution. **b.** A formal training session, especially for medical students. **c.** Any institution that provides special advice or training. 4. ____________

RELATED WORDS **clinical** *adjective;* **clinically** *adverb*

EXAMPLE Boston's Joslin *Clinic* specializes in the treatment of diabetes.

5. **contagious** (kən-tā′jəs) *adjective* **a.** Spread by indirect or direct contact; catching; infectious. **b.** Carrying disease. 5. ____________

RELATED WORDS **contagiously** *adverb;* **contagiousness** *noun*

EXAMPLE In the Middle Ages, the highly *contagious* bubonic plague caused more deaths than wars did.

6. **convalescence** (kŏn′və-lĕs′əns) *noun* The time needed to return to health after illness, injury, or surgery. 6. ____________

RELATED WORDS **convalesce** *verb;* **convalescent** *adjective;* **convalescent** *noun*

EXAMPLE Today doctors feel that daily exercise after an operation speeds up a patient's *convalescence.*

7. **endurance** (ĕn-do͝or′əns) *noun* The ability to last or survive under strain, stress, or use; long-lasting strength. 7. ____________

USAGE NOTE Some nouns may also be used as adjectives: "The Iditarod is an *endurance* test."

RELATED WORD **endure** *verb*

EXAMPLE The Iditarod, a 1049-mile dog-sled race, is an exhausting test of *endurance* for both driver and dog team.

8. **paralysis** (pə-răl′ĭ-sĭs) *noun* **a.** The loss of feeling in, or ability to move, a part of the body. **b.** A lack of ability to act normally (for example, because of fear or uncertainty). 8. ____________

USAGE NOTE The plural of the word *paralysis* is *paralyses.*

RELATED WORDS **paralytic** *adjective;* **paralytic** *noun;* **paralyze** *verb*

EXAMPLE Cases of polio, a disease sometimes causing *paralysis* of arms and legs, are rare today.

9. **soothe** (so͞o*th*) *verb* To relieve by calming or comforting. 9. ____________

RELATED WORDS **soothing** *adjective;* **soothingly** *adverb*

EXAMPLE Being held seemed to *soothe* the crying baby.

10. **thrive** (thrīv) *verb* **a.** To grow or do well. **b.** To be successful. 10. ____________

EXAMPLE To *thrive,* most plants need water and sunlight.

Copyright © Houghton Mifflin Company. All rights reserved.

Name ______________________________ Date ______________

Exercise 1 Matching Words and Definitions

Match the definition in Column B with the word in Column A. Write the letter of the correct definition on the answer line.

Column A	*Column B*
1. convalescence	a. very sharp or severe; keen
2. thrive	b. the loss of feeling or of ability to move
3. soothe	c. very sensitive to certain things
4. acute	d. to relieve by calming or comforting
5. paralysis	e. to relieve by making more bearable
6. endurance	f. spread by contact; catching
7. contagious	g. long-lasting strength
8. clinic	h. the time needed to return to health after illness, injury, or surgery
9. alleviate	i. a specialized institution or training session
10. allergic	j. to grow or do well

1. ______
2. ______
3. ______
4. ______
5. ______
6. ______
7. ______
8. ______
9. ______
10. ______

Exercise 2 Using Words Correctly

Each of the following questions contains an italicized vocabulary word. Choose the correct answer to the question, and write *Yes* or *No* on the answer line.

1. Does skipping meals *alleviate* hunger? 1. ______
2. Is chicken pox *contagious?* 2. ______
3. Does *convalescence* take place before an operation? 3. ______
4. If you are *allergic* to something, do you react badly to it? 4. ______
5. Do long-distance runners need *endurance?* 5. ______
6. Do worms have *acute* intelligence? 6. ______
7. Would good soup *soothe* hunger pains? 7. ______
8. Can stage fright cause speech *paralysis?* 8. ______
9. Would you find doctors at a *clinic?* 9. ______
10. If a business *thrives,* does its owner worry? 10. ______

Exercise 3 Choosing the Best Definition

For each italicized vocabulary word in the following sentences, write the letter of the best definition on the answer line.

1. See your doctor if you have *acute* chest pains. 1. ______
   a. sharp **b.** odd **c.** pretty **d.** mild

Copyright © 1988 Houghton Mifflin Company. All rights reserved.

2. What is the best way to *soothe* itching from poison ivy? 2. ________
a. cure **b.** treat **c.** calm **d.** catch

3. Both laughter and gloom are *contagious.* 3. ________
a. catching **b.** serious **c.** common **d.** natural

4. For three weeks after the accident, Jill had some *paralysis* in her arm. 4. ________
a. problems **b.** numbness **c.** itching **d.** shock

5. In its new home, the once skinny puppy *thrived.* 5. ________
a. worsened **b.** sickened **c.** grew **d.** wiggled

6. What is the usual period of *convalescence* for a broken leg? 6. ________
a. hospitalization **b.** surgery **c.** bill **d.** recovery

7. Doctors questioned whether the sick person had enough *endurance* to get through an operation. 7. ________
a. intelligence **b.** stubbornness **c.** cash **d.** strength

8. When it comes to surprise quizzes, I am certainly *allergic.* 8. ________
a. sensitive **b.** afraid **c.** understanding **d.** quick

9. Continuing aid is needed to *alleviate* famine in Africa. 9. ________
a. lessen **b.** treat **c.** erase **d.** hide

10. Every month Sal has a tennis *clinic.* 10. ________
a. open competition **c.** injury
b. exam **d.** training session

Exercise 4 Using Different Forms of Words

Decide which form of the vocabulary word in parentheses best completes the sentence. The form given may be correct. Write your answer on the answer line.

1. Flat-roofed houses cannot __?__ heavy snowfall. *(endurance)* 1. ________

2. Maria had to __?__ at home for a few days after having her tonsils out. *(convalescence)* 2. ________

3. The bat hears so __?__ that it can detect insects in flight. *(acute)* 3. ________

4. Gentle exercise helps in the __?__ of muscle stiffness. *(alleviate)* 4. ________

5. Julio's cough needed prompt __?__ attention. *(clinic)* 5. ________

6. The class's recycling business began to __?__ after the radio station provided free advertising. *(thrive)* 6. ________

7. Gentle waves lapped __?__ against my sunburned legs. *(soothe)* 7. ________

8. The committee members were __?__ by their failure to agree. *(paralysis)* 8. ________

9. "With a dust __?__ like mine, shouldn't I skip cleaning my room?" Andrea asked her mother. *(allergic)* 9. ________

10. Lou giggled so __?__ that the whole class was soon roaring with laughter. *(contagious)* 10. ________

Copyright © 1988 Houghton Mifflin Company. All rights reserved.

Name ______________________________ Date ______________

Reading Comprehension

Each numbered sentence in the following passage contains an italicized vocabulary word or related form. After you read the passage, you will complete an exercise.

Test-Tube Skin

Double disaster hit the Selby family on July 1, 1983. Glen Selby, six, and his brother Jamie, five, were burned over nearly 97 percent of their bodies. (1) Both suffered the most ***acute*** kind of burn, which is known as "third-degree" because all three layers of skin are injured.

Until recently, such injuries were almost always fatal. (2) A body simply could not ***endure*** what followed. Shock always hit. (3) In addition, the already weakened body became infected by anything ***contagious*** in the air. The few who did survive faced lives of extreme pain. (4) Although not victims of ***paralysis,*** they often moved stiffly because of skin or muscle damage.

(5) Today, however, the Selby boys are ***thriving.*** (6) Their successful ***convalescence*** is due to speedier and safer skin-graft techniques. (7) This development is ***soothing*** news for the families of burn victims as well as for the victims themselves.

Grafting is the attaching of one part of a living thing onto another. When skin is grafted, healthy skin replaces damaged skin. (8) Since most bodies are ***allergic*** to "foreign" parts, doctors now use the victims' own skin. Yet how could they in a case like the Selbys', when so much skin is damaged?

All it took for the Selby boys was the uninjured 3 percent. Tiny scraps of healthy skin were cut off, separated into cells, and bathed in a chemical for fast growth. The new skin was again separated and allowed to grow until there were enough matchbook-size patches to begin covering wounds. The result was a new skin, a bit shinier, pinker, and smoother than the old, but also flexible.

In view of the Selby case, the medical community has good reason to be enthusiastic about skin grafting. When disaster strikes, despair need not follow. (9) ***Clinics*** like the Shriners Burns Institutes are there to help, better and faster than before. (10) Now doctors can truly ***alleviate*** suffering — by giving back normal life.

Reading Comprehension Exercise

Each of the following statements corresponds to a numbered sentence in the passage. Each statement contains a blank and is followed by four answer choices. Decide which choice fits best in the blank. The word or phrase that you choose must express roughly the same meaning as the italicized word in the passage. Write the letter of your choice on the answer line.

1. The Selby boys suffered __?__ burns over most of their bodies. 1. ________
   a. large **b.** severe **c.** scattered **d.** mild

2. Burn victims usually could not __?__ deadly aftereffects. 2. ________
   a. expect **b.** attack **c.** survive **d.** prevent

3. __?__ diseases swiftly attacked an already weakened body. 3. ________
   a. Infectious **b.** Serious **c.** Childhood **d.** Rare

Copyright © 1988 Houghton Mifflin Company. All rights reserved.

4. Stiffness, not __?__, was a common aftereffect in burns. 4. ______
   a. severe aching c. loss of feeling
   b. loss of memory d. increased limpness

5. The Selby boys are now __?__. 5. ______
   a. walking successfully c. giving clinics
   b. continuing treatments d. doing well

6. A new skin-graft technique helped their __?__. 6. ______
   a. recovery b. comfort c. attitude d. appearance

7. Faster and more complete recovery is __?__ news for burn victims and their families. 7. ______
   a. surprising b. comforting c. alarming d. important

8. Patients react __?__ to skin grafts from others. 8. ______
   a. happily b. well c. swiftly d. badly

9. Special __?__ continue to treat victims like the Selbys. 9. ______
   a. hospitals b. meetings c. schools d. students

10. Skin grafting can __?__ suffering and give much hope. 10. ______
   a. shorten b. treat c. lessen d. improve

Practice with Analogies

An analogy compares word pairs that are related in some way. An analogy can be expressed in a sentence or with colons (the single colon means "is to" and the double colon means "as").

Fast is to quick as start is to begin.
FAST : QUICK : : start : begin

STRATEGY To complete an analogy, find the relationship between the words in the first pair. The second pair must have the same relationship. *Quick* is a synonym for *fast,* and *start* is a synonym for *begin.* The relationship is word/synonym. Here are some other relationships.

See pages 52 and 86 for some other strategies to use with analogies.

RELATIONSHIP	EXAMPLE
word/antonym	generous : stingy
class/member of class	horse : Clydesdale
size	pond : ocean
cause/effect	virus : illness
worker/place of work	mechanic : garage

DIRECTIONS On the answer line, write the vocabulary word that completes each analogy.

1. Energy is to energetic as allergy is to __?__. 1. ______
2. Cease is to stop as __?__ is to flourish. 2. ______
3. Rejoice is to grieve as __?__ is to upset. 3. ______
4. Pledge is to promise as lessen is to __?__. 4. ______
5. Actor is to theater and doctor is to __?__. 5. ______
6. Weight lifter is to strength as runner is to __?__. 6. ______

Copyright © Houghton Mifflin Company. All rights reserved.

Lesson 6

The Roots *-vid-* and *-vis-*

Lesson 6 WORD LIST

This is the first of several lessons on word roots. Most roots in English come from two languages, Latin or early Greek. The roots *-vid-* and *-vis-* are two forms of the Latin word meaning "to see." Words containing "view" are also related to the same Latin ancestor. They branched off from a French form of *-vid-*.

You are already familiar with many words stemming from this lesson's roots. For example, what does a good *provider* see to? If your *vision* is poor, which sense is in trouble? Why does a jury need to see *evidence?* Why are graphs and charts called *visual aids?*

To get the most out of this lesson, look closely at each word's parts and also at the kind of seeing defined. What kind of "sight" is involved: eyesight? foresight? insight? Does the list refer to a viewer or to a view? Does it suggest an actual picture or a mental picture? Does it deal with eyes or ideas?

WORD LIST
- improvise
- revision
- video
- viewpoint
- visible
- visionary
- visor
- vista
- visual
- visualize

DEFINITIONS

After you have studied the definitions and example for each vocabulary word, write the word on the line to the right.

1. **improvise** (ĭm′prə-vīz′) *verb* To make up, invent, or perform on the spot. 1. ____________

   RELATED WORD **improvisation** *noun*

   EXAMPLE Given only three notes, Grace can *improvise* a melody on the piano in five minutes.

2. **revision** (rĭ-vĭzh′ən) *noun* **a.** A corrected or improved version, especially of written work. **b.** A change. 2. ____________

   RELATED WORD **revise** *verb*

   EXAMPLE Does this *revision* of the travel guide have up-to-date food and hotel prices?

3. **video** (vĭd′ē-ō′) *adjective* Relating to the picture part of television. *noun* **a.** Television. **b.** The picture part of a television program. 3. ____________

   EXAMPLE The *video* controls are under the volume button.

Copyright © 1988 Houghton Mifflin Company. All rights reserved.

4. **viewpoint** (vyo͞o'point') *noun* A particular way of looking or thinking about something; point of view. 4. ______

EXAMPLE The "Letters" section of a newspaper is a good place to find differing, even clashing, *viewpoints* on a topic.

5. **visible** (vĭz'ə-bəl) *adjective* **a.** Capable of being seen. **b.** Easily noticed; clear; apparent. 5. ______

RELATED WORDS **visibility** *noun;* **visibly** *adverb*

EXAMPLE The planet Venus is *visible* without a telescope.

6. **visionary** (vĭzh'ə-nĕr'ē) *adjective* **a.** Imaginary; fanciful. **b.** Able to see beyond the present. *noun* A dreamer; someone who can see beyond the present. 6. ______

RELATED WORD **vision** *noun*

EXAMPLE Was Henry Ford's timing of the Model T car *visionary* or just plain lucky?

7. **visor** (vī'zər) *noun* **a.** Something that sticks out, such as on a cap or windshield, to protect the eyes. **b.** The movable part of a helmet. 7. ______

EXAMPLE Most cars today have tinted glass instead of a *visor.*

8. **vista** (vĭs'tə) *noun* **a.** A distant or far-reaching view, especially one seen through an opening. **b.** A mental view of a series of events. 8. ______

EXAMPLE The barn opened onto an endless *vista* of ripe wheat.

9. **visual** (vĭzh'o͞o-əl) *adjective* **a.** Relating to the sense of sight. **b.** Done by means of vision. 9. ______

RELATED WORD **visually** *adverb*

EXAMPLE "Always maintain *visual* contact with your audience," advised the acting coach.

10. **visualize** (vĭzh'o͞o-ə-līz') *verb* To form a mental picture of. 10. ______

RELATED WORD **visualization** *noun*

EXAMPLE Try to *visualize* a finished photo before taking it.

Copyright © 1988 Houghton Mifflin Company. All rights reserved.

Name ______________________________ Date ____________

Exercise 1 Completing Definitions

On the answer line, write the word from the vocabulary list that best completes each definition.

1. A corrected or changed version of something is a __?__. 1. ________
2. A hat brim to protect the eyes from weather is a __?__. 2. ________
3. Something that relates to the sense of sight is said to be __?__. 3. ________
4. Something imaginary, especially if related to the future, is __?__. 4. ________
5. The picture is the __?__ part of a telecast. 5. ________
6. To see something in your mind is to __?__ it. 6. ________
7. Something that is easily seen is __?__. 7. ________
8. To create something on the spot is to __?__ it. 8. ________
9. Your way of looking at something is your __?__. 9. ________
10. A distant or far-reaching view is a __?__. 10. ________

Exercise 2 Using Words Correctly

Decide whether the italicized vocabulary word has been used correctly in the sentence. On the answer line, write *Correct* for correct use and *Incorrect* for incorrect use.

1. When saluting, the nervous recruit knocked his *vista* sideways. 1. ________
2. Nothing beyond the car hood was *visible* in the fog. 2. ________
3. Adjust the *video* controls; the sound is breaking my eardrums! 3. ________
4. Binoculars and telescopes are *visual* aids. 4. ________
5. *Visionaries* who spoke of human flight were once thought mad. 5. ________
6. Usually the *revision* of a paper comes before the outline. 6. ________
7. When I like a book, I *visualize* myself as its hero. 7. ________
8. Draw a straight line to connect the three *viewpoints.* 8. ________
9. To build a model, check the pieces and *improvise* each step. 9. ________
10. The knight breathed and saw through slits in his *visor.* 10. ________

Exercise 3 Choosing the Best Word

Decide which vocabulary word or related form best completes the sentence, and write the letter of your choice on the answer line.

1. The talk-show host invited __?__ different from her own. 1. ________
   a. revisions **b.** videos **c.** vistas **d.** viewpoints

Copyright © 1988 Houghton Mifflin Company. All rights reserved.

2. In the background of the portrait was a mountain __?__. 2. ______
a. vista b. visual c. visionary d. improvisation

3. Shelly entertained us by __?__ cymbals from pot lids. 3. ______
a. visualizing b. improvising c. revising d. visionary

4. After checking his paper, Andy made only one __?__. 4. ______
a. revision b. video c. visor d. viewpoint

5. The practical Ben Franklin also had a __?__ side. 5. ______
a. video b. visible c. visionary d. revised

6. Skilled plastic surgeons leave barely __?__ scars. 6. ______
a. visible b. visionary c. visual d. improvised

7. Jill found it hard to __?__ the scene described in the book. 7. ______
a. revise b. visualize c. visible d. improvise

8. The motorcycle officer raised her __?__ and said, "License?" 8. ______
a. video b. visor c. viewpoint d. visionary

9. Smoke signals are a form of __?__ communication. 9. ______
a. visionary b. improvised c. revised d. visual

10. Can you name someone who is a stage, screen, and __?__ star? 10. ______
a. visionary b. visual c. visible d. video

Exercise 4 Using Different Forms of Words

Decide which form of the vocabulary word in parentheses best completes the sentence. The form given may be correct. Write your answer on the answer line.

1. Courses in __?__ are required in acting school. *(improvise)* 1. ______
2. That cover is __?__ superb, but is the book any good? *(visual)* 2. ______
3. Let's consider other __?__ before taking a vote. *(viewpoint)* 3. ______
4. Hal __?__ camp life in an unrealistic way. *(visualize)* 4. ______
5. Shana's skiing improved __?__ over vacation. *(visible)* 5. ______
6. When clouds parted, breathtaking __?__ appeared. *(vista)* 6. ______
7. Something is wrong with the __?__ part of the television set. *(video)* 7. ______
8. The work helmet had a __?__ from forehead to chin. *(visor)* 8. ______
9. Mrs. Waugh, do you think I should __?__ my poem? *(revision)* 9. ______
10. The Panama Canal took great __?__, then hard work. *(visionary)* 10. ______

Copyright © 1988 Houghton Mifflin Company. All rights reserved.

Name ________________________________ Date ____________

Reading Comprehension

Each numbered sentence in the following passage contains an italicized vocabulary word or related form. After you read the passage, you will complete an exercise.

Georgia O'Keeffe: American Artist

In 1899, when twelve, Georgia O'Keeffe blurted out to a friend, "I'm going to be an artist." (1) She never ***revised*** those words. (2) Today, the world of the ***visual*** arts is richer for it.

In 1887, the year O'Keeffe was born, the Senate denied women the right to vote. By law or custom, other rights were also denied. (3) Then, for example, a career as a female artist was nearly unthinkable, even for a ***visionary.***

In life and art, however, O'Keeffe had a talent for being different. (4) She ***visualized*** a bold style and pursued her dream.

In her twenties, when teaching art in Texas, O'Keeffe fell in love with the Southwest. (5) Its wide-open ***vistas,*** bold sun, and sharp contrasts matched her own style. Later in life she would call New Mexico home.

Life in Texas left its mark on her. (6) The young teacher would paint for hours under the hot sun, unprotected by umbrella or sun ***visor.*** Not surprisingly, her painting became flooded with light and seemed larger than life.

O'Keeffe's art falls into groups. (7) Not ***improvisations,*** her paintings are products of what the artist herself referred to as her "single-track mind. I work on an idea for a long time. It's like getting acquainted . . . and I don't get acquainted easily." When in New York, she painted many skyscrapers and, to make busy New Yorkers notice, huge flowers. Notice they did. In 1923 a series of six lilies fetched an unheard-of $25,000.

Changing times were mirrored in changing topics: skyscrapers, flowers, bones, roads, clouds, and — as sight dimmed — shadows.

The sale of the lilies set a lifelong pattern of high pricing. O'Keeffe and her husband hated to part with their "children" and would ask awesome rates to discourage buyers they disliked. Still, the paintings sold.

(8) Valuing privacy, the artist kept personal ***visibility*** low. (9) She accepted only a few offers to exhibit or to appear on ***video*** specials, all the while continuing to paint and to encourage young artists.

(10) O'Keeffe's unusual ***viewpoint*** was consistent with her high standards. She once destroyed forty paintings with "Of course I destroy my old paintings. Do you keep all your old hats?"

Like her art, O'Keeffe was a truly American original. She died in 1986, at the age of ninety-eight.

Please turn to the next page.

Copyright © 1988 Houghton Mifflin Company. All rights reserved.

Reading Comprehension Exercise

Each of the following statements corresponds to a numbered sentence in the passage. Each statement contains a blank and is followed by four answer choices. Decide which choice fits best in the blank. The word or phrase that you choose must express roughly the same meaning as the italicized word in the passage. Write the letter of your choice on the answer line.

1. Georgia O'Keeffe never __?__ her early career plans. 1. ________
   a. changed **b.** found **c.** knew **d.** lost

2. The world of the __?__ arts has been enriched. 2. ________
   a. mechanical **b.** navigational **c.** musical **d.** viewed

3. At that time a career as a female artist was very unusual, even for a __?__. 3. ________
   a. dreamer **c.** wealthy person
   b. professor **d.** gifted person

4. O'Keeffe __?__ a bold personal style. 4. ________
   a. expected **b.** imagined **c.** disliked **d.** feared

5. The __?__ in the Southwest matched O'Keeffe's personality. 5. ________
   a. views **b.** buildings **c.** flowers **d.** tourists

6. Young O'Keeffe painted outside without a(n) __?__. 6. ________
   a. easel **b.** sunshade **c.** audience **d.** care

7. Her carefully produced paintings were not __?__. 7. ________
   a. popular **c.** done without planning
   b. expensive **d.** well planned

8. The artist kept personal __?__ low. 8. ________
   a. appearances **b.** reviews **c.** sightseeing **d.** needs

9. She rarely appeared on __?__ programs. 9. ________
   a. art **b.** television **c.** western **d.** foreign

10. O'Keeffe's __?__ may be considered a little unusual. 10. ________
    a. personality **b.** prices **c.** outlook **d.** career

Writing Assignment

Imagine that you are a famous artist or crafter and that a reporter is interviewing you for the local newspaper. She says, "Tell us something about the way you work." Using five words from this lesson, write a paragraph in which you explain your method of working. Underline each word that you use.

Copyright © 1988 Houghton Mifflin Company. All rights reserved.

Name ______________________ Date ______________

Dictionary Skills

Finding the Right Definition

Many words listed in a dictionary have more than one definition. When you look up a word, you must decide which definition best fits the sentence in which you heard or read the word. Here are two strategies to help you choose the right definition.

STRATEGIES

1. *Read all of the definitions in an entry.* In order to find the right definition, you need to know all of the possibilities. Suppose you came across the word *dissolution* in this sentence:

   After the *dissolution* of their partnership, Mr. Jones and Mr. LaSalle each went into business for himself.

   First you would find the word in a dictionary and read each of the three definitions.

   dis•so•lu•tion (dĭs′ə-lo͞o′shən) *n.* **1.** The act or process of breaking up into parts; disintegration. **2.** An act of ending a formal or legal bond or tie; annulment; termination: *dissolution of a contract; dissolution of a marriage.* **3.** The act or process of changing from a solid to a liquid.

2. *Read the sentence to yourself, substituting each definition for the word in question.* Include only important words in each definition. Your second such sentence is the only one that would make sense: "After the *ending of the formal bond* of their partnership, Mr. Jones and Mr. LaSalle each went into business for himself." The second definition is therefore the right one.

Exercise Finding the Right Definition

Using dictionary entries at the end of this exercise, write the correct definition of the italicized word in each of the following sentences. Then write a sentence of your own in which you use the word according to the same definition.

1. He will reach his *majority* next year.

   DEFINITION ______________________

   SENTENCE ______________________

Please turn to the next page.

Copyright © 1988 Houghton Mifflin Company. All rights reserved.

2. At our school girls are in the *majority*.

DEFINITION ______________________________

SENTENCE ______________________________

3. The carving Grandmother gave my parents is *exquisite*.

DEFINITION ______________________________

SENTENCE ______________________________

4. He detected the wrong notes because of his *exquisite* ear for music.

DEFINITION ______________________________

SENTENCE ______________________________

5. The gloves were designed *expressly* for very cold weather.

DEFINITION ______________________________

SENTENCE ______________________________

6. The baby sitter *expressly* told Judy to stay in the house.

DEFINITION ______________________________

SENTENCE ______________________________

7. The elderly *couple* were loved by everyone in the neighborhood.

DEFINITION ______________________________

SENTENCE ______________________________

8. You will succeed if you *couple* imagination and dedication.

DEFINITION ______________________________

SENTENCE ______________________________

cou•ple (kŭp′əl) *n.* **1.** Two things of the same kind; a pair. **2.** A man and woman united in some way, as by marriage. **3.** *Informal.* A small but indefinite number; a few; several: *a couple of days.* —*v.* **cou•pled, cou•pling. 1.** To link together; attach; join: *couple cars of a train. Intelligence coupled with hard work accounted for her success.* **2.** To link (physical systems, especially electric circuits) so that energy is transferred from one to the other.

ex•press•ly (ĭk-sprĕs′lē) *adv.* **1.** Especially; particularly: *a ship designed expressly for exploring the Arctic waters.* **2.** Without any doubt; definitely; plainly; explicitly: *The rules expressly forbid it.*

ex•qui•site (ĕk′skwĭz-ĭt) *or* (ĭk-skwĭz′ĭt) *adj.* **1.** Of special beauty, charm, elegance, etc.: *an exquisite vase.* **2.** Intense; keen: *He takes exquisite pleasure in his meals.* **3.** Keenly sensitive; discriminating: *She has exquisite taste in art.* **—ex′qui•site•ly** *adv.*

ma•jor•i•ty (mə-jôr′ĭ-tē) *or* (-jŏr′-) *n., pl.* **ma•jor•i•ties. 1.** The greater number or part of something; a number more than half of a total: *the majority of the class.* **2.** The excess of a greater number over a smaller number; margin: *won by a majority of 5,000 votes.* **3.** The status of having reached the age of legal responsibility.

 Copyright © Houghton Mifflin Company. All rights reserved.

Lesson 7

Movement

Lesson 7 WORD LIST

Words are like broadcasting systems. A poor system sends weak signals. The better the system, the stronger the signal. Well-chosen words send strong signals and clear messages that listeners or readers can receive without difficulty.

A sharply focused word leaves a strong impression. As you compare the choices in the following sentences, ask yourself which word or phrase is more vivid.

> A horse *goes/gallops.*
> The ballerina *danced/spun.*
> I *sat/slumped* in my seat.

Like the verbs above, most words in this lesson are vivid. Try picturing the movements described in some of them. Which words are the easiest to see in your mind?

WORD LIST

brisk
fleet
linger
mingle
nimble
perpetual
saunter
scurry
stride
totter

DEFINITIONS

After you have studied the definitions and example for each vocabulary word, write the word on the line to the right.

1. **brisk** (brĭsk) *adjective* **a.** Lively; energetic. **b.** Sharp or keen in speech or manner. **c.** Refreshing. 1. ______________

   RELATED WORDS **briskly** *adverb;* **briskness** *noun*

   EXAMPLE My grandparents take a *brisk* walk every evening.

2. **fleet** (flēt) *adjective* Moving swiftly; rapid. *noun* A group of vehicles, such as taxis or fishing boats. 2. ______________

   RELATED WORD **fleetness** *noun*

   EXAMPLE Gazelles and cheetahs are *fleet* animals.

3. **linger** (lĭng′gər) *verb* **a.** To delay in leaving. **b.** To remain alive; last. 3. ______________

   RELATED WORD **lingeringly** *adverb*

   EXAMPLE The movie's ending *lingered* in my mind.

4. **mingle** (mĭng′gəl) *verb* **a.** To become mixed or blended. **b.** To mix in or join with others. 4. ______________

   EXAMPLE The smells of pine and lilies *mingled* in the air.

Copyright © 1988 Houghton Mifflin Company. All rights reserved.

5. **nimble** (nĭm′bəl) *adjective* **a.** Moving quickly and lightly. **b.** Clever; quick-thinking. 5. ____________

RELATED WORDS **nimbleness** *noun;* **nimbly** *adverb*

EXAMPLE Speed typists must have *nimble* fingers.

6. **perpetual** (pər-pĕch′o͞o-əl) *adjective* **a.** Continuing without interruption; constant. **b.** Lasting a very long time or forever. 6. ____________

RELATED WORD **perpetually** *adverb*

EXAMPLE Mosquitoes are a *perpetual* nuisance to summer campers.

7. **saunter** (sôn′tər) *verb* To walk in a relaxed and carefree way; stroll. 7. ____________

EXAMPLE Under a lazy summer sun, children played in the sand, and couples *sauntered* along the beach.

8. **scurry** (skûr′ē) *verb* To run hurriedly; scamper. 8. ____________

EXAMPLE Hearing steps, the quail chicks *scurried* for cover.

MEMORY CUE *Scurry* suggests *hurry.*

9. **stride** (strīd) *noun* **a.** A long step or the distance covered in such a step. **b.** A step forward; an advance. *verb* To walk energetically and with long steps. 9. ____________

EXAMPLE A toddler must run to keep up with an adult's *stride.*

10. **totter** (tŏt′ər) *verb* **a.** To sway as if about to fall. **b.** To walk unsteadily. **c.** To seem about to collapse. 10. ____________

RELATED WORD **tottery** *adjective*

EXAMPLE Babies learning to walk *totter* whenever they stand.

Copyright © Houghton Mifflin Company. All rights reserved.

Name ______________________________ Date ____________

Exercise 1 Matching Words and Definitions

Match the definition in Column B with the word in Column A. Write the letter of the correct definition on the answer line.

Column A	Column B
1. perpetual	a. to stroll
2. linger	b. to sway as if about to fall; walk unsteadily
3. mingle	c. to run hurriedly; scamper
4. brisk	d. moving swiftly; rapid
5. nimble	e. continuing without interruption; constant
6. fleet	f. a long step; a step forward
7. totter	g. lively; sharp; refreshing
8. saunter	h. to delay in leaving
9. scurry	i. moving quickly and lightly
10. stride	j. to mix or blend; join in

1. ________
2. ________
3. ________
4. ________
5. ________
6. ________
7. ________
8. ________
9. ________
10. ________

Exercise 2 Using Words Correctly

Each of the following questions contains an italicized vocabulary word. Choose the correct answer to the question, and write *Yes* or *No* on the answer line.

1. At 95°F is the air *brisk?* 1. ________
2. Do firefighters *saunter* to a fire? 2. ________
3. Can whales *stride?* 3. ________
4. Do good hosts *mingle* with their guests? 4. ________
5. Are magicians *fleet* of hand? 5. ________
6. Is a dizzy person likely to *totter?* 6. ________
7. Are gymnasts *nimble?* 7. ________
8. Can lightning *linger?* 8. ________
9. Is the movement of the earth *perpetual?* 9. ________
10. Can a glacier *scurry?* 10. ________

Exercise 3 Choosing the Best Word

Decide which vocabulary word or related form best expresses the meaning of the italicized word or phrase in the sentence. On the answer line, write the letter of the correct choice.

1. Shall we *stroll* through the park? 1. ________
   a. stride **b.** saunter **c.** totter **d.** mingle

Copyright © 1988 Houghton Mifflin Company. All rights reserved.

2. A good lawyer must have a *quick and clever* mind. 2. ________
a. tottery b. fleet c. nimble d. brisk

3. Away the kitten *scampered,* chasing a tennis ball. 3. ________
a. sauntered b. strode c. scurried d. lingered

4. The elderly woman answered the reporter's questions in a *lively* way. 4. ________
a. brisk b. perpetual c. lingering d. scurry

5. Adam *swayed as if about to fall* on his new skates. 5. ________
a. sauntered b. lingered c. scurried d. tottered

6. Marathon runners need endurance; sprinters need *swiftness.* 6. ________
a. fleetness b. briskness c. strides d. nimbleness

7. Stew should simmer for a long time so that its flavors *blend.* 7. ________
a. linger b. scurry c. mingle d. saunter

8. Because they grow so quickly, puppies are *constantly* hungry. 8. ________
a. perpetually b. lingeringly c. nimbly d. briskly

9. One pool rule is "No *staying around* after dark." 9. ________
a. lingering b. mingling c. sauntering d. tottering

10. Penicillin was a huge *advance* in the battle against infection. 10. ________
a. saunter b. totter c. stride d. fleet

Exercise 4 Using Different Forms of Words

Decide which form of the vocabulary word in parentheses best completes the sentence. The form given may be correct. Write your answer on the answer line.

1. Clocked at 65 mph, the cheetah is known for its __?__. *(fleet)* 1. ________
2. All of the runners __?__ cleared the first hurdle. *(nimble)* 2. ________
3. Little Katie glanced __?__ at the toy store window. *(linger)* 3. ________
4. Sea travel makes some people weak and __?__. *(totter)* 4. ________
5. Faking confidence, Dana __?__ up to the microphone. *(stride)* 5. ________
6. Sometimes __?__ seems a little like rudeness. *(brisk)* 6. ________
7. Instead of running, the thief __?__ with the crowd. *(mingle)* 7. ________
8. The heart __?__ pumps blood throughout the body. *(perpetual)* 8. ________
9. __?__ through the desert preserve, they saw many kinds of cacti. *(saunter)* 9. ________
10. "__?__," Dad yelled, "or you'll miss the bus!" *(scurry)* 10. ________

Copyright © 1988 Houghton Mifflin Company. All rights reserved.

Name ______________________________ Date ____________

Reading Comprehension

Each numbered sentence in the following passage contains an italicized vocabulary word or related form. After you read the passage, you will complete an exercise.

Smokejumpers: Airborne Firefighters

(1) Since the days of the bucket brigade, great ***strides*** have been made in firefighting. Most colonial firefighters were volunteers. Today's firefighters are professionals and even specialists. Among the most specialized are smokejumpers — those who fight forest fires.

(2) Not everyone is willing to jump from a low-flying plane, land near a raging fire, and ***scurry*** to put it out. It takes a special breed of person.

The most important requirement for being a smokejumper is excellent physical condition. Endurance and strength are absolutely necessary. Trainees must also learn wilderness survival and advanced firefighting techniques.

(3) Since they often land in thickly forested areas, smokejumpers face the ***perpetual*** problem of tangled parachute lines. (4) It takes ***nimbleness*** to free oneself from treetops.

Smokejumpers must also be able to work alone. (5) While the city firefighter is backed by a whole ***fleet*** of support vehicles, a smokejumper patrols long stretches of forest on foot, carrying up to a hundred pounds of special equipment.

(6) Although a forest fire may seem to die, it can ***linger***. (7) Small fires must be kept from ***mingling*** with nearby brush. (8) In an already dry area, a ***brisk*** wind can quickly fan a blazing bonfire. (9) Smokejumpers must race, not ***saunter***, from one checkpoint to the next.

Even after a fire is dead, smokejumpers are not out of danger. They must still find their way out of the wilderness. (10) Often, almost numb with exhaustion, they ***totter*** into pickup points and collapse.

For anyone who has wanted to be an athlete, skydiver, explorer, and firefighter, smokejumping is the perfect career.

Please turn to the next page.

Copyright © 1988 Houghton Mifflin Company. All rights reserved.

Reading Comprehension Exercise

Each of the following statements corresponds to a numbered sentence in the passage. Each statement contains a blank and is followed by four answer choices. Decide which choice fits best in the blank. The word or phrase that you choose must express roughly the same meaning as the italicized word in the passage. Write the letter of your choice on the answer line.

1. Since colonial days, great __?__ have been made in firefighting. 1. ________
   a. profits b. advances c. discoveries d. mistakes

2. Smokejumpers must land near a fire and __?__ to put it out. 2. ________
   a. fight bravely c. move ahead
   b. plan carefully d. run hurriedly

3. Catching parachute lines in trees is a(n) __?__ problem. 3. ________
   a. constant b. annoying c. everyday d. confusing

4. It takes __?__ to get untangled from a treetop landing. 4. ________
   a. high intelligence c. ability to think and move quickly
   b. brute strength d. fancy footwork

5. The city firefighter is often backed by a support __?__. 5. ________
   a. group b. engine c. ladder d. ambulance

6. A seemingly dead forest fire can __?__. 6. ________
   a. smoke b. stay alive c. go underground d. jump

7. The __?__ of small fires and bushes may spell disaster. 7. ________
   a. growing b. mixing c. touching d. smoking

8. A(n) __?__ wind can turn a small fire into an enormous blaze. 8. ________
   a. icy b. light c. active d. sudden

9. Fires move fast, and smokejumpers cannot simply __?__ from one point to the next. 9. ________
   a. walk b. stroll c. move d. parachute

10. As they reach the pickup point, smokejumpers often __?__. 10. ________
    a. get a second wind c. write reports
    b. take great strides d. seem to stumble

Writing Assignment

Imagine that you are participating in a national or international sports event. Write a letter to a friend in which you tell about the part of the event that was most important to you. Use at least five words from this lesson and underline each one.

Copyright © 1988 Houghton Mifflin Company. All rights reserved.

Lesson 8

Appearance and Texture

A single word can mean very different things, depending on context. For example, the word *rough* describes different qualities when applied to movement, gems, and cloth. Horseplay is always *rough.* A diamond is *rough* only before it is cut and polished. Wool does not start out *rough* but may end up that way. So, depending on context, *rough* may mean "rowdy," "natural," or "scratchy"!

Like *rough,* many words about appearance and texture lead double lives. For example, three list words answer these riddles:

How is a *dull knife* like a *sharp tongue?* Both are __?__.
How is *rock salt* like *bad manners?* Both are __?__.
How is our *sun* like a *big smile?* Both are __?__.

If the answers have not already come to you, read on.

WORD LIST
blunt
coarse
dense
dingy
iridescent
opaque
radiant
sheen
tinge
transparent

DEFINITIONS

After you have studied the definitions and example for each vocabulary word, write the word on the line to the right.

1. **blunt** (blŭnt) *adjective* **a.** Not sharp or pointed; dull-edged. **b.** Straightforward, even cutting (as a remark). *verb* **a.** To make dull. **b.** To weaken.

   RELATED WORDS **bluntly** *adverb;* **bluntness** *noun*

   EXAMPLE The knife was too *blunt* to slice tomatoes.

   1. ______________

2. **coarse** (kôrs) *adjective* **a.** Not fine in texture. **b.** Rough; scratchy; harsh. **c.** Impolite in manner or speech; crude.

   RELATED WORDS **coarsely** *adverb;* **coarseness** *noun*

   EXAMPLE "Which kind of sandpaper do you want," asked the salesperson, "extra fine, fine, medium, or *coarse?*"

   2. ______________

   MEMORY CUE *Coarse* is an adjective. *Course* is a noun: "As the main *course,* we had a delicious salad made from *coarse* wheat."

3. **dense** (dĕns) *adjective* **a.** Very thick. **b.** Tightly packed together; crowded. **c.** Thickheaded; stupid.

   RELATED WORDS **densely** *adverb;* **density** *noun*

   EXAMPLE Anyone hiking in a *dense* forest should always carry a compass because landmarks are difficult to spot.

   3. ______________

Copyright © 1988 Houghton Mifflin Company. All rights reserved.

4. **dingy** (dĭn′jē) *adjective* **a.** Dirty; grimy. **b.** Dull; dreary. 4. ____________

RELATED WORD **dinginess** *noun*

EXAMPLE The puppy's favorite place to sleep was a cardboard box with a *dingy* old blanket.

5. **iridescent** (ĭr′ĭ-dĕs′ənt) *adjective* Having shiny and rainbowlike colors. 5. ____________

RELATED WORD **iridescence** *noun*

EXAMPLE Many butterflies have jewel-like, *iridescent* wings.

6. **opaque** (ō-pāk′) *adjective* **a.** Not letting light through. **b.** Unclear or muddled, as a piece of writing. 6. ____________

RELATED WORDS **opacity** *noun;* **opaquely** *adverb*

EXAMPLE Plaster walls, aluminum foil, and heavy window shades are all *opaque;* objects cannot be seen through them.

USAGE NOTE *Opaque* materials do not always block out all light, but they block out enough so that objects on the other side cannot be identified.

7. **radiant** (rā′dē-ənt) *adjective* **a.** Giving out light or heat. **b.** Filled with happiness, joy, or love. **c.** Glowing; bright. 7. ____________

RELATED WORDS **radiance** *noun;* **radiantly** *adverb;* **radiate** *verb;* **radiator** *noun*

EXAMPLE The sun, lamps, hot-water bottles, and heaters are all *radiant* objects.

8. **sheen** (shēn) *noun* Shine; brightness. 8. ____________

EXAMPLE Danny waxed and polished his car until it had a mirrorlike *sheen.*

9. **tinge** (tĭnj) *noun* **a.** A tint; a trace of color. **b.** A hint of feeling, such as jealousy, regret, or sadness. *verb* **a.** To tint. **b.** To affect slightly. 9. ____________

EXAMPLE The red in that raincoat has a *tinge* of orange.

10. **transparent** (trăns-pâr′ənt) *adjective* **a.** Letting light through. **b.** Easily understood; obvious. 10. ____________

RELATED WORDS **transparency** *noun;* **transparently** *adverb*

EXAMPLE Window glass, plastic wrap, and sheer curtains are all *transparent.*

Copyright © 1988 Houghton Mifflin Company. All rights reserved.

Name ______________________________ Date ____________

Exercise 1 Writing Correct Words

On the answer line, write the word from the vocabulary list that fits each definition.

1. Giving out light or heat 1. ____________
2. Dirty or grimy; dull or dreary 2. ____________
3. A hint of color or feeling 3. ____________
4. Having shiny and rainbowlike colors 4. ____________
5. Shine; brightness 5. ____________
6. Not fine in texture; rough, scratchy, or harsh 6. ____________
7. Not letting light through 7. ____________
8. Not sharp or pointed; dull-edged 8. ____________
9. Very thick; tightly packed together; crowded 9. ____________
10. Letting light through 10. ____________

Exercise 2 Using Words Correctly

Decide whether the italicized vocabulary word has been used correctly in the sentence. On the answer line, write *Correct* for correct use and *Incorrect* for incorrect use.

1. The warehouse windows had been painted with an *opaque* paint so that people could not see in. 1. ____________
2. Another word for "teen-ager" is *iridescent.* 2. ____________
3. "Don't be silly," said Jennifer. "Of *coarse* I'll be at the party!" 3. ____________
4. Silks usually have a brighter *sheen* than wools. 4. ____________
5. Jake tried to *blunt* his way through the essay test. 5. ____________
6. Carry a map, compass, and extra food if you plan to go hiking in an area with *dense* forest. 6. ____________
7. That pinpoint star is actually a *radiant* sphere larger than our own sun! 7. ____________
8. Shampoo advertisements usually promise soft, *dingy* hair. 8. ____________
9. We could see shadows of fish beneath the almost *transparent* ice in the brook. 9. ____________
10. Betty felt a strong *tinge* of pain when she sprained her ankle. 10. ____________

Copyright © 1988 Houghton Mifflin Company. All rights reserved.

Exercise 3 Choosing the Best Word

Decide which vocabulary word or related form best expresses the meaning of the italicized word or phrase in the sentence. On the answer line, write the letter of the correct choice.

1. Brass can be treated with a clear coating to keep its *brightness*. 1. ________
   a. iridescence **b.** coarseness **c.** sheen **d.** transparency
2. The jade was so thin that it was almost *letting light through*. 2. ________
   a. transparent **b.** tinged **c.** radiant **d.** opaque
3. Barcelona, Spain, is a *thickly* populated city. 3. ________
   a. coarsely **b.** dingy **c.** densely **d.** bluntly
4. The baby's smile was *full of warmth and light*. 4. ________
   a. dingy **b.** radiant **c.** iridescent **d.** opaque
5. Strawberries give cereal and milk a red *tint*. 5. ________
   a. tinge **b.** radiance **c.** sheen **d.** iridescence
6. Teeth of a chain saw will become *dull* after long, heavy use. 6. ________
   a. dingy **b.** coarse **c.** blunt **d.** tinged
7. No good detective story has an *obvious* solution. 7. ________
   a. opaque **b.** blunt **c.** transparent **d.** iridescent
8. In sunlight an oily puddle has *shiny and rainbowlike* colors. 8. ________
   a. tinged **b.** dense **c.** opaque **d.** iridescent
9. At that beach the sand is *not fine in texture*. 9. ________
   a. dingy **b.** coarse **c.** dense **d.** blunt
10. A century ago, many children labored in *dreary* textile mills. 10. ________
    a. coarse **b.** tinged **c.** radiant **d.** dingy

Exercise 4 Using Different Forms of Words

Decide which form of the vocabulary word in parentheses best completes the sentence. The form given may be correct. Write your answer on the answer line.

1. "Like my hat?" I asked. "Looks silly," Sis said __?__. *(blunt)* 1. ________
2. A population __?__ of fifty people per square mile is low. *(dense)* 2. ________
3. Chrome has a much higher __?__ than rubber. *(sheen)* 3. ________
4. This oil lamp seems to __?__ as much heat as light! *(radiant)* 4. ________
5. Is turquoise blue __?__ with green or vice versa? *(tinge)* 5. ________
6. Mr. DeHoyos said, "Choose your art project material for __?__, not for color." *(opaque)* 6. ________
7. Swearing or other __?__ is not allowed. *(coarse)* 7. ________
8. Diamonds are rated for __?__ as well as for color, size, and cut. *(transparent)* 8. ________

Copyright © 1988 Houghton Mifflin Company. All rights reserved.

Name ______________________________ Date ______________

9. The male peacock's tail feathers have a brilliant __?__. *(iridescent)* 9. ______________

10. Edward Steichen's photos recorded the __?__ of the living conditions of newly arrived immigrants in city slums. *(dingy)* 10. ______________

Reading Comprehension

Each numbered sentence in the following passage contains an italicized vocabulary word or related form. After you read the passage, you will complete an exercise.

Plastic: The Miracle Material

Plastic isn't so much an invention as a series of developments, some planned and some accidental. The birth of the plastics industry is usually dated from the development of Bakelite in 1909. Before then, however, other important products had been produced.

In 1869 John W. Hyatt of Albany, New York, accidentally invented celluloid. He was looking for artificial ivory for billiard balls!

(1) Today's wide choice of ***iridescent*** fabrics has roots in other research. In 1884 a Frenchman had already developed an artificial fiber called "viscose." In time this material would be able to take much brighter dyes than most natural fibers.

In 1908 a Swiss inventor developed cellophane. (2) It is an ancestor of today's ***transparent*** plastics.

The first widely usable plastic got its name from Leo H. Baekland, another New Yorker. He stumbled across Bakelite when looking for a better varnish. The chemist R. W. Seabury pointed out the material's wonderful molding qualities. When heated, it would soften but not melt. When cooled, it would keep any texture given it while hot. (3) A ***coarse*** surface in the mold would reappear in reverse on the cooled object. (4) Bakelite would take any shape, from pointed to ***blunt.***

The new plastic would not conduct heat or carry electric current. (5) Bakelite was ideal, then, for products in which ***radiant*** heat or electric shock was a problem. Some kitchen appliances and telephones are still made of Bakelite or related materials.

(6) The first plastics were ***opaque.*** By the mid-1930s, however, technology had made use of early discoveries and produced clear plastics.

Researchers developed many different types of plastic before they discovered its inner structure. (7) We now know that plastic is made up of huge chains of ***densely*** packed atomic particles, called "polymers." These polymers are what make plastic so strong.

(8) The ***dingy*** laboratories of early researchers are a far cry from today's modern facilities and their achievements. (9) The next time you marvel at the ***sheen*** of a new car, think of Baekland and the others who made plastics possible. (10) Let your wonder be ***tinged*** with admiration for all their work.

Reading Comprehension Exercise

Each of the following statements corresponds to a numbered sentence in the passage. Each statement contains a blank and is followed by four answer choices. Decide which choice fits best in the blank. The word or phrase that you choose must express roughly the same meaning as the italicized word in the passage. Write the letter of your choice on the answer line.

1. Today there is a wide choice of __?__ artificial fabrics. 1. ______________
   a. rainbowlike **b.** youthful **c.** cheap **d.** dreary

Copyright © 1988 Houghton Mifflin Company. All rights reserved.

2. Cellophane was an early __?__ plastic. 2. ______
a. lightweight b. see-through c. heavy d. colorful

3. Even __?__ surfaces could be molded in Bakelite. 3. ______
a. painted b. shiny c. slippery d. rough

4. It could be easily molded into shapes with pointed or __?__ edges. 4. ______
a. different b. thin c. sharp d. flat

5. Bakelite was ideal for products in which __?__ heat was a problem. 5. ______
a. glowing b. gas c. decreasing d. oil

6. Early plastics did not __?__. 6. ______
a. let light through
b. feel smooth to the touch
c. conduct electricity
d. offer protection from fire

7. Polymers are chains of __?__ packed atomic particles. 7. ______
a. loosely b. slowly c. closely d. carefully

8. Today's laboratories are very different from the __?__ workrooms of early experimenters. 8. ______
a. cheerful b. dreary c. old-fashioned d. city

9. The __?__ of a new car has been made possible by research in plastics. 9. ______
a. price b. appearance c. glossiness d. texture

10. Let your wonder be __?__ with admiration for the work of these scientists. 10. ______
a. multiplied b. colored c. underlined d. divided

Practice with Analogies

STRATEGY Watch out for reversed elements in analogies.

See pages 32 and 86 for some other strategies to use with analogies.

INCORRECT Tree is to leaf as hoof is to horse.
CORRECT Tree is to leaf as horse is to hoof.

DIRECTIONS On the answer line, write the letter of the phrase that best completes the analogy. Some of the items use the strategy above.

1. Tinge is to tint as 1. ______
(A) royal is to king (B) hue is to shade (C) paint is to brush
(D) incorrect is to inaccurate

2. Dense is to thick as 2. ______
(A) wild is to tame (B) doctor is to stethoscope
(C) genuine is to fake (D) commonplace is to ordinary

3. Tight is to loose as 3. ______
(A) blunt is to sharp (B) curtain is to opaque
(C) coarse is to scratchy (D) dingy is to grimy

4. Sandpaper is to rough as 4. ______
(A) smooth is to glass (B) warm is to cold (C) glass is to smooth
(D) ice is to water

5. Dingy is to filthy as 5. ______
(A) black is to white (B) clean is to spotless (C) seldom is to often
(D) colt is to horse

Copyright © Houghton Mifflin Company. All rights reserved.

Words from Spanish

Have you ever played WHAT IF? Historians often do. What if Columbus had, as planned, landed in China in 1492? What if Moctezuma II had conquered Cortés in 1520? What if the Spanish Armada had defeated the British navy in 1588? What if France had kept the land between the Mississippi and the Rockies in 1803?

If key events had turned out otherwise, this book might not be in English. It would probably be in either French or Spanish.

Although English did become the language of the United States, Spanish and French have left their marks. Spanish influence is still strong. In this lesson you will learn some Spanish words that have made their way into English.

WORD LIST

bolero
escapade
fiesta
guerrilla
lariat
mesa
mustang
poncho
siesta
stampede

DEFINITIONS

After you have studied the definitions and example for each vocabulary word, write the word on the line to the right.

1. **bolero** (bō-lâr′ō) *noun* **a.** A fast Spanish dance. **b.** The music for a bolero. **c.** A short jacket of Spanish origin, worn open at the front. 1. ____________

   EXAMPLE The steps of the *bolero* include the "walk," the "sudden stop," and several sharp turns done to a snappy triple rhythm.

2. **escapade** (ĕs′kə-pād′) *noun* A carefree or reckless, sometimes illegal, adventure. 2. ____________

   EXAMPLE Adventure lovers will be spellbound by the *escapades* in *A Connecticut Yankee in King Arthur's Court.*

3. **fiesta** (fē-ĕs′tə) *noun* **a.** A festival or religious holiday. **b.** Any celebration. 3. ____________

   EXAMPLE The *fiesta,* which included parades, a banquet, dancing, and games, lasted all weekend.

Copyright © 1988 Houghton Mifflin Company. All rights reserved.

4. **guerrilla** (gə-rĭl′ə) *noun* A member of an unofficial military group that fights an enemy army through threats or sudden raids by small bands, usually with the support of local people. *adjective* Related to the guerrilla style of fighting.

EXAMPLE Some colonial American soldiers were *guerrillas*.

4. ____________

5. **lariat** (lăr′ē-ət) *noun* A long rope with an adjustable loop at one end, used for catching horses and cattle; a lasso.

EXAMPLE Throwing a *lariat* takes strength and practice.

5. ____________

6. **mesa** (mā′sə) *noun* A flat-topped hill or small plateau with steep sides.

EXAMPLE The *mesa* is a common land formation in the American Southwest.

6. ____________

7. **mustang** (mŭs′tăng′) *noun* A wild horse of the North American plains, descended from Spanish horses.

EXAMPLE The *mustang* has much greater strength and endurance than an eastern showhorse.

7. ____________

8. **poncho** (pŏn′chō) *noun* **a.** A blanketlike cloak with a head hole in the center. **b.** A raincoat in the same style.

EXAMPLE A *poncho* can be many things: cloak, blanket, tent, umbrella, or even saddle cloth.

8. ____________

9. **siesta** (sē-ĕs′tə) *noun* **a.** An afternoon rest or nap. **b.** Any nap.

EXAMPLE In southern European and Latin American towns, the air conditioner has not brought an end to the wonderful custom of an afternoon *siesta*.

9. ____________

10. **stampede** (stăm-pēd′) *noun* **a.** A sudden racing of startled animals, especially cattle or horses. **b.** A sudden rush or mass movement of people. *verb* To cause or be in a stampede.

EXAMPLE A bolt of lightning can turn a calmly grazing herd into a deadly *stampede*.

10. ____________

ETYMOLOGY NOTE The Spanish *estampida* ("uproar") comes ultimately from a Germanic word meaning "to stamp"; noise and stamping feet are major elements of a stampede.

Copyright © Houghton Mifflin Company. All rights reserved.

Name ______________________________ Date ____________

Exercise 1 Completing Definitions

On the answer line, write the word from the vocabulary list that best completes the definition.

1. A small plateau with steep sides is a(n) __?__. 1. ________
2. An afternoon rest or nap is a(n) __?__. 2. ________
3. The __?__ is a fast Spanish dance. 3. ________
4. Someone who is a member of an unofficial military group may be a(n) __?__. 4. ________
5. A festival or religious holiday is a(n) __?__. 5. ________
6. A reckless, and sometimes illegal, adventure is a(n) __?__. 6. ________
7. A(n) __?__ is a blanketlike cloak with a head hole. 7. ________
8. Another word for lasso is __?__. 8. ________
9. The sudden racing of a herd of startled animals is a(n) __?__. 9. ________
10. A wild or half-wild North American horse descended from Spanish horses is a(n) __?__. 10. ________

Exercise 2 Using Words Correctly

Decide whether the italicized vocabulary word has been used correctly in the sentence. On the answer line, write *Correct* for correct use and *Incorrect* for incorrect use.

1. The heat made me so sleepy I took a *siesta* instead of biking. 1. ________
2. Tortillas made out of *mesa* flour are the best kind. 2. ________
3. A brilliant display of fireworks marked the end of the *fiesta*. 3. ________
4. Who ordered the hamburger with onions, hot peppers, relish, and *mustang?* 4. ________
5. The zoo had baboons, chimpanzees, and a rare white *guerrilla*. 5. ________
6. Get out your *ponchos;* that cloud means rain! 6. ________
7. Every Sunday, Dad grabs the funnies to catch up on the latest *escapades* of his favorite characters. 7. ________
8. Mom says she gets exhausted just watching the *bolero*. 8. ________
9. The yearly *stampede* of the Nile River turns dry farmland green. 9. ________
10. His *lariat* spinning, the cowhand roped the runaway horse. 10. ________

Copyright © 1988 Houghton Mifflin Company. All rights reserved.

Exercise 3 Choosing the Best Definition

For each italicized vocabulary word in the following sentences, write the letter of the best definition on the answer line.

1. We followed the sounds of dance music to reach the *fiesta*. 1. ________
   a. ballroom **b.** meal **c.** celebration **d.** holiday

2. Sara wore a beautiful handmade *poncho* from Peru. 2. ________
   a. loose dress **b.** felt hat **c.** silver belt **d.** cloak

3. "Here comes the *stampede!*" said a clerk as the store opened. 3. ________
   a. panic **b.** mob **c.** police **d.** beef

4. Pancho Villa, a Mexican *guerrilla*, lived from 1877 until 1923. 4. ________
   a. army captain **b.** bandit **c.** zoo keeper **d.** unofficial soldier

5. Instead of studying, Lenny dreamed of a fishing *escapade*. 5. ________
   a. surprise **b.** adventure **c.** trip **d.** holiday

6. Nan modeled her designer jeans, blouse, and matching *bolero*. 6. ________
   a. Spanish-style hat **b.** shawl **c.** jacket **d.** fan

7. Many Spanish people end the noon meal with an hour-long *siesta*. 7. ________
   a. nap **b.** dessert **c.** swim **d.** exercise period

8. When not in use, a *lariat* hangs looped from the saddlehorn. 8. ________
   a. branding iron **b.** rope **c.** ten-gallon hat **d.** saddlebag

9. It takes weeks of patience to tame a *mustang*. 9. ________
   a. stray dog **b.** wildcat **c.** wild horse **d.** moose

10. Some *mesas* have names, like New Mexico's Mesa Encantada. 10. ________
    a. flat hills **b.** deep canyons **c.** earthquakes **d.** forests

Exercise 4 Using Different Forms of Words

Decide which form of the vocabulary word in parentheses best completes the sentence. The form given may be correct. Write your answer on the answer line.

1. When in Spain, Tom bought several __?__ as gifts. *(bolero)* 1. ________
2. __?__ still roam the western plains. *(mustang)* 2. ________
3. __?__ have many uses on the open range. *(lariat)* 3. ________
4. __?__ are fascinating examples of erosion. *(mesa)* 4. ________
5. Sports tragedies have been caused by __?__, panicky fans. *(stampede)* 5. ________
6. __?__ still play an important role in village life. *(fiesta)* 6. ________
7. For Wu the trip to the theme park was an exciting __?__. *(escapade)* 7. ________
8. After Sunday dinner Dad yawned and said, "Ah, __?__ time." *(siesta)* 8. ________
9. Sudden raids are a feature of __?__ warfare. *(guerrilla)* 9. ________
10. The first __?__ were probably two blankets joined. *(poncho)* 10. ________

Copyright © 1988 Houghton Mifflin Company. All rights reserved.

Name ________________________________ Date ____________

Reading Comprehension

Each numbered sentence in the following passage contains an italicized vocabulary word. After you read the passage, you will complete an exercise.

A Family Inheritance

After my grandmother Rivera died, my mother cried a lot and then took a plane to Mexico City, where my grandmother had been living for the past ten years.

My mother returned to California a week later with greetings from many relatives I had never met and two trunks of things that had belonged to my grandparents.

Mother took Grandma's trunk into her bedroom and left Grandpa's trunk in the living room. (1) She said she was tired and needed to take a ***siesta.***

I was eager to examine the contents of the trunk, as I thought it would help me to know my grandparents better. I had been very young when they lived in California. My mother often told me that my grandparents had lived an exciting life. I wanted to find out for myself.

I opened the trunk that had the initials *E.R.G.*, which stood for Esteban Rivera-Gonzalez, the name of my adventurous grandfather. (2) The first thing I noticed inside the trunk was a large, faded ***poncho.*** I imagined my grandfather wearing it as he rode a horse across his ranch lands. (3) Coiled on top of the poncho was a ***lariat,*** silvered by sun and age. Curious, I reached for it and then I twirled it above my head. (4) How many calves had this lariat pulled off the cliffs of windswept ***mesas?*** (5) How many bucking ***mustangs*** had it tamed?

My imaginings grew wilder. (6) Soon I pictured Grandpa lassoing and stopping longhorn cattle as they ***stampeded*** in his direction. Now, as I picked up a pair of spurs, I could read the letters *E.R.G.* engraved in them. (7) Each new souvenir triggered an exciting ***escapade.*** (8) I could picture a small army of ***guerrillas*** relentlessly chasing Grandpa during his early years as a soldier. Of course, he easily outwitted them. (9) Events in Grandpa's life were jostling one another like people in a noisy crowd at a ***fiesta.*** If only I could picture my grandmother the way I was seeing my grandfather!

Suddenly, somewhere behind me, was the faint whirring of castanets. I spun around. (10) Silhouetted against the window in the early evening twilight was a dancer, frozen in the final pose of the ***bolero!***

This time, my imagination had taken me too far. I remembered the stories my mother had told me — of how my grandmother, as a young woman, had danced the bolero.

"Grandma," I barely dared to whisper.

With castanets held high, the shadowy silhouette turned into the light, becoming a real person — my mother.

"Just me," she said. "You know, Elena, it helps me to look through Grandma's things and remember what an eventful life she led."

I sighed. "I wish I'd had a chance to know her better."

My mother smiled. "You remind me of her," she said, gently taking the spurs from my hand. "Your grandmother Rivera also had a wonderful imagination."

Please turn to the next page.

Copyright © 1988 Houghton Mifflin Company. All rights reserved.

Reading Comprehension Exercise

Each of the following statements corresponds to a numbered sentence in the passage. Each statement contains a blank and is followed by four answer choices. Decide which choice fits best in the blank. The word or phrase that you choose must express roughly the same meaning as the italicized word in the passage. Write the letter of your choice on the answer line.

1. While Mother took a __?__, Elena went through Grandpa Rivera's trunk. 1. ________
   a. break b. message c. snooze d. walk

2. A __?__ was inside the old trunk. 2. ________
   a. silver belt c. hat with a feather
   b. designer sheet d. loose cape

3. At the very top of the trunk was a __?__. 3. ________
   a. wreath b. souvenir c. rope d. snake

4. Had it been used to rescue calves from cliffs of windswept __?__? 4. ________
   a. plateaus b. towers c. canyons d. mountains

5. Had it tamed bucking __?__? 5. ________
   a. sheep b. buffalo c. cattle d. horses

6. Elena imagined Grandpa as he lassoed __?__ longhorn cattle. 6. ________
   a. raging b. valuable c. western d. frightening

7. Each souvenir suggested another __?__. 7. ________
   a. narrow escape c. historical event
   b. heroic act d. wild adventure

8. Next, Elena imagined __?__ running after her grandfather. 8. ________
   a. soldiers b. bandits c. fans d. ranchers

9. In Elena's mind events were as jumbled as bodies in a crowd at a __?__. 9. ________
   a. carnival b. wedding c. theater d. parade

10. Outlined against the window was a woman in a __?__ pose. 10. ________
    a. modeling b. bored c. dance d. dressmaker's

Writing Assignment

Write a paragraph of copy for an advertisement about travel in Mexico or one of the southwestern states. Describe the sights that every tourist should see. In your advertisement use at least five words from this lesson. Underline them or use special printing to emphasize them. If you wish, cut out pictures from magazines or newspaper travel pages to illustrate your paragraph.

Copyright © 1988 Houghton Mifflin Company. All rights reserved.

Name ______________________________ Date ______________

Test-Taking Skills

Synonym Tests

Vocabulary tests often include a section on identifying **synonyms**—words that have nearly the same meaning. *Hole* and *cavity* are synonyms; so are *praise* and *acclaim*. Here are five strategies for taking synonym tests.

STRATEGIES

1. *Read all of the choices before selecting an answer.*
2. *To narrow your choice, eliminate answers that are obviously wrong.*

   Despite the bravery of the firefighters, all efforts to save the forest were *futile*.
   a. successful **b.** obscure **c.** useless **d.** assistance

   Assistance can be eliminated because it is the wrong part of speech—a noun, not an adjective. *Successful* does not make sense in the sentence. With only two choices remaining, you can see that *useless* makes sense in the sentence and is therefore the correct answer.
3. *Do not let an antonym in the answer choices confuse you.* In the sentence about the forest fire, *successful* is an **antonym**—a word that means the opposite of another word.
4. *Watch for choices that have been added to mislead you.* There may be words that sound somewhat like the word in the test item.

   The musicians gave a benefit performance to show their *compassion* for the people made homeless by the earthquake.
   a. synthetic **b.** sympathy **c.** confidence **d.** belief

   Even though *confidence* sounds a bit like *compassion*, it is not the correct answer.
5. *Study the sentence for clues to the correct meaning of the word.*

   He watched the pelican *plummet* from the sky to catch the fish.
   a. swim **b.** dive **c.** roam **d.** climb

   The pelican plummets *from* the sky *to* the water. *Swim* and *climb* cannot be correct. Since *roam* does not make sense in the item, *dive* must be the correct choice.

Please turn to the next page.

Copyright © 1988 Houghton Mifflin Company. All rights reserved.

Exercise **Identifying Synonyms**

Choose the synonym of the italicized word in each sentence. Write the letter of the synonym on the answer line.

1. We watched the mountain goats *ascend* the cliff. 1. ________
   a. hurdle **b.** climb **c.** sturdy **d.** walk
2. The committee did a *prodigious* amount of work on the project. 2. ________
   a. poor **b.** noticeably **c.** immerse **d.** immense
3. The man's *haggard* appearance shocked his friends. 3. ________
   a. hairy **b.** ugly **c.** weird **d.** exhausted
4. The administrator's *judicious* decision pleased everyone. 4. ________
   a. wise **b.** happy **c.** humorous **d.** nasty
5. We got tickets to the rock concert *gratis.* 5. ________
   a. early **b.** easily **c.** free **d.** nearby
6. The personalities of the club members are *diverse.* 6. ________
   a. intelligent **b.** similar **c.** different **d.** colorful
7. Tanya was *commended* for her prize-winning science project. 7. ________
   a. praised **b.** criticized **c.** worried **d.** outstanding
8. The unkind remark *disconcerted* Meredith. 8. ________
   a. self-conscious **b.** embarrassed **c.** amused **d.** harassed
9. On their last night together, the campers sang with *gusto.* 9. ________
   a. eager **b.** enthusiasm **c.** taste **d.** rigor
10. Leslie's eyes were *furtive* as she stole a glance at the hiding place. 10. ________
    a. merry **b.** gloom **c.** miffed **d.** shifty
11. Because time for the meeting was limited, Ms. Murphy gave a *succinct* account of her visit to Big Bend National Park. 11. ________
    a. interesting **b.** long **c.** brief **d.** illustrated
12. Nearly everyone agrees that health care is an issue of *primary* importance. 12. ________
    a. first **b.** little **c.** less **d.** greater
13. Because of poor grades, Calvin's name was *deleted* from the list. 13. ________
    a. lost **b.** omitted **c.** chosen **d.** missing
14. The private investigator's document was placed in the *confidential* files. 14. ________
    a. long-term **b.** short-term **c.** appropriate **d.** secret
15. Although they studied the evidence carefully, the jury members came to an *erroneous* conclusion. 15. ________
    a. correct **b.** incorrect **c.** unclear **d.** surprising

Copyright © 1988 Houghton Mifflin Company. All rights reserved.

Lesson 10

Friends and Foes

Making friends is very important to most of us. We develop qualities that will cause other people to like us. For example, a warm smile and a sympathetic manner are positive qualities that attract friends.

Some people seem to have a natural talent for making friends; others, unfortunately, do not. Often, unfriendly behavior is entirely unintentional. One person may act in an unfriendly or hostile way without realizing that he or she is offending others. Another person may be painfully shy. This quality of shyness may cause the person to avoid others, and such behavior is then misinterpreted as unfriendliness.

The words in this lesson describe both friendly and unfriendly behavior. Learning these words should give you a better understanding of the behavior of the people around you.

WORD LIST
aloof
amiable
antisocial
betray
enmity
recluse
responsive
rival
solitary
treacherous

DEFINITIONS

After you have studied the definitions and example for each vocabulary word, write the word on the line to the right.

1. **aloof** (ə-lo͞of′) *adjective* Reserved; distant, especially in relations with others: *an aloof person.* *adverb* Apart; at a distance but within view: *to stand aloof.*

   RELATED WORD **aloofness** *noun*

   EXAMPLE Most of the class mistook the new student's *aloof* manner for snobbishness.

   1. ____________

2. **amiable** (ā′mē-ə-bəl) *adjective* **a.** Good-natured; friendly. **b.** Pleasant; agreeable: *an amiable group.*

   RELATED WORDS **amiability** *noun;* **amiably** *adverb*

   EXAMPLE *Amiable* people often make good salespersons.

   2. ____________

   USAGE NOTE *Amity*, a related noun meaning "peaceful relations" or "friendship," is an antonym of *enmity* (p. 62).

3. **antisocial** (ăn′tē-sō′shəl) *adjective* **a.** Avoiding the company of others; not social; unfriendly. **b.** Against society: *robbery and other antisocial acts.*

   EXAMPLE Some people who seem *antisocial* may just be very shy or nervous.

   3. ____________

Copyright © Houghton Mifflin Company. All rights reserved.

4. **betray** (bĭ-trā′) *verb* **a.** To commit treason against; be a traitor to: *betray one's country.* **b.** To be disloyal or unfaithful to (a cause or a friend). **c.** To give away; reveal: *Careless errors betrayed haste.* 4. ______

RELATED WORDS **betrayal** *noun;* **betrayer** *noun*

EXAMPLE During World War II, Vidkun Quisling *betrayed* his country and was called a traitor by the people of Norway.

5. **enmity** (ĕn′mĭ-tē) *noun* Deep hatred, as between enemies or bitter opponents; hostility. 5. ______

EXAMPLE In the play *Romeo and Juliet,* long-lasting *enmity* between the Montague and Capulet families causes the death of their children.

MEMORY CUE *En*mity exists between *en*emies; the *n* comes before the *m* in *enmity.*

6. **recluse** (rĕk′lo͞os) *noun* A person who withdraws from society; hermit. 6. ______

RELATED WORD **reclusive** *adjective*

EXAMPLE When he died, very few people knew anything about Howard Hughes except that he was a billionaire and a *recluse.*

7. **responsive** (rĭ-spŏn′sĭv) *adjective* Reacting quickly to a suggestion, request, influence, or problem; sympathetic. 7. ______

RELATED WORDS **respond** *verb;* **response** *noun;* **responsively** *adverb;* **responsiveness** *noun*

EXAMPLE A *responsive* doctor senses immediately what a patient wants to know.

8. **rival** (rī′vəl) *noun* **a.** A competitor; someone who tries to outdo another. **b.** Someone or something that equals or matches another: *a performance without rival.* *adjective* Being a rival; competing. *verb* **a.** To try to equal or outdo; compete. **b.** To be a match for. 8. ______

RELATED WORD **rivalry** *noun*

EXAMPLE Who will be *rivals* in the next World Series?

9. **solitary** (sŏl′ĭ-tĕr′ē) *adjective* **a.** Without the company of others: *solitary work.* **b.** Single; lone: *a solitary pine.* **c.** Far away from society; remote: *a solitary cabin in the wilderness.* 9. ______

RELATED WORD **solitude** *noun*

EXAMPLE A forest ranger's job is *solitary* but satisfying.

USAGE NOTE *Solitary* and *solitude* express singleness: "*solitary* traveler" or "liking *solitude.*" Use other words for "lonely" or "loneliness."

10. **treacherous** (trĕch′ər-əs) *adjective* **a.** Disloyal; traitorous: *a treacherous friend.* **b.** Dangerous, unsafe: *treacherous surf.* 10. ______

RELATED WORDS **treacherously** *adverb;* **treachery** *noun*

EXAMPLE Gossip is not just mean — it is *treacherous.*

Copyright © Houghton Mifflin Company. All rights reserved.

Name ______________________________ Date __________

Exercise 1 Matching Words and Definitions

Match the definition in Column B with the word in Column A. Write the letter of the correct definition on the answer line.

1. ________
2. ________
3. ________
4. ________
5. ________
6. ________
7. ________
8. ________
9. ________
10. ________

Column A	*Column B*
1. antisocial	**a.** good-natured; friendly
2. treacherous	**b.** a person who withdraws from society
3. solitary	**c.** reserved; distant in manner
4. aloof	**d.** avoiding the company of others; against society
5. enmity	**e.** to commit treason against; be disloyal; reveal
6. recluse	**f.** without the company of others; lone
7. rival	**g.** deep hatred; hostility
8. responsive	**h.** reacting quickly to a suggestion, request, influence, or problem; sympathetic
9. amiable	**i.** a competitor; the equal or match of someone
10. betray	**j.** disloyal; dangerous

Exercise 2 Using Words Correctly

Each of the following statements contains an italicized vocabulary word. Decide whether the sentence is true or false, and write *True* or *False* on the answer line.

1. A deaf person is *responsive* to most sounds. 1. ________
2. For a wonderful party, invite only *antisocial* people. 2. ________
3. The Bermuda Triangle is a *treacherous* area for ships. 3. ________
4. A person who avoids the company of others may be called a *recluse.* 4. ________
5. Reading is usually a *solitary* activity. 5. ________
6. Gifts are usually a sign of *enmity.* 6. ________
7. To be good at a target-shooting sport, you must be *amiable.* 7. ________
8. All people who live in tall apartment houses are *aloof.* 8. ________
9. Some spies *betray* their own country. 9. ________
10. Friends may be *rivals.* 10. ________

Exercise 3 Choosing the Best Definition

For each italicized vocabulary word or related form in the following sentences, write the letter of the best definition on the answer line.

1. "Grace has a talent," said Frank, "for disagreeing so *amiably!*" 1. ________
   a. frequently **b.** good-naturedly **c.** quickly **d.** nastily

Copyright © 1988 Houghton Mifflin Company. All rights reserved.

2. The *solitary* bear gazed longingly from its own cage to a cavernous area where a family of bears frolicked happily. 2. ________
a. lone **b.** large **c.** friendly **d.** lively

3. The weather on mountaintops can change *treacherously* fast. 3. ________
a. dangerously **b.** terribly **c.** amazingly **d.** criminally

4. Grief turns the hero of *Silas Marner* into a *recluse.* 4. ________
a. criminal **b.** companion **c.** stowaway **d.** hermit

5. Locking oneself in one's room can be an *antisocial* act. 5. ________
a. unfriendly **b.** necessary **c.** angry **d.** thoughtless

6. The nurse checked often to see whether the patient was *responsive.* 6. ________
a. comfortable **b.** in pain **c.** sympathetic **d.** reacting

7. *Enmities* can be handed down from generation to generation. 7. ________
a. Diseases **b.** Hatreds **c.** Riches **d.** Feelings

8. Trembling hands *betrayed* the speaker's nervousness. 8. ________
a. hurt **b.** helped **c.** hid **d.** showed

9. "Why must I always be so *aloof?*" wailed the fun-loving prince. 9. ________
a. well-behaved **c.** apart from others
b. on public view **d.** closely watched

10. Lack of *rivalry* between identical twins is said to be quite common. 10. ________
a. sameness **b.** competition **c.** personality **d.** equality

Exercise 4 Using Different Forms of Words

Decide which form of the vocabulary word in parentheses best completes the sentence. The form given may be correct. Write your answer on the answer line.

1. The __?__ Emily Dickinson wrote almost two thousand poems. *(recluse)* 1. ________
2. Insulting guests is an example of __?__ behavior. *(antisocial)* 2. ________
3. The __?__ of the dentist calmed the child. *(amiable)* 3. ________
4. Giving away a friend's secret is a __?__ of trust. *(betray)* 4. ________
5. Can your fire department __?__ to an alarm in three to five minutes? *(responsive)* 5. ________
6. An understandable __?__ exists between cats and mice. *(enmity)* 6. ________
7. Do you prefer studying with friends or in __?__? *(solitary)* 7. ________
8. Cats, unlike dogs, have a reputation for __?__. *(aloof)* 8. ________
9. Central and North high schools have a longtime __?__. *(rival)* 9. ________
10. History shows that rulers died from palace __?__ as well as from disease, war, and old age. *(treacherous)* 10. ________

Copyright © 1988 Houghton Mifflin Company. All rights reserved.

Name ______________________________ Date __________

Reading Comprehension

Each numbered sentence in the following passage contains an italicized vocabulary word or related form. After you read the passage, you will complete an exercise.

Snakes: Friends or Foes?

There is no question about it. Reptiles have a bad reputation. Is it deserved?

If a cat keeps mice and other rodents away from crops and stored grain, it is prized. A monkey that dies for science has mourners. Even the ugly watchdog gets respect.

But what about the lowly snake? Is it praised, mourned, or respected? The answer is NO, even though the snake is an excellent mouser, does its bit for science, and even works as a security guard.

(1) Believe it or not, a Virginian once hired an ***amiable*** boa constrictor to guard his business. In Sweden three deadly snakes in a display case guarded a sapphire worth $500,000. (2) In neither case did the snakes ***betray*** their employers' confidence. Both employers accurately judged fear of snakes an effective weapon against crime.

(3) Why do so many people feel such ***enmity*** toward snakes? There are two main reasons. The snake has been cast as a villain since storytelling began. Also, some snakes *are* deadly (about eight out of every hundred kinds). People rightly fear rattlers, cottonmouths, and vipers.

However, snakes can and do help save human lives. A strong painkiller called "cobroxin" is made from cobra poison. Venom milked from the Russell's viper helps keep hemophiliacs alive. Hemophilia is a disease in which blood does not clot properly. A cut or a bad bruise can lead to death by bleeding. (4) Medicine made from the viper venom speeds up the clotting ***response,*** saving lives.

Under natural conditions, snakes are no threat. (5) They are ***reclusive*** creatures. (6) This ***aloofness*** is natural. (7) For them, it is not the least bit ***antisocial.*** (8) Leaving their burrows, caves, or trees only for warmth or food, snakes lead a ***solitary*** life. "Food" means insects, rodents, and other snakes, which are eaten whole.

While we may not admire the snake's manners, we can admire its beauty. (9) The variety in color and pattern among reptiles is ***rivaled*** only by that of birds.

From time to time, the snake has been a respected symbol. A serpent flag with the motto "Don't tread on me!" waved from colonial ships. Since ancient times, a sword with two snakes wound around it has been a symbol of the medical profession.

For good and bad reasons, then, the snake is an object of fascination. (10) In all fairness, its one-sided reputation for ***treachery*** is not entirely deserved.

Please turn to the next page.

Copyright © 1988 Houghton Mifflin Company. All rights reserved.

Reading Comprehension Exercise

Each of the following statements corresponds to a numbered sentence in the passage. Each statement contains a blank and is followed by four answer choices. Decide which choice fits best in the blank. The word or phrase that you choose must express roughly the same meaning as the italicized word in the passage. Write the letter of your choice on the answer line.

1. A business executive once hired a(n) __?__ snake as a security guard. 1. ________
   a. friendly b. ugly c. deadly d. lovable
2. The "watchsnakes" did not __?__ their employers. 2. ________
   a. please b. deserve c. slide out from under d. fail
3. Snakes bring out a great __?__ in people. 3. ________
   a. hostility b. anger c. admiration d. fascination
4. Thanks to the Russell's viper, the clotting __?__ of hemophiliacs' blood is quickened. 4. ________
   a. medicine b. disease c. reaction d. problem
5. Snakes are __?__ animals. 5. ________
   a. shy b. sociable c. dangerous d. hermitlike
6. The snake's __?__ is natural, not learned. 6. ________
   a. dislike for society c. love of trees
   b. distant manner d. sociability
7. Snakes cannot be said to be genuinely __?__. 7. ________
   a. criminal b. lonely c. unfriendly d. poisonous
8. They simply prefer to live __?__. 8. ________
   a. outdoors b. in houses c. alone d. in burrows
9. The varied beauty of reptiles is __?__ only by that of birds. 9. ________
   a. matched b. unequaled c. known d. disliked
10. The snake's reputation for __?__ is not completely fair. 10. ________
    a. variety b. traitorousness c. usefulness d. aggressiveness

Practice with Analogies

See pages 32, 52, and 86 for some strategies to use with analogies.

DIRECTIONS On the answer line, write the vocabulary word that completes each analogy.

1. Happy is to sad as friendly is to __?__. 1. ________
2. Costly is to expensive as dangerous is to __?__. 2. ________
3. Recluse is to reclusive as response is to __?__. 3. ________
4. Thief is to steal as traitor is to __?__. 4. ________
5. Two is to double as one is to __?__. 5. ________
6. Suitor is to woo as __?__ is to compete. 6. ________

Copyright © Houghton Mifflin Company. All rights reserved.

Lesson 11

The Law

When a law is made, it establishes rules for acceptable and unacceptable behavior. Putting the law into practice and interpreting it are not so simple, however. In law, definitions are extremely important. Lives have been ruined and millions of dollars won over the interpretation of a few words.

The words that you see below are some of the most familiar law terms. They are used mainly in connection with courtroom procedures. Learning them should help you understand books, movies, and television programs about the law.

WORD LIST

bankrupt
defendant
evident
fugitive
just
larceny
lenient
testimony
verdict
witness

DEFINITIONS

After you have studied the definitions and example for each vocabulary word, write the word on the line to the right.

1. **bankrupt** (băngk′rŭpt′) *adjective* **a.** Declared by law unable to pay one's debts. **b.** Completely without money. **c.** Lacking in some way or quality: *bankrupt in manners.* *verb* To cause to become bankrupt. 1. ______________

RELATED WORD **bankruptcy** *noun*

EXAMPLE The property of a *bankrupt* person may be divided among those to whom he or she owes money.

2. **defendant** (dĭ-fĕn′dənt) *noun* The person against whom a legal action is brought: *defendant in a murder trial.* 2. ______________

RELATED WORDS **defend** *verb;* **defender** *noun;* **defense** *noun;* **defensible** *adjective*

EXAMPLE The lawyer asked the *defendant* to explain where he was on the night of the car accident.

3. **evident** (ĕv′ĭ-dənt) *adjective* Easily seen or understood; obvious; clear. 3. ______________

RELATED WORDS **evidence** *noun;* **evidently** *adverb*

EXAMPLE After five scoreless innings, it was *evident* that the teams were well matched.

4. **fugitive** (fyōō′jĭ-tĭv) *noun* A person who runs away or flees from the law: *a fugitive from justice.* *adjective* Running away or fleeing: *a fugitive convict.* 4. ____________

EXAMPLE Eight men formed a posse to help the sheriff find the dangerous *fugitive.*

5. **just** (jŭst) *adjective* **a.** Honest; fair: *a just ruler.* **b.** Suitable or proper: *a just cause.* *adverb* **a.** Exactly: *It was just as you said.* **b.** At that instant: *just then.* 5. ____________

RELATED WORDS **justice** *noun;* **justly** *adverb*

EXAMPLE The judge was greatly respected for her *just* decisions.

6. **larceny** (lär′sə-nē) *noun* The crime of taking away and keeping another's property; stealing; theft. 6. ____________

RELATED WORD **larcenous** *adjective*

EXAMPLE After hearing statements from the bank tellers, the jury found the young woman guilty of *larceny.*

7. **lenient** (lē′nē-ənt) *adjective* **a.** Inclined to forgive; merciful: *a lenient judge.* **b.** Not strict or demanding; generous: *lenient rules.* 7. ____________

RELATED WORDS **leniency** *noun;* **leniently** *adverb*

EXAMPLE The *lenient* baby sitter let Josh watch television even after he had surprised her with his pet snake.

8. **testimony** (tĕs′tə-mō′nē) *noun* **a.** A spoken or written statement or declaration given under oath, especially in court. **b.** Any evidence in support of a fact; proof. 8. ____________

RELATED WORD **testify** *verb*

EXAMPLE The gardener's *testimony* was very important in the puzzling case of the kidnapped French poodle.

9. **verdict** (vûr′dĭkt) *noun* **a.** The decision reached by a jury at the end of a trial. **b.** A conclusion or judgment: *waiting for the verdict of history.* 9. ____________

EXAMPLE We could not predict whether the jury's *verdict* would be "guilty" or "innocent."

10. **witness** (wĭt′nĭs) *noun* **a.** Someone who testifies in court. **b.** Someone who has heard or seen something. **c.** Someone who signs an official document. *verb* **a.** To be present at; see: *to witness a volcanic eruption.* **b.** To act as a witness: *to witness the signing of a will.* 10. ____________

EXAMPLE The statements of the *witnesses* to the accident disagreed in one very important detail.

Copyright © 1988 Houghton Mifflin Company. All rights reserved.

Name ______________________________ Date __________

Exercise 1 Completing Definitions

On the answer line, write the word from the vocabulary list that best completes each definition.

1. Someone who has been accused of a crime is a __?__. 1. __________
2. A person who flees from the law is a __?__. 2. __________
3. Unlawfully taking property from another is the crime of __?__. 3. __________
4. __?__ is a statement given under oath. 4. __________
5. Something that is __?__ is obvious. 5. __________
6. The __?__ of a jury is its decision about a defendant's innocence or guilt. 6. __________
7. An individual or a company that cannot pay its debts may be declared __?__. 7. __________
8. A(n) __?__ decision is fair or suitable. 8. __________
9. Someone who has the power to punish but instead acts mercifully is __?__. 9. __________
10. Someone who testifies in court or sees something happen is a __?__. 10. __________

Exercise 2 Using Words Correctly

Each of the following questions contains an italicized vocabulary word. Choose the correct answer to the question, and write *Yes* or *No* on the answer line.

1. Does a *verdict* of "not guilty" mean a jail sentence for the defendant? 1. __________
2. Would the *testimony* of an eyewitness be important in court? 2. __________
3. Would you expect someone who is *bankrupt* to lend money to others? 3. __________
4. Do honest people avoid *larceny?* 4. __________
5. Is a lifetime prison sentence for the theft of a quart of milk *just?* 5. __________
6. If you were a *witness* at a wedding, might you sign the marriage certificate? 6. __________
7. Would a *fugitive* be comfortable in the presence of the police? 7. __________
8. If something is *evident,* can it be easily understood? 8. __________
9. Would a librarian be considered *lenient* if he occasionally allowed people to return overdue books without charging them fines? 9. __________
10. Does the *defendant* in a court of law decide if someone is guilty or not guilty? 10. __________

Copyright © 1988 Houghton Mifflin Company. All rights reserved.

Exercise 3 Choosing the Best Definition

For each italicized vocabulary word in the following sentences, write the letter of the best definition on the answer line.

1. The play *Twelve Angry Men* shows how jury members reach a *verdict*. 1. ________
   a. judgment **b.** recess **c.** solution **d.** destination

2. Some students thought that the cafeteria rules were not *lenient* enough. 2. ________
   a. rigid **b.** clear **c.** flexible **d.** structured

3. After examining the contents of his piggy bank, Bobby announced that he was *bankrupt*. 3. ________
   a. overjoyed **c.** financially ruined
   b. disappointed **d.** in need of a new bank

4. In the 1800s the Underground Railroad helped *fugitive* slaves. 4. ________
   a. working **b.** runaway **c.** clever **d.** educated

5. Few people *witness* Halley's Comet twice in a lifetime. 5. ________
   a. write about **b.** describe **c.** see **d.** forget

6. Perry Mason, the lawyer-hero of a mystery series, rarely fails to prove the innocence of a *defendant*. 6. ________
   a. guilty person **b.** accused person **c.** judge **d.** suspect

7. The difference between "petty" and "grand" *larceny* is in the value of the property involved. 7. ________
   a. crime **c.** destruction by fire
   b. destruction by flood **d.** theft

8. The doctor's *testimony* established the time of the victim's death. 8. ________
   a. notes **b.** tests **c.** statement **d.** defense

9. "It is not *evident* to me that higher life exists on other planets," said the professor. 9. ________
   a. obvious **b.** necessary **c.** reasonable **d.** important

10. "Finding homes for abandoned animals is a *just* cause for you to devote your time to," Tom's mother said. 10. ________
    a. thankless **b.** suitable **c.** poor **d.** difficult

Exercise 4 Using Different Forms of Words

Decide which form of the vocabulary word in parentheses best completes the sentence. The form given may be correct. Write your answer on the answer line.

1. The witness to the accident was asked to __?__ in court. *(testimony)* 1. ____________
2. Agatha Christie could __?__ be called the "Queen of Mystery Writers." *(just)* 2. ____________
3. The judge showed __?__ toward the shoplifter. *(lenient)* 3. ____________
4. Frequent declarations of __?__ are not good for business. *(bankrupt)* 4. ____________
5. __?__ is needed to prove guilt. *(evident)* 5. ____________

Copyright © 1988 Houghton Mifflin Company. All rights reserved.

Name ______________________________ Date ____________

6. The store detective noted Alfred's __?__ behavior. *(larceny)* 6. ____________

7. In the winter of 1888, Easterners __?__ "a record blizzard." *(witness)* 7. ____________

8. The __?__ was out: the new dance was a nationwide hit. *(verdict)* 8. ____________

9. The __?__ hid in a cave in the mountain. *(fugitive)* 9. ____________

10. In chess, checkmate occurs when a player cannot __?__ a king. *(defendant)* 10. ____________

Reading Comprehension

Each numbered sentence in the following passage contains an italicized vocabulary word. After you read the passage, you will complete an exercise.

O. Henry: American Short Story Writer

In 1897 prison doors slammed shut on William Sidney Porter. In 1901 they opened, and out he walked with a new name and a second chance. (1) The one-time ***fugitive*** turned that chance into lasting fame.

Porter (1862–1910) was born in North Carolina. When he was three, his mother died, and he went to live with relatives who educated him and encouraged him to read.

In 1892, because of poor health, Porter was sent to a Texas ranch. There he soaked up not only the sun but also stories. For two years he listened to the tales of cowhands, drifters, and outlaws.

In 1894 Porter went to Austin, Texas. There a series of misfortunes struck. The woman he married was sickly. Their baby died. His humor magazine was not successful. Porter decided to quit his job as a bank teller and work in Houston for a newspaper. After his departure the Austin bank accused Porter of stealing money. (2) He was then forced to return to Austin and stand trial for ***larceny.*** (3) From the beginning of the trial, it was ***evident*** that the case against Porter was not very strong. Sloppy bookkeeping may have been more to blame than larcenous behavior. (4) The bank officials' ***testimony*** did not seem highly damaging. (5) Still, there were few ***witnesses*** to speak in Porter's defense. (6) The jury returned a ***verdict*** of guilty. (7) The ***defendant,*** William Sidney Porter, lost.

(8) Convinced that he had not been treated in a ***just*** manner, Porter managed to escape the law and to flee Austin. However, when he returned to visit his dying wife, he was arrested.

(9) Porter was such a model prisoner that a ***lenient*** judge reduced the five-year jail sentence to three. Those years served Porter well. He began to write at breakneck speed, rarely stopping to revise. It was at this time that he took the pen name O. Henry. Porter borrowed his new name from a kindly prison guard.

National magazines were eager to buy his stories. By 1904 a book of short stories, *Cabbages and Kings,* was published. Thirteen other collections followed quickly.

(10) O. Henry died almost ***bankrupt,*** but he left a wealth of over six hundred stories. Like his stories O. Henry's life was brief and marked by sudden twists of fate. It is especially fitting, then, that O. Henry stories are known for their surprise endings.

Please turn to the next page.

Copyright © 1988 Houghton Mifflin Company. All rights reserved.

Reading Comprehension Exercise

Each of the following statements corresponds to a numbered sentence in the passage. Each statement contains a blank and is followed by four answer choices. Decide which choice fits best in the blank. The word or phrase that you choose must express roughly the same meaning as the italicized word in the passage. Write the letter of your choice on the answer line.

1. The writer O. Henry was once a(n) __?__. 1. ________
   a. escapee from justice **c.** hardened criminal
   b. crime reporter **d.** prison guard

2. In Austin, Texas, he stood trial for __?__. 2. ________
   a. bribery **b.** murder **c.** theft **d.** slander

3. It was __?__ that the case against Porter was weak. 3. ________
   a. untrue **b.** clear **c.** doubtful **d.** fortunate

4. __?__ about Porter did not seem very harmful. 4. ________
   a. Stories **b.** Publicity **c.** Statements **d.** Arguments

5. Porter had few __?__ for him. 5. ________
   a. people who wrote **c.** people who testified
   b. people who bought supplies **d.** people who raised money

6. The jury returned with the __?__ that Porter was guilty. 6. ________
   a. decision **b.** sentence **c.** confession **d.** suspect

7. The __?__, William Sidney Porter, did not win. 7. ________
   a. accused **b.** lawyer **c.** reporter **d.** criminal

8. Porter fled because he felt he had not been treated in a(n) __?__ manner. 8. ________
   a. kindly **b.** fair **c.** helpful **d.** equal

9. A(n) __?__ judge reduced Porter's sentence. 9. ________
   a. angry **b.** forgetful **c.** harsh **d.** merciful

10. O. Henry died almost __?__. 10. ________
    a. famous **b.** bitter **c.** wealthy **d.** penniless

Writing Assignment

Imagine yourself as a writer for a dramatic television show that has a lawyer as the main character. In a paragraph or two, write about a courtroom situation that could be expanded into an interesting episode for the show. Use five words from this lesson and underline each one.

Copyright © 1988 Houghton Mifflin Company. All rights reserved.

Lesson 12

The Root *-meter-*

The Greek root *-meter-*, meaning "measure," may already look familiar to you. In our language it is an independent word that has several different meanings. *Meter* stands for a unit of measure equal to about 39.37 inches. It is also a rhythm pattern in music or poetry.

All of the words in this lesson contain either the root *-meter-* or one of its related forms, *-metr-* and *-metry*. In each case *the other part* of the word tells what is being measured. For example, a thermometer measures heat, while a speedometer measures speed. Watch and listen for words with the root *-meter-*, as they will help you in your study of mathematics and science.

WORD LIST
altimeter
barometer
diameter
geometry
kilometer
metric
metronome
micrometer
odometer
perimeter

DEFINITIONS

After you have studied the definitions and example for each vocabulary word, write the word on the line to the right.

1. **altimeter** (ăl-tĭm'ĭ-tər) *noun* An instrument that measures the height at which an object, such as an aircraft, is located. 1. ____________

   EXAMPLE The pilot used an *altimeter* to determine the position of the airplane.

2. **barometer** (bə-rŏm'ĭ-tər) *noun* **a.** An instrument that measures the air pressure of the atmosphere and is widely used in the study and forecasting of weather. **b.** Something that shows a change; an indicator: *Wealth is sometimes considered a barometer of success.* 2. ____________

   RELATED WORDS **barometric** *adjective;* **barometrically** *adverb*

   EXAMPLE The television announcer checked the *barometer* before giving the weather forecast.

3. **diameter** (dī-ăm'ĭ-tər) *noun* **a.** A straight line segment that passes through the center of a circle or sphere with both of its ends on the boundary. **b.** The length of such a line. 3. ____________

   EXAMPLE The *diameter* of a circle cuts it exactly in half.

Copyright © 1988 Houghton Mifflin Company. All rights reserved.

4. **geometry** (jē-ŏm′ĭ-trē) *noun* The branch of mathematics dealing with measurements and relationships of points, lines, angles, surfaces, and shapes. 4. ________

RELATED WORDS **geometric, geometrical** *adjectives;* **geometrically** *adverb*

EXAMPLE When she studied *geometry,* Martha learned how to measure and draw angles correctly.

5. **kilometer** (kĭl′ə-mē′tər) *noun* A unit of length equal to 1000 meters, or about 0.6214 mile. 5. ________

EXAMPLE The driving distance between Chicago and Milwaukee is about 145 *kilometers.*

6. **metric** (mĕt′rĭk) *adjective* Referring to a system of weights and measures based on units of 10, 100, and 1000. 6. ________

RELATED WORDS **meter** *noun;* **metrical** *adjective*

EXAMPLE The *metric* system is based on two measurements, the meter for length and the kilogram for weight.

7. **metronome** (mĕt′rə-nōm′) *noun* An instrument used to mark time in steady beats at various speeds. 7. ________

EXAMPLE To practice his piano piece, Eric set the *metronome* at "presto," or about 192 beats per minute.

8. **micrometer** (mī-krŏm′ĭ-tər) *noun* An instrument used for measuring very small distances. 8. ________

EXAMPLE When part of a microscope, a *micrometer* can measure the thickness of a cell wall.

9. **odometer** (ō-dŏm′ĭ-tər) *noun* An instrument that measures distance traveled by a vehicle. 9. ________

EXAMPLE A car *odometer* is based on the number of times a wheel rotates per mile or kilometer.

10. **perimeter** (pə-rĭm′ĭ-tər) *noun* **a.** The sum of the lengths of the segments that form the sides of a geometrical figure such as a polygon or circle. **b.** The outer boundary of such a figure. **c.** The outer limits of an area. 10. ________

EXAMPLE Jerry measured all sides of the table and then totaled the measurements to find its *perimeter.*

Copyright © Houghton Mifflin Company. All rights reserved.

Name ______________________________ Date ______________

Exercise 1 Matching Words and Definitions

Match the definition in Column B with the word in Column A. Write the letter of the correct definition on the answer line.

Column A	Column B
1. micrometer	a. instrument that measures height
2. kilometer	b. straight line through the center of a circle
3. altimeter	c. instrument measuring atmospheric pressure
4. geometry	d. the boundary length of a geometrical figure
5. barometer	e. a unit of length equal to 1000 meters
6. metric	f. instrument measuring distance traveled
7. odometer	g. instrument marking time in steady beats
8. metronome	h. instrument measuring very small distances
9. diameter	i. referring to a system of measurement
10. perimeter	j. a branch of mathematics that deals with points, lines, angles, surfaces, and shapes

1. ________
2. ________
3. ________
4. ________
5. ________
6. ________
7. ________
8. ________
9. ________
10. ________

Exercise 2 Using Words Correctly

Each of the following questions contains an italicized vocabulary word. Choose the correct answer to the question, and write *Yes* or *No* on the answer line.

1. Does a *metronome* help a musician practice? 1. ________
2. Can you walk the *perimeter* of a square without turning any corners? 2. ________
3. Is an *altimeter* needed in a sports car? 3. ________
4. Does a *barometer* measure blood pressure? 4. ________
5. Is *geometry* the study of rocks and mountains? 5. ________
6. Does the *diameter* of a circle pass through the circle's center? 6. ________
7. Can weight be measured in the *metric* system? 7. ________
8. Is a *kilometer* a measure of weight? 8. ________
9. Does an *odometer* measure speed? 9. ________
10. Could you measure the width of a single hair with a *micrometer?* 10. ________

Exercise 3 Choosing the Best Definition

For each italicized vocabulary word in the following sentences, write the letter of the best definition on the answer line.

1. If given the *diameter* of a circle, you can calculate the circle's area. 1. ________
   a. line through the center **c.** distance around the edge
   b. smaller section **d.** exact location

Copyright © 1988 Houghton Mifflin Company. All rights reserved.

2. Calvin checked the *barometer* and then decided to carry an umbrella. 2. ________

a. atmospheric air-pressure measurer c. weight measurer
b. altitude measurer d. angle measurer

3. A clockwork *metronome* works by means of a double pendulum with a movable upper weight. 3. ________

a. chime b. second hand c. time beater d. level

4. Finding the length of a side of a square is easy if you know the *perimeter* of that square. 4. ________

a. planned construction c. corner angle
b. length of the diagonal d. sum of the lengths of the segments

5. When traveling in Europe, tourists must think in *kilometers.* 5. ________

a. distance measurements of 1000 meters
b. distance measurements of 1.58 miles
c. distance measurements of 500 meters
d. distance measurements of .5 miles

6. Because the plane's *altimeter* was broken, the landing was difficult. 6. ________

a. speed measurer c. mileage measurer
b. altitude measurer d. cabin-pressure measurer

7. Many countries in the world have already adopted the *metric* system. 7. ________

a. gold-backed c. credit-card
b. measured on the basis of units of ten d. computer-data

8. The research scientist relied on her *micrometer.* 8. ________

a. mileage measurer c. small-distance measurer
b. altitude measurer d. speed measurer

9. Euclid, a Greek scholar who lived around 300 B.C., organized and systematized the *geometry* then known. 9. ________

a. earth-science information c. medical facts
b. mathematics of areas and shapes d. life-science information

10. We used the car *odometer* to keep track of our vacation route. 10. ________

a. speed measurer c. air-pressure measurer
b. height measurer d. distance measurer

Exercise 4 Using Different Forms of Words

Decide which form of the vocabulary word in parentheses best completes the sentence. The form given may be correct. Write your answer on the answer line.

1. In Europe speed limits are posted in __?__, not miles. *(kilometer)* 1. ________

2. You can find the __?__ of a circle by doubling the length of the radius. *(diameter)* 2. ________

3. "The __?__ pressure is falling fast," warned the forecaster. "Snow is coming." *(barometer)* 3. ________

4. One of the passengers in the hot-air balloon checked the __?__ to determine the altitude. *(altimeter)* 4. ________

Copyright © 1988 Houghton Mifflin Company. All rights reserved.

Name ______________________________ Date ______________

5. The student needed to work out the math problem ___?___. *(geometry)* 5. ______________

6. A home gas ___?___ usually has four dials. *(metric)* 6. ______________

7. We built a fence around the ___?___ of our vegetable garden. *(perimeter)* 7. ______________

8. It is illegal for car dealers to turn back ___?___. *(odometer)* 8. ______________

9. Piano teachers often use ___?___ with beginning students. *(metronome)* 9. ______________

10. The scientist ordered several ___?___ for his laboratory. *(micrometer)* 10. ______________

Reading Comprehension

Each numbered sentence in the following passage contains an italicized vocabulary word. After you read the passage, you will complete an exercise.

Measuring Devices — Past and Present

An 1870 mathematics textbook asks students these questions: How many leagues in nine miles? How many pints in eight gills? How many quarters in twelve nails?

In 1870 a fourth grader would have answered these questions correctly. Today students use other terms to discuss measurements.

Current systems of measurement for everything from line length to air pressure are based on centuries of scientific investigation. Our debt to the ancients goes very far back.

(1) For example, ***geometry,*** now a commonly taught high school math course, was created more than two thousand years ago. Euclid, a Greek mathematician, worked out and recorded rules for figuring out lengths and areas of flat or solid shapes. (2) These rules included a way to calculate the ***perimeter*** of a circle. (3) Euclid wrote that all one needed was a formula and the ***diameter*** of the circle.

The measurement of time also has ancient origins. Until a few hundred years ago, people had only undependable sun clocks and water clocks. Time calculations became more accurate when inventors developed clocks that were based on weighted motion. (4) The ***metronome*** is an example of a time-marking device that uses a weight. Today digital clocks have made time silent.

(5) In 1789 the procedure for weighing and measuring lengths was challenged by the introduction of the ***metric*** system. At this time many people felt that the measurement system of feet and inches was too difficult to use. They claimed that the numbers twelve and thirty-six, which measure the inches in the foot and the yard, were hard to multiply and divide. In the metric system, measurement is based on easily calculated numbers such as 100 and 1000. (6) For example, a ***kilometer*** is the length of 1000 meters. Many countries, such as Canada, show mileage from town to town or city to city in kilometers. Throughout the world countries have already adopted or are adopting the metric system for everyday use. In the United States, the metric system is used for some measurements.

Great advances have also been made in measuring weather. (7) Thermometers gauge air temperature, while ***barometers*** help to predict storms by measuring the air pressure of the atmosphere. (8) In addition, barometers are a part of ***altimeters,*** which are so important in airplane navigation.

Automobile drivers have also benefited from scientific progress in measurement. (9) To answer the question "When are we going to get there?" tired parents still look at the car ***odometer.***

(10) As scientists continue to investigate new and better systems of measurement for all areas of life, they will be aided by such devices as the ***micrometer,*** that precise instrument capable of measuring things that are invisible to the human eye.

Please turn to the next page.

Copyright © 1988 Houghton Mifflin Company. All rights reserved.

Reading Comprehension Exercise

Each of the following statements corresponds to a numbered sentence in the passage. Each statement contains a blank and is followed by four answer choices. Decide which choice fits best in the blank. The word or phrase that you choose must express roughly the same meaning as the italicized word in the passage. Write the letter of your choice on the answer line.

1. The creator of __?__ is the Greek scholar Euclid. 1. ________
   a. temperature measurement c. modern mathematics
   b. astronomy d. shape measurement

2. He showed a way to measure the __?__ a circle. 2. ________
   a. distance around b. width of c. angle of d. depth of

3. One needs to know the circle's __?__. 3. ________
   a. area b. density c. line dividing it in half d. angle

4. A __?__ operates by using a weight. 4. ________
   a. temperature-measuring device c. device to measure mileage
   b. time-marking device d. device to measure angles

5. In 1789 a new system of measuring __?__ was developed. 5. ________
   a. length and weight b. air pressure c. temperature d. height

6. On road signs some countries use __?__ instead of miles. 6. ________
   a. air pressure c. metric distances
   b. freeway warnings d. temperatures

7. A(n) __?__ makes it possible to predict storms. 7. ________
   a. air-pressure measurer c. speed gauge
   b. mileage measurer d. height gauge

8. A(n) __?__ indicates an airplane's height. 8. ________
   a. speed gauge c. air-pressure measurer
   b. altitude measurer d. mileage measurer

9. A(n) __?__ can help drivers calculate when a trip will end. 9. ________
   a. oil gauge c. mileage gauge
   b. temperature gauge d. cruise-control button

10. Research scientists are aided by the __?__. 10. ________
    a. small-distance measurer c. computer chip
    b. small wrench d. metric ruler

Writing Assignment

What kind of measuring devices do the members of your family use at home, in school, or on the job? List these devices and choose the three that you think are most useful. Write a paragraph entitled "Three Measuring Devices We Can't Live Without" in which you explain why these devices are so necessary. Include at least four words from this lesson and underline each one.

Copyright © 1988 Houghton Mifflin Company. All rights reserved.

Name ______________________________ Date ______________

Test-Taking Skills

TEST-TAKING SKILLS

Antonym Tests

Besides a section on synonyms, vocabulary tests frequently have one on identifying antonyms. **Antonyms** are words with opposite meanings. *Good* and *bad* are antonyms, as are *few* and *many*. An antonym test asks you to identify the antonym of a word in a sentence. Here are five strategies for taking such a test.

STRATEGIES

1. *Be sure to read all of the choices before answering the test item.*
2. *Narrow your choices by eliminating answers that are obviously wrong.*

   The dirt road was *blocked* for hours by a fallen tree.
   a. suddenly **b.** opposed **c.** barred **d.** opened

   You can eliminate *suddenly* because it is the wrong part of speech. *Opposed* does not make sense as a choice. This process of elimination leaves two choices to consider.
3. *Do not be misled by a synonym in the answer choices.* In the sample test item about the dirt road, *blocked* and *barred* are synonyms—words that have nearly the same meaning. The correct choice is the antonym, *opened.*
4. *Be alert for other misleading choices.* Words that sound somewhat alike are sometimes given in the answer choices. In the sample test above, *opened* and *opposed* might be confused by someone reading too hastily. As you have seen, however, *opposed* is not the correct choice.
5. *Study the sentence for clues to the meaning of the word.*

   The *minute* computer chip can fit on your fingertip.
   a. tiny **b.** invisible **c.** large **d.** partial

   Since the chip fits on a fingertip, it must be very small. The opposite of very small is large, so the correct answer must be *c*.

Please turn to the next page.

Copyright © 1988 Houghton Mifflin Company. All rights reserved.

Exercise Identifying Antonyms

Choose the antonym of the italicized word in each sentence. Write the letter of the correct choice on the answer line.

1. The plane flew upward to get over the *lofty* peak. 1. ________
   a. steep b. jagged c. distant d. low
2. *Murky* waters hid the sunken ship. 2. ________
   a. clear b. chilly c. calm d. northern
3. The *arduous* work exhausted the entire crew. 3. ________
   a. abrupt b. busy c. easy d. difficult
4. Manuel's *lucid* explanation helped me to understand the math problem. 4. ________
   a. long b. quiet c. first d. confusing
5. The winner's happiness was *evident* to everyone. 5. ________
   a. obvious b. hidden c. hideous d. silly
6. Unfortunately the runner *fumbled* the ball. 6. ________
   a. rubbed b. saw c. grasped d. kicked
7. A *novice* skier should first learn how to come to a stop. 7. ________
   a. beginner b. young c. brave d. expert
8. Belinda spoke *candidly* about her reasons for quitting the team. 8. ________
   a. hastily b. much c. dishonestly d. popularly
9. Only I could hear what Gloria was *murmuring.* 9. ________
   a. muttering b. shouting c. intending d. gesturing
10. The beautiful day made me feel *lighthearted.* 10. ________
    a. worried b. depressing c. uninterested d. old
11. The actress *declined* to give an interview to the press. 11. ________
    a. agreed b. wished c. argued d. refused
12. The clothing fashions of today may seem *obsolete* tomorrow. 12. ________
    a. uninteresting b. strange c. up-to-date d. old
13. Famous in the world of sports, the *coveted* trophy is awarded annually. 13. ________
    a. valuable b. unwanted c. admired d. polished
14. The television program about federal spending to reduce air pollution was considered *controversial* by many viewers. 14. ________
    a. boring b. interesting c. shocking d. acceptable
15. After it was taken over by another firm, the James Company *relinquished* control of the design of its products. 15. ________
    a. regained b. strengthened c. lost d. exercised

Copyright © 1988 Houghton Mifflin Company. All rights reserved.

Lesson 13

Anger and Forgiveness

Lesson 13 WORD LIST

Everyone has had the experience of being angry. People express anger differently, as demonstrated in the following example.

> Sandra made a conscious effort not to frown, but every time she thought about Jill she wanted to scream. Instead, Sandra sat reading a book, being careful not to let anyone know how she was feeling.
>
> Jill still couldn't believe that Sandra had acted so insensitively. The rage welled up inside of her until it exploded, and she found herself yelling at the first person who dared to enter her room uninvited: her younger brother.

Both Sandra and Jill are feeling anger, but they are reacting to this emotion in different ways. Some of the words in this lesson deal with kinds of anger — from blind rage to the quiet, brooding variety. Other words refer to the end of anger, which often leads to forgiveness. Learning these words should give you a better understanding of people — in and out of literature.

WORD LIST

appease
assuage
belligerent
condone
indignant
infuriate
reconcile
resent
retaliate
wrath

DEFINITIONS

After you have studied the definitions and example for each vocabulary word, write the word on the line to the right.

1. **appease** (ə-pēz′) *verb* To calm or soothe, especially by giving in to demands. 1. ____________

   RELATED WORD **appeasement** *noun*

   EXAMPLE A settlement was made to *appease* the workers' demands for higher wages.

2. **assuage** (ə-swāj′) *verb* **a.** To lessen the force or pain of: *to assuage a widow's grief.* **b.** To satisfy or quench: *to assuage a child's thirst for knowledge.* 2. ____________

   RELATED WORD **assuagement** *noun*

   EXAMPLE Marla's mother tried to *assuage* her daughter's anxiety on the first day of school.

Copyright © 1988 Houghton Mifflin Company. All rights reserved.

3. **belligerent** (bə-lĭj′ər-ənt) *adjective* **a.** Quick to fight or argue; hostile: *a belligerent person.* **b.** Of, pertaining to, or engaged in warfare: *belligerent powers.* *noun* A nation fighting a war.

RELATED WORDS **belligerence** *noun;* **belligerently** *adverb*

EXAMPLE The referee gave both *belligerent* hockey players ten-minute penalties.

3. ____________

ETYMOLOGY NOTE *Bellum* is the Latin word meaning "war." *Bellicose,* a related word, is stronger than *belligerent* and means "warlike in manner or temperament."

4. **condone** (kən-dōn′) *verb* To forgive, overlook, or disregard (an offense) without protest or blame.

EXAMPLE "I can tolerate many things," explained the teacher, "but I cannot *condone* cheating under any circumstances."

4. ____________

5. **indignant** (ĭn-dĭg′nənt) *adjective* Feeling or showing anger about something unjust, mean, or unworthy.

RELATED WORDS **indignantly** *adverb;* **indignation** *noun*

EXAMPLE John became *indignant* after the store manager refused to refund his money for a carton of spoiled milk.

5. ____________

6. **infuriate** (ĭn-fyo͝or′ē-āt′) *verb* To make furious; enrage.

EXAMPLE A last-minute penalty call against the goalkeeper *infuriated* the coach.

6. ____________

7. **reconcile** (rĕk′ən-sīl′) *verb* **a.** To restore friendship between: *to reconcile former friends.* **b.** To bring (oneself) to accept: *to reconcile oneself to a loss.* **c.** To bring into harmony or agreement: *to reconcile different points of view.*

RELATED WORD **reconciliation** *noun*

EXAMPLE Janet gave a party, hoping to *reconcile* Sue and Ann.

7. ____________

8. **resent** (rĭ-zĕnt′) *verb* To feel angry or bitter about.

RELATED WORDS **resentful** *adjective;* **resentfully** *adverb;* **resentment** *noun*

EXAMPLE The employee *resented* being treated without respect.

8. ____________

9. **retaliate** (rĭ-tăl′ē-āt′) *verb* To return like for like; pay back in kind: *to retaliate against an attack.*

RELATED WORDS **retaliation** *noun;* **retaliatory** *adjective*

EXAMPLE In the 1930s many factory workers *retaliated* against low wages with peaceful sit-down strikes.

9. ____________

10. **wrath** (răth) *noun* Violent, resentful anger; rage.

RELATED WORDS **wrathful** *adjective;* **wrathfully** *adverb;* **wrathfulness** *noun*

EXAMPLE Mythology is full of stories of mortals who challenge or defy the gods and then suffer their *wrath.*

10. ____________

MEMORY CUE We feel *wr*ath when we've been *wr*onged.

Copyright © Houghton Mifflin Company. All rights reserved.

Name ______________________________ Date ______________

Exercise 1 Matching Words and Definitions

Match the definition in Column B with the word in Column A. Write the letter of the correct definition on the answer line.

1. ________
2. ________
3. ________
4. ________
5. ________
6. ________
7. ________
8. ________
9. ________
10. ________

Column A	Column B
1. belligerent	a. to lessen the force or pain of
2. indignant	b. to forgive, overlook, or disregard (an offense)
3. wrath	c. to return like for like; pay back in kind
4. assuage	d. quick to fight or argue; hostile
5. resent	e. violent, resentful anger; rage
6. reconcile	f. to feel angry or bitter about
7. infuriate	g. to make furious; enrage
8. retaliate	h. to calm by giving in to demands
9. appease	i. to restore friendship between; bring (oneself) to accept
10. condone	j. feeling anger about something unjust

Exercise 2 Using Words Correctly

Each of the following statements contains an italicized vocabulary word. Decide whether the sentence is true or false, and write *True* or *False* on the answer line.

1. Most schools do not *condone* gum chewing in class. 1. ________
2. *Belligerent* people make friends easily. 2. ________
3. An apology and an honest smile can help *appease* anger. 3. ________
4. Teen-agers *resent* being treated like babies. 4. ________
5. Medals are given to *retaliate* for bravery. 5. ________
6. *Wrath* describes the situation of being wrapped up in oneself. 6. ________
7. A person who is *infuriated* is speechless with joy. 7. ________
8. Someone who is wrongfully arrested has a right to feel *indignant.* 8. ________
9. An insult is sure to *assuage* hurt feelings. 9. ________
10. If you hope to *reconcile* friends, you might encourage them to discuss their differences. 10. ________

Exercise 3 Choosing the Best Word

Decide which vocabulary word or related form best expresses the meaning of the italicized word or phrase in the sentence. On the answer line, write the letter of the correct choice.

1. Helen *came to accept* the loss of her pet rabbit. 1. ________
   a. retaliated **b.** reconciled herself to **c.** condoned **d.** assuaged

Copyright © 1988 Houghton Mifflin Company. All rights reserved.

2. Tim, always *ready to start a fight,* was often in the principal's office. 2. ________
a. appeased b. indignant c. belligerent d. condoning

3. Mom and Dad rarely *purposely overlook* my staying out late. 3. ________
a. assuage b. resent c. condone d. appease

4. The matador's red cape *enraged* the bull. 4. ________
a. infuriated b. reconciled c. appeased d. assuaged

5. In 1773, when the British refused to drop the tea tax, Bostonians *paid them back* by dumping tea into Boston Harbor. 5. ________
a. condoned b. appeased c. retaliated d. resented

6. The Boston Tea Party earned for Massachusetts the *great rage* of the British Parliament. 6. ________
a. reconciliation b. wrath c. appeasement d. assuagement

7. At the First Continental Congress, the colonists formally expressed their *feeling of anger toward injustices.* 7. ________
a. retaliation b. appeasement c. reconciliation d. indignation

8. The colonists *felt bitterness toward* foreign rule. 8. ________
a. resented b. reconciled c. infuriated d. condoned

9. The losers were *made calm* only when a rematch was scheduled. 9. ________
a. resented b. retaliated c. infuriated d. appeased

10. Making new friends *lessened* Sal's feeling of homesickness. 10. ________
a. assuaged b. resented c. condoned d. retaliated

Exercise 4 Using Different Forms of Words

Decide which form of the vocabulary word in parentheses best completes the sentence. The form given may be correct. Write your answer on the answer line.

1. The fishers decided against __?__ for the accidental cutting of their nets. *(retaliate)* 1. ________

2. __?__ his sister, Tommy turned off the television set. *(infuriate)* 2. ________

3. "__?__ bad behavior makes your job more difficult," the veteran baby sitter told the newcomer. *(condone)* 3. ________

4. Ronald __?__ his desire to learn more about ancient Greece by reading three books on the subject. *(assuage)* 4. ________

5. The old friends celebrated their __?__ by exchanging gifts. *(reconcile)* 5. ________

6. "Is your goal __?__?" the reporter asked the President. *(appease)* 6. ________

7. "__?__ has no place on the tennis court," said the coach. *(belligerent)* 7. ________

8. Bobby replied __?__ to his older sister's accusation. *(indignant)* 8. ________

9. Brenda hid her __?__ at missing her favorite television show. *(resent)* 9. ________

10. In a __?__ voice, the lawyer explained why the defendant should be put in jail. *(wrath)* 10. ________

Copyright © 1988 Houghton Mifflin Company. All rights reserved.

Name ______________________________ Date ____________

Reading Comprehension

Each numbered sentence in the following passage contains an italicized vocabulary word or related form. After you read the passage, you will complete an exercise.

Aesculapius: A Great Healer

Lightning, some people say, never strikes twice. The Greek mythological character of Aesculapius, however, was touched by lightning — more than once.

According to a Greek myth, Aesculapius' mother died after her son's birth. Aesculapius was then taken by his father, Apollo, who turned the baby over to the wise and kindly Chiron to bring up in his cave on Mount Pelion. Chiron was a centaur, a creature with the head and arms of a man and the body of a horse. Some shepherds showed some interest in the infant, but they were frightened by a bolt of lightning from Aesculapius' body.

This lightning bolt was significant. **(1)** It was the sign of Zeus, that ***belligerent*** god of the sky who was also Apollo's father and Aesculapius' grandfather.

Apollo was the god of medicine. It was fitting that Apollo had chosen Chiron as guardian, for the centaur also knew much about herbs and medicines.

Soon Aesculapius outshone his teacher. He could cure anyone. There was only one challenge left. Could he bring the dead back to life? With the help of the goddess Athena, Aesculapius succeeded in bringing back to life a man named Hippolytus.

(2) Upon hearing the news of his grandson's feat, Zeus was ***infuriated.*** **(3)** He reacted ***indignantly*** to the idea that Aesculapius would dare to bring someone back to life. **(4)** Zeus' anger was not easily ***assuaged.*** **(5)** He deeply ***resented*** any meddling with the Olympian order, and the dead were, in a way, his business. They were ruled by Hades, his brother and god of the Underworld.

(6) To get even for his grandson's act, Zeus let loose the full fury of his ***wrath,*** killing Aesculapius with a thunderbolt. **(7)** Enraged, Apollo ***retaliated*** by killing the Cyclopes, the creatures who forged the thunderbolts for Zeus. **(8)** Unable to ***condone*** the killing of the Cyclopes, Zeus struck again. He sentenced Apollo to one year on earth as a servant.

Meanwhile, Olympians spoke up in behalf of Aesculapius. **(9)** Their efforts at ***appeasement*** eventually did win over Zeus. **(10)** In a grudging act of ***reconciliation,*** Zeus honored Aesculapius, placing him in the sky as the star formation called the Serpent Holder.

Reading Comprehension Exercise

Each of the following statements corresponds to a numbered sentence in the passage. Each statement contains a blank and is followed by four answer choices. Decide which choice fits best in the blank. The word or phrase that you choose must express roughly the same meaning as the italicized word in the passage. Write the letter of your choice on the answer line.

1. Lightning was one sign of the __?__ god Zeus. 1. ________
   a. domineering **b.** quick to fight **c.** gigantic **d.** powerful

2. Zeus was __?__ by Aesculapius' behavior. 2. ________
   a. upset **b.** enraged **c.** amused **d.** terrified

Copyright © 1988 Houghton Mifflin Company. All rights reserved.

3. Zeus reacted ___?___ to Aesculapius' deed. 3. ________
a. angrily b. carelessly c. unhappily d. in a terrified way

4. Zeus' anger was not easily ___?___. 4. ________
a. relieved b. controlled c. dealt with d. noticed

5. The chief god of Olympus ___?___ the meddling of outsiders. 5. ________
a. was suspicious of c. was bitter about
b. was ignorant of d. secretly enjoyed

6. Zeus let loose all of his ___?___. 6. ________
a. horses b. patience c. curiosity d. rage

7. Apollo ___?___ Zeus for his son's death. 7. ________
a. apologized to c. paid back
b. asked pardon from d. blamed

8. Zeus could not ___?___ the death of the Cyclopes. 8. ________
a. judge b. understand c. blame d. overlook

9. Olympians were finally successful in their attempts at ___?___. 9. ________
a. peace-making b. remembering c. winning d. punishing

10. Making Aesculapius a star formation was an act of ___?___. 10. ________
a. restored harmony b. recognition c. mourning d. shame

Practice with Analogies

STRATEGY Check grammatical relationships. If the given words are a noun-verb pair, the answer must be a noun-verb pair. Eliminate choices that don't match grammatically.

See pages 32 and 52 for some other strategies to use with analogies.

INCORRECT Microscope is to magnify as telescope is to far.
CORRECT Microscope is to magnify as radar is to detect.

DIRECTIONS On the answer line, write the letter of the phrase that best completes the analogy. Some of the items use the strategy explained above.

1. Fear is to fright as 1. ________
(A) condone is to oppose (B) wrath is to rage
(C) resent is to indignant (D) appease is to alarm

2. Argue is to reconcile as 2. ________
(A) offend is to apologize (B) happy is to smile
(C) defend is to attorney (D) injure is to hurt

3. Appease is to calm as 3. ________
(A) tie is to tight (B) acrobat is to trampoline
(C) danger is to escape (D) discover is to find

4. Enemy is to belligerent as 4. ________
(A) flexible is to gymnast (B) banquet is to feast
(C) necessary is to essential (D) genius is to intelligent

5. Annoy is to infuriate as 5. ________
(A) shout is to whisper (B) anger is to please (C) like is to adore
(D) coat is to hanger

Copyright © Houghton Mifflin Company. All rights reserved.

Lesson 14

Stops and Delays

One of the first words we learn is *stop.* It is an important everyday word. Parents use the word *stop* as a warning to small children. Young children use the word in childhood games. As children progress in their development, they discover a variety of words to describe different kinds of stopping. Some of these words deal with delay or being behind schedule. As you study the words below, notice the kind of situation each vocabulary word describes and the cause for each stop or delay.

WORD LIST

adjourn
cease
decisive
detain
hinder
prolong
repress
shackle
tarry
undermine

DEFINITIONS

After you have studied the definitions and example for each vocabulary word, write the word on the line to the right.

1. **adjourn** (ə-jûrn′) *verb* **a.** To stop or put off until another time. **b.** To move from one place to another: *Guests adjourned to the living room.* 1. ________

RELATED WORD **adjournment** *noun*

EXAMPLE Congress *adjourned* on Wednesday.

2. **cease** (sēs) *verb* **a.** To put an end to; discontinue: *The factory ceased production.* **b.** To come to an end; stop: *The noise ceased.* *noun* The stopping of something. 2. ________

RELATED WORDS **ceaseless** *adjective;* **ceaselessly** *adverb*

EXAMPLE The parrot *ceased* talking when its cage was covered.

3. **decisive** (dĭ-sī′sĭv) *adjective* **a.** Having the power to settle something; conclusive: *a decisive argument.* **b.** Characterized by decision and firmness: *a decisive person.* 3. ________

RELATED WORDS **decisively** *adverb;* **decisiveness** *noun*

EXAMPLE "The Badgers have scored a *decisive* victory over the Cougars!" the newscaster stated enthusiastically.

Copyright © 1988 Houghton Mifflin Company. All rights reserved.

4. **detain** (dĭ-tān′) *verb* **a.** To delay by holding back; keep from proceeding. **b.** To keep in custody; confine. 4. ______________

RELATED WORD **detainment** *noun*

EXAMPLE The loudspeaker announced, "Flight 131 has been *detained* by bad weather in Chicago and will be an hour late."

5. **hinder** (hĭn′dər) *verb* To get in the way of; hamper; interfere with. 5. ______________

RELATED WORD **hindrance** *noun*

EXAMPLE Wind and rain *hindered* the search party.

6. **prolong** (prə-lông′) *verb* To stretch out in time or extent; lengthen; extend: *to prolong a vacation.* 6. ______________

RELATED WORD **prolongation** *noun*

EXAMPLE It is unwise to *prolong* waits between dental checkups.

7. **repress** (rĭ-prĕs′) *verb* **a.** To control by holding back; restrain; stifle: *to repress a laugh.* **b.** To control by crushing: *to repress a rebellion.* **c.** To keep from the conscious mind: *to repress an unhappy memory.* 7. ______________

RELATED WORDS **repression** *noun;* **repressive** *adjective*

EXAMPLE When Trina saw the *A* on her math paper, she could not *repress* a squeal of delight.

8. **shackle** (shăk′əl) *verb* **a.** To keep from moving freely; restrict; hamper. **b.** To chain to. *noun* **a.** A metal ring put around the ankle or wrist and attached to a chain. **b.** Anything that confines or restrains: *the shackles of ignorance.* 8. ______________

EXAMPLE Dan worked so hard on his report that he felt *shackled* to his desk.

9. **tarry** (tăr′ē) *verb* **a.** To delay or be late in going or coming; linger. **b.** To stay temporarily: *to tarry in Mexico.* 9. ______________

EXAMPLE "Do not *tarry* on your way to the dinner table," Mother joked.

10. **undermine** (ŭn′dər-mīn′) *verb* To weaken bit by bit; drain; disable. 10. ______________

EXAMPLE Never getting enough sleep *undermined* Rodney's health.

Copyright © 1988 Houghton Mifflin Company. All rights reserved.

Name ____________________ Date ____________

Exercise 1 Completing Definitions

On the answer line, write the word from the vocabulary list that best completes each definition.

1. To stop or discontinue is to __?__. 1. ________
2. To interfere or get in the way of is to __?__. 2. ________
3. To hold back by stifling or crushing is to __?__. 3. ________
4. To delay in leaving or to stay temporarily is to __?__. 4. ________
5. Something that is conclusive or characterized by decision or firmness is __?__. 5. ________
6. To put off until another time is to __?__. 6. ________
7. To lengthen in time or extent is to __?__. 7. ________
8. To __?__ is to restrict greatly. 8. ________
9. To delay by holding back is to __?__. 9. ________
10. To weaken or drain away slowly is to __?__. 10. ________

Exercise 2 Using Words Correctly

Each of the following questions contains an italicized vocabulary word. Choose the correct answer to the question, and write *Yes* or *No* on the answer line.

1. Should a judge be a *decisive* person? 1. ________
2. Could working in a restaurant *hinder* someone's ability to stay on a diet? 2. ________
3. Does regular exercise usually *undermine* someone's health? 3. ________
4. If a hockey game goes into overtime, is it *prolonged?* 4. ________
5. Might members of an old-fashioned chain gang be *shackled* together? 5. ________
6. Would most students be happy if final exams *ceased?* 6. ________
7. Can a bus be *detained* by bad weather? 7. ________
8. If you *tarry* over breakfast, will you eat quickly? 8. ________
9. Is school *adjourned* for blizzards or hurricanes? 9. ________
10. Does a United States President have the right to *repress* freedom of speech? 10. ________

Copyright © 1988 Houghton Mifflin Company. All rights reserved.

Exercise 3 Choosing the Best Definition

For each italicized vocabulary word in the following sentences, write the letter of the best definition on the answer line.

1. When Mr. Nellis retires, he will *cease* working. 1. ________
   a. delay **b.** begin **c.** stop **d.** enjoy
2. Millions of immigrants were *detained* at Ellis Island. 2. ________
   a. fed **b.** questioned **c.** helped **d.** delayed
3. Not studying *hindered* Paul's chances of doing well on the test. 3. ________
   a. hampered **b.** increased **c.** helped **d.** added to
4. The seniors *repressed* shouts of joy until the graduation ended. 4. ________
   a. shortened **b.** imitated **c.** stifled **d.** gave
5. It was the coach's habit to *tarry* after practice. 5. ________
   a. scold **b.** linger **c.** give advice **d.** joke
6. Because of a *prolonged* illness, the student repeated third grade. 6. ________
   a. delayed **b.** unusual **c.** serious **d.** lengthy
7. Our candidate won a *decisive* victory. 7. ________
   a. conclusive **b.** narrow **c.** questionable **d.** early
8. Used to casual clothes, Danny felt *shackled* in a suit and tie. 8. ________
   a. important **b.** nervous **c.** embarrassed **d.** restricted
9. Judge Brewster *adjourned* the court session at four o'clock. 9. ________
   a. addressed **b.** began **c.** extended **d.** brought to a close
10. Too much criticism *undermines* self-confidence. 10. ________
    a. develops **b.** tunnels **c.** weakens **d.** strengthens

Exercise 4 Using Different Forms of Words

Decide which form of the vocabulary word in parentheses best completes the sentence. The form given may be correct. Write your answer on the answer line.

1. Some people talk __?__ on the telephone. *(cease)* 1. ________
2. Millie's unexpected __?__ caused her to miss the party. *(detain)* 2. ________
3. The Ortegas __?__ their stay in Ontario. *(prolong)* 3. ________
4. In the end people usually rebel against __?__ treatment. *(repress)* 4. ________
5. Will Congress vote on the bill before summer __?__? *(adjourn)* 5. ________
6. The prisoners were __?__ and put into the dungeon. *(shackle)* 6. ________
7. __?__ by rough seas, the channel swimmer gave up. *(hinder)* 7. ________
8. __?__ on the way to her piano lesson made Laura late. *(tarry)* 8. ________
9. Erosion __?__ the foundation of the beach house. *(undermine)* 9. ________
10. Because of the new manager's __?__, the firm prospered. *(decisive)* 10. ________

Copyright © Houghton Mifflin Company. All rights reserved.

Name ______________________________ Date ____________

Reading Comprehension

Each numbered sentence in the following passage contains an italicized vocabulary word or related form. After you read the passage, you will complete an exercise.

Harriet Tubman: Early Freedom Fighter

As a girl Harriet Tubman (1820–1913) escaped from slavery. (1) As a woman she dedicated herself to helping others escape the ***shackles*** of slavery and to assisting other African Americans to gain the right to vote.

Harriet Tubman was one of the most daring conductors of what was known as the Underground Railroad. This term did not refer to an actual railroad, but to a nationwide network of homes, back roads, rivers, and tunnels that stretched from the Deep South to Canada. (2) Its workers shared one goal: to ***undermine*** and eventually eliminate the institution of slavery.

In her efforts to help several hundred slaves escape, Mrs. Tubman made nineteen dangerous trips into the South. She often said, "I never run my train off the track, and I never lost a passenger."

While leading the frightened but determined slaves along the path to freedom, Mrs. Tubman was helped by secret supporters who offered their homes and barns to the weary travelers. (3) It was often necessary for the fleeing slaves to ***adjourn*** to a new location without much warning.

Calm and levelheaded, Harriet Tubman worked well under these emergency conditions. (4) For her the unexpected appearance of a slave catcher was only a temporary ***hindrance.*** (5) When a slave catcher appeared, Mrs. Tubman might do something bold like letting several chickens loose and then ***tarrying*** conspicuously while trying to capture them. The slave catcher would usually decide that she was a harmless old woman.

(6) Mrs. Tubman's constant struggle was complicated by the existence of the ***repressive*** Fugitive Slave Act, which had been passed in 1850. This law gave slave catchers the right to arrest runaway slaves in free territory. The law also stated that citizens must cooperate. Because of this act, runaway slaves were no longer safe once they reached the northern states. (7) They were forced to ***prolong*** their lengthy journey, not able to find safety until they reached Canada.

Because of this act, some previously helpful citizens withdrew their aid. Others, actively sympathetic to the cause, continued to help the runaway slaves at great risk to themselves. (8) For example, angry citizens of Oberlin, Ohio, once forcibly ***detained*** a slave catcher at an inn while his captive ran away.

The conclusion of the Civil War in 1865 ended the need for an Underground Railroad, but it did not end Mrs. Tubman's activities. (9) Until her death in 1913, she never ***ceased*** helping African Americans in their struggle for equal rights. (10) She argued ***decisively*** that they must not be prevented from voting. For Harriet Tubman the fight for equality and freedom was never-ending.

Please turn to the next page.

Copyright © Houghton Mifflin Company. All rights reserved.

Reading Comprehension Exercise

Each of the following statements corresponds to a numbered sentence in the passage. Each statement contains a blank and is followed by four answer choices. Decide which choice fits best in the blank. The word or phrase that you choose must express roughly the same meaning as the italicized word in the passage. Write the letter of your choice on the answer line.

1. Harriet Tubman tried to help other slaves escape the ___?___ of slavery. 1. __________
   a. institution b. ignorance c. restraints d. condition

2. ___?___ the institution of slavery was the goal of the Underground Railroad. 2. __________
   a. Strengthening c. Weakening
   b. Avoiding d. Contributing to

3. Runaway slaves often had to ___?___ rapidly. 3. __________
   a. run b. move c. talk d. act

4. For Harriet Tubman a slave catcher was only a momentary ___?___. 4. __________
   a. obstacle b. reality c. disaster d. incident

5. To distract a slave catcher, Mrs. Tubman might ___?___ conspicuously. 5. __________
   a. talk b. walk c. sing d. linger

6. The ___?___ Fugitive Slave Act added to Mrs. Tubman's struggle. 6. __________
   a. insulting b. restraining c. unfair d. poorly written

7. The act ___?___ the journeys of the escaping slaves. 7. __________
   a. extended b. speeded c. stopped d. complicated

8. Some Ohio citizens once ___?___ a slave catcher so his captive could escape. 8. __________
   a. chased b. punished c. jailed d. delayed

9. Harriet Tubman never ___?___ helping blacks gain equal rights. 9. __________
   a. avoided b. seriously tried c. stopped d. thought of

10. She argued ___?___ that blacks should not be kept from voting. 10. __________
    a. conclusively b. loudly c. at length d. carefully

Writing Assignment

Imagine yourself as a newspaper reporter who writes an advice column. You have just received the following letter: "My best friend is having a party, but I can't go because I have already accepted another invitation for the same night. I want to tell my friend, but I'm afraid she'll get mad at me. Tired of Delaying." Using at least four words from this lesson, answer this letter in a paragraph or two. Underline each word.

Copyright © 1988 Houghton Mifflin Company. All rights reserved.

Lesson 15

Music and Sound

This lesson is based on words related to music and sound. Some of the words describe certain kinds of music or groups of music makers. Others deal with qualities of sound. You will find that some of the words have meanings that go beyond music.

When studying the definitions that follow, try to hear any sound described and to visualize how it is produced. How many people are involved? Are they playing instruments or singing or both? Is the sound produced music, language, or just noise?

WORD LIST

ballad
choral
lyric
opera
resonant
rhythm
serenade
shrill
symphony
tenor

DEFINITIONS

After you have studied the definitions and example for each vocabulary word, write the word on the line to the right.

1. **ballad** (băl′əd) *noun* **a.** A poem, often intended to be sung, that tells a story in a simple manner. **b.** A popular song, usually romantic or sentimental, that tells a story in several verses. 1. ______________

SEE *serenade.*

RELATED WORD **balladeer** *noun*

EXAMPLE Some American *ballads* were first sung in Britain.

2. **choral** (kôr′əl) *adjective* Related to a chorus or choir; written for performance by a chorus. 2. ______________

RELATED WORD **chorister** *noun*

EXAMPLE Many of the *choral* works of Johann Sebastian Bach (1685–1750) are still sung today.

3. **lyric** (lĭr′ĭk) *adjective* **a.** Of poetry that is a direct, often song-like expression of the poet's thoughts and feelings. **b.** Having a high, sweet singing voice: *a lyric soprano.* *noun* **a.** A lyric poem. **b.** *Usually plural.* The words of a song. 3. ______________

RELATED WORDS **lyrical** *adjective;* **lyrically** *adverb;* **lyricism** *noun*

EXAMPLE The *lyric* poems of Edgar Allan Poe could be set to music.

Copyright © Houghton Mifflin Company. All rights reserved.

4. **opera** (ŏp′ər-ə) *noun* A dramatic play in which most or all of the words are sung. 4. ____________

RELATED WORD **operatic** *adjective*

EXAMPLE *Operas* are usually large productions, with dancers, expensive costumes, and spectacular scenery.

5. **resonant** (rĕz′ə-nənt) *adjective* Having a rich, full, pleasing sound; vibrating: *a resonant concert hall.* 5. ____________

RELATED WORDS **resonance** *noun;* **resonate** *verb*

EXAMPLE One of the qualities valued in radio announcers is a *resonant* voice.

6. **rhythm** (rĭ*th*′əm) *noun* **a.** A repeated pattern of strong and weak beats, as in music or poetry. **b.** A characteristic sound or motion: *the steady rhythm of a healthy heartbeat.* **c.** A natural cycle: *the rhythm of the tides.* 6. ____________

RELATED WORDS **rhythmic** *adjective;* **rhythmically** *adverb*

EXAMPLE "One, two, three, this isn't me," muttered Trish as she tried to dance in time to the *rhythm* of the waltz.

7. **serenade** (sĕr′ə-nād′) *noun* **a.** A musical piece that honors or expresses love for someone: *a lover's serenade.* **b.** A certain kind of piece written for a small group of instruments. *verb* To sing a love song to someone. 7. ____________

EXAMPLE "That's a *serenade* to spring," joked my uncle as we walked past a pond full of croaking frogs.

USAGE NOTE A ballad (p. 93) *tells a story,* even a love story, but a serenade, intended to be played or sung outdoors at night, *expresses* love.

8. **shrill** (shrĭl) *adjective* High-pitched and piercing. *verb* To utter in a piercing manner. 8. ____________

RELATED WORDS **shrillness** *noun;* **shrilly** *adverb*

EXAMPLE When the *shrill* wail of a siren sounded, the traffic split as if cut by a knife.

9. **symphony** (sĭm′fə-nē) *noun* **a.** A long piece, usually of four sections, written for an orchestra. **b.** A large professional orchestra. 9. ____________

RELATED WORD **symphonic** *adjective*

EXAMPLE To be able to play all *symphonies,* a professional orchestra should keep one hundred musicians on its payroll.

10. **tenor** (tĕn′ər) *noun* **a.** The highest natural adult male voice. **b.** A person having such a voice. **c.** The general meaning or intention of something written or spoken: *the tenor of her remarks.* *adjective* Relating to a tenor range: *a tenor aria.* 10. ____________

EXAMPLE The Italian singer Luciano Pavarotti is a *tenor.*

Copyright © Houghton Mifflin Company. All rights reserved.

Name ______________________________ Date ____________

Exercise 1 Writing Correct Words

On the answer line, write the word from the vocabulary list that fits each definition.

1. A long piece, usually of four sections, written for an orchestra; a large professional orchestra — 1. __________
2. A poem, often intended to be sung, that tells a story in a simple manner — 2. __________
3. The highest natural adult male voice; the general meaning of something written or spoken — 3. __________
4. Related to a chorus or choir; written for performance by a chorus — 4. __________
5. High-pitched; piercing — 5. __________
6. Of poetry that is direct and songlike — 6. __________
7. A repeated pattern of strong and weak beats, as in music or poetry — 7. __________
8. A musical piece that honors or expresses love for someone — 8. __________
9. Having a rich, full, pleasing sound; vibrating — 9. __________
10. A dramatic play in which most or all of the words are sung — 10. __________

Exercise 2 Using Words Correctly

Each of the following questions contains an italicized vocabulary word. Choose the correct answer to the question, and write *Yes* or *No* on the answer line.

1. Would you order a *choral* arrangement from a flower shop? — 1. ________
2. Does a male opera singer with a very low voice sing *tenor?* — 2. ________
3. Is it pleasant to listen to a singer with a *shrill* voice? — 3. ________
4. Is a *resonant* voice desirable for stars of musical comedy? — 4. ________
5. If your voice has a *lyric* quality to it, will you probably be accepted in the school choir? — 5. ________
6. When balloonists want to rise, do they throw *ballads* overboard? — 6. ________
7. Should a musician be experienced in order to play a *symphony?* — 7. ________
8. Is a *serenade* a good type of song to march to? — 8. ________
9. Should a drummer have a good sense of *rhythm?* — 9. ________
10. Is an *opera* longer than a song? — 10. ________

Copyright © 1988 Houghton Mifflin Company. All rights reserved.

Exercise 3 Choosing the Best Word

Decide which vocabulary word or related form best completes the sentence, and write the letter of your choice on the answer line.

1. "I am going to play a(n) __?__ for my fiancée," Arthur said, grabbing his guitar. 1. ________
   a. serenade **b.** opera **c.** choral **d.** symphony

2. Choruses still sing many of J. S. Bach's __?__ works. 2. ________
   a. symphonic **b.** rhythmic **c.** choral **d.** resonant

3. Lew sang "The __?__ of John Henry," about a railroad worker. 3. ________
   a. Opera **b.** Symphony **c.** Serenade **d.** Ballad

4. The __?__ call of a bird woke us with a start on the first morning of the camping trip. 4. ________
   a. symphonic **b.** operatic **c.** shrill **d.** tenor

5. Some __?__ feature live horses and cannons onstage. 5. ________
   a. symphonies **b.** operas **c.** serenades **d.** ballads

6. Crowds flocked to hear the sweet voice of the __?__ soprano. 6. ________
   a. lyric **b.** shrill **c.** rhythmic **d.** resonant

7. In ragtime piano music, the melody is syncopated against a steady __?__ in the bass. 7. ________
   a. resonance **b.** symphony **c.** tenor **d.** rhythm

8. It takes a good ear to hear all the instruments played in a __?__. 8. ________
   a. ballad **b.** serenade **c.** symphony **d.** lyric

9. The __?__ of the lawyer's letter was threatening. 9. ________
   a. rhythm **b.** tenor **c.** lyricism **d.** resonance

10. The big, rich tone of the __?__ violin matched its price tag, $120,000! 10. ________
    a. choral **b.** tenor **c.** resonant **d.** rhythmic

Exercise 4 Using Different Forms of Words

Decide which form of the vocabulary word in parentheses best completes the sentence. The form given may be correct. Write your answer on the answer line.

1. After the feast a __?__ sang about Robin Hood. *(ballad)* 1. ________
2. Tom plays __?__ saxophone in the school band. *(tenor)* 2. ________
3. Glee club members sang a variety of __?__ music. *(choral)* 3. ________
4. Members of the __?__ orchestra were required to play a wide variety of selections. *(symphony)* 4. ________
5. The speaker, her voice rising and falling __?__, held everyone spellbound. *(lyric)* 5. ________
6. In the movie the pirate __?__ the princess. *(serenade)* 6. ________
7. An __?__ voice may take a long time to develop. *(opera)* 7. ________

Copyright © 1988 Houghton Mifflin Company. All rights reserved.

Name ______________________________ Date ______________

8. At noon the factory whistle __?__ announced lunch hour. *(shrill)* 8. ______________

9. The pounding of waves __?__ through the ocean cave. *(resonant)* 9. ______________

10. __?__ hoofbeats broke the silence. *(rhythm)* 10. ______________

Reading Comprehension

Each numbered sentence in the following passage contains an italicized vocabulary word or related form. After you read the passage, you will complete an exercise.

Orpheus and Eurydice: Victims of Love

(1) The Greek mythological story of Orpheus and Eurydice has the type of plot that a writer of ***ballads*** might find inspiring. (2) Indeed, this particular myth has captured the imagination of many artists, including Christoph Gluck (1714–1787), who based an ***opera*** on the famous story. (3) The opera's ***lyricism*** successfully recaptures the lovers' joy and grief.

(4) Orpheus was a musician and poet whose ***resonant*** voice was unmatched. (5) The songs he played on a simple lyre had more impact than a ***symphony*** performed by a large orchestra. His music could charm wild beasts and make even rocks and trees follow him. It seemed to give him godlike powers.

On one occasion Orpheus' music saved the lives of Jason and the Argonauts, who were sailing dangerously close to the rocks where the Sirens lived. (6) According to myth, the enchanting love songs of these evil ***choristers*** lured ship captains and their crews toward the rocks, where they found only a watery grave. (7) Miraculously, Orpheus' singing was so powerful that it drowned out these deadly ***serenades.***

After the Argonaut adventure, Orpheus fell deeply in love with, and married, the beautiful maiden Eurydice.

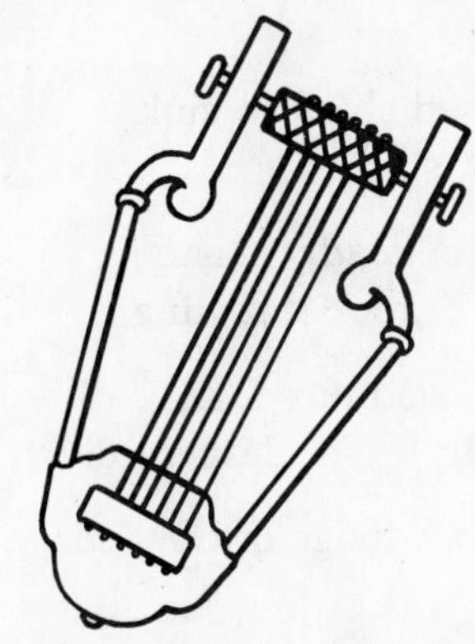

Just after their marriage, Eurydice was running from danger and failed to see a snake in her path. It bit her. (8) She cried out ***shrilly*** and then died.

Once dead, Eurydice went to the Underworld, or Hades. Like most of the other dead, she became a *shade,* someone who loses all memory and feeling. Orpheus was heartbroken by this chain of events and vowed to get Eurydice back. He used his music to do so, accomplishing the impossible three times.

First, he charmed his way into Hades. (9) Next, the shades, supposedly lacking all feelings, flocked to hear his ***rhythmic*** melodies. Finally, he melted the cold heart of Hades, god of the Underworld, who promised to release Eurydice on one condition.

(10) The ***tenor*** of the bargain was that Orpheus agreed not to look back to see if Eurydice was following him on the long trail leading out of the Underworld. He promised not to glance at her until they reached earth.

Keeping this in mind, the pair set off, with Orpheus singing happily and being careful to keep his eyes straight ahead. All went well until Orpheus reached the end of the trail and stepped joyfully into the daylight. Thinking that Eurydice was right behind him, Orpheus turned too soon — only to see his beloved wife slip back into the darkness.

"Farewell," he heard her murmur.

From then on, the singer's life was filled with sorrow. He soon died and was never able to rejoin Eurydice. Instead, he went to the heavens, immortalized as the musical constellation Lyra.

Please turn to the next page.

Copyright © 1988 Houghton Mifflin Company. All rights reserved.

Reading Comprehension Exercise

Each of the following statements corresponds to a numbered sentence in the passage. Each statement contains a blank and is followed by four answer choices. Decide which choice fits best in the blank. The word or phrase that you choose must express roughly the same meaning as the italicized word in the passage. Write the letter of your choice on the answer line.

1. The story of Orpheus and Eurydice would make a good __?__. 1. ________
   a. fairy tale   b. movie   c. novel   d. storytelling song

2. Christoph Gluck wrote a __?__ about it. 2. ________
   a. biography   c. dramatic play with music
   b. book of poetry   d. series of articles

3. The __?__ of the music recaptures the lovers' joy and grief. 3. ________
   a. emotional quality   c. turning point
   b. complicated plot   d. descriptive character

4. Orpheus had a very __?__ voice. 4. ________
   a. sophisticated   b. harsh   c. rich   d. unusual

5. His songs had greater influence than a __?__. 5. ________
   a. book of poems   c. short novel
   b. long musical piece   d. dramatic play

6. The Sirens were vicious __?__ who caused ships to sink. 6. ________
   a. rocks   b. monsters   c. spies   d. singers

7. Orpheus kept the Argonauts safe from the deadly __?__. 7. ________
   a. love songs   b. looks   c. traps   d. rock-throwing

8. After being bitten by a snake, Eurydice cried out __?__. 8. ________
   a. for help   b. piercingly   c. excitedly   d. desperately

9. The shades gathered to listen to the __?__ songs of Orpheus. 9. ________
   a. long   c. highly entertaining
   b. favorite   d. regular beat of the

10. The __?__ of the bargain was that Orpheus could not look back while leading Eurydice out of Hades. 10. ________
    a. general meaning   c. final result
    b. hidden danger   d. high point

Writing Assignment

In an imaginary letter to a parent or another adult, explain why your favorite musical group or your favorite type of music is worth listening to. In one paragraph give at least two general reasons to support your claim. Provide a specific example for each general reason. Use five vocabulary words from this lesson and underline each one.

 Copyright © 1988 Houghton Mifflin Company. All rights reserved.

Name ______________________ Date ______________________

READING SKILLS

Reading Skills

Context Clues

When you read, you sometimes encounter unfamiliar words. You can use the other words in a sentence—the **context**—as clues to the definition of the word you don't know. These word clues are called **context clues.** Read the following sentence and see if you can define *hilarious* by using context clues.

Everyone laughed at Carlos's *hilarious* story.

Since everyone laughed, the story must be funny. Therefore, *hilarious* must mean "funny." The following procedure will help you use the context to guess the meaning of an unfamiliar word.

PROCEDURE

1. *Read the sentence completely.*
2. *Use the other words in the sentence as clues to the meaning of the word you don't know.*
3. *Reread the sentence to see if your definition of the word makes sense.*
4. *Check your definition by looking up the word in a dictionary.*

Exercise **Using Context Clues**

Use context clues to define the italicized word in each of the following sentences. *Step 1:* Write your own definition of the word. *Step 2:* Write the dictionary definition of the word. Choose the definition that best fits the way the word is used in the sentence. *Step 3:* Write a sentence of your own in which you use the word correctly.

1. Few of us believed her *incredible* story.

YOUR DEFINITION ______________________

DICTIONARY DEFINITION ______________________

SENTENCE ______________________

Please turn to the next page.

Copyright © 1988 Houghton Mifflin Company. All rights reserved.

2. Mai could see only fuzzy shapes through the window that frost had made *translucent.*

YOUR DEFINITION ______________________________

DICTIONARY DEFINITION ______________________________

SENTENCE ______________________________

3. Once a *pauper,* DeSayle was now a lord with a huge estate.

YOUR DEFINITION ______________________________

DICTIONARY DEFINITION ______________________________

SENTENCE ______________________________

4. The *ornate* furniture seemed out of place in the simple house.

YOUR DEFINITION ______________________________

DICTIONARY DEFINITION ______________________________

SENTENCE ______________________________

5. During storms the rocky islands are a *menace* to ships.

YOUR DEFINITION ______________________________

DICTIONARY DEFINITION ______________________________

SENTENCE ______________________________

6. The woodcutter's progress through the forest was *hampered* by thickets.

YOUR DEFINITION ______________________________

DICTIONARY DEFINITION ______________________________

SENTENCE ______________________________

7. The iceberg was nearly split in two by a *crevice.*

YOUR DEFINITION ______________________________

DICTIONARY DEFINITION ______________________________

SENTENCE ______________________________

8. Since our funds were *insufficient,* we could not take the trip.

YOUR DEFINITION ______________________________

DICTIONARY DEFINITION ______________________________

SENTENCE ______________________________

Copyright © 1988 Houghton Mifflin Company. All rights reserved.

Lesson 16

Activity and Inactivity

The states of activity and inactivity are a natural part of life. People work or play, then rest. Many animals actively look for food in the warm months and then hibernate during the cold ones. After centuries of inactivity, a volcano erupts unexpectedly. Each of these examples is part of the natural pattern of motion and rest.

As you study the words, picture the activities they describe. Ask yourself these questions: Can this word be applied to a person, an animal, a thing, or an idea? Does it describe activity or inactivity? Finally, could this word be used to describe your own active or inactive states?

WORD LIST

dormant
energetic
industrious
loiter
lull
restless
sluggish
spry
strenuous
vigor

DEFINITIONS

After you have studied the definitions and example for each vocabulary word, write the word on the line to the right.

1. **dormant** (dôr′mənt) *adjective* **a.** Temporarily inactive but capable of renewed activity. **b.** In an inactive, sleeplike condition during which life processes slow down or are suspended: *a dormant snake.* 1. ______________

   RELATED WORD **dormancy** *noun*

   EXAMPLE The villagers nervously studied the *dormant* volcano, looking for signs of life.

2. **energetic** (ĕn′ər-jĕt′ĭk) *adjective* Full of energy; peppy; lively. 2. ______________

   RELATED WORDS **energetically** *adverb;* **energize** *verb;* **energy** *noun*

   EXAMPLE "I'm exhausted after baby-sitting for those *energetic* twins!" exclaimed Julie.

3. **industrious** (ĭn-dŭs′trē-əs) *adjective* Hard-working. 3. ______________

   RELATED WORDS **industrialize** *verb;* **industriously** *adverb;* **industriousness** *noun*

   EXAMPLE *Industrious* students do good work and finish it on time.

Copyright © 1988 Houghton Mifflin Company. All rights reserved.

4. **loiter** (loi′tər) *verb* **a.** To stand idly about; linger. **b.** To proceed slowly or with many stops. 4. ______________

RELATED WORD **loiterer** *noun*

EXAMPLE The mother told her child not to *loiter* but to come directly home after school.

5. **lull** (lŭl) *noun* A temporary lessening of activity or noise: *a lull in the storm.* *verb* **a.** To cause to sleep or rest; soothe. **b.** To trick into trusting: *to lull victims with smooth talk.* 5. ______________

EXAMPLE The musicians tuned their instruments during the *lull* between pieces.

6. **restless** (rĕst′lĭs) *adjective* **a.** Unable to relax, rest, or be still: *a restless child.* **b.** Without rest or sleep: *a restless night.* **c.** Never still or motionless: *a restless sea.* 6. ______________

RELATED WORDS **restlessly** *adverb;* **restlessness** *noun*

EXAMPLE When strangers approached, the dog became *restless* and would not sit quietly at his owner's side.

7. **sluggish** (slŭg′ĭsh) *adjective* **a.** Showing little movement or activity: *sluggish water.* **b.** Lacking in alertness or energy; dull; lazy: *a sluggish response.* **c.** Slow to perform or respond. 7. ______________

RELATED WORDS **sluggishly** *adverb;* **sluggishness** *noun*

EXAMPLE Horns blared during the *sluggish* rush-hour traffic.

8. **spry** (sprī) *adjective* Active; nimble; lively; brisk. 8. ______________

RELATED WORDS **spryly** *adverb;* **spryness** *noun*

EXAMPLE "When I am sixty, I hope I am as *spry* as Grandmother Diaz is at eighty!" said Dad.

9. **strenuous** (strĕn′yo͞o-əs) *adjective* **a.** Requiring great effort, energy, or exertion. **b.** Vigorously active. 9. ______________

MEMORY CUE You must *strain* to do something *strenuous.*

RELATED WORDS **strenuously** *adverb;* **strenuousness** *noun*

EXAMPLE Moving a heavy piece of furniture is a *strenuous* task.

10. **vigor** (vĭg′ər) *noun* **a.** Physical energy or strength. **b.** Strong feeling; enthusiasm or intensity. 10. ______________

RELATED WORDS **vigorous** *adjective;* **vigorously** *adverb*

EXAMPLE The tennis champion played the game with great *vigor.*

Copyright © Houghton Mifflin Company. All rights reserved.

Name ______________________________ Date ______________

Exercise 1 Completing Definitions

On the answer line, write the word from the vocabulary list that best completes each definition.

1. An active or nimble person is said to be ___?___. 1. ________
2. To be peppy or lively is to be ___?___. 2. ________
3. A temporary lessening of activity is a ___?___. 3. ________
4. People who work hard can be described as ___?___. 4. ________
5. Something that shows little movement or someone who lacks alertness is ___?___. 5. ________
6. Someone who is full of physical energy or strength has ___?___. 6. ________
7. Someone who stands idly about is said to ___?___. 7. ________
8. Something that is temporarily inactive is in a ___?___ state. 8. ________
9. Something that requires great effort or energy is ___?___. 9. ________
10. Someone who is unable to relax or be still might be described as ___?___. 10. ________

Exercise 2 Using Words Correctly

Each of the following questions contains an italicized vocabulary word. Choose the correct answer to the question, and write *Yes* or *No* on the answer line.

1. Is a person *loitering* if he or she runs from place to place? 1. ________
2. Could bad dreams cause someone to have a *restless* night? 2. ________
3. Could you say that a rock is full of *vigor?* 3. ________
4. Is it accurate to call a champion hitter a *sluggish* player? 4. ________
5. Is a *dormant* something that you wipe your feet on? 5. ________
6. Could you say there is a *lull* in a storm if the rain stops? 6. ________
7. Is climbing a steep mountain with a forty-pound pack on your back a *strenuous* activity? 7. ________
8. After you soap a car, do you *spry* the soap off and then apply wax? 8. ________
9. Is someone who watches television all day an *industrious* person? 9. ________
10. Is a person who exercises constantly considered *energetic?* 10. ________

Copyright © 1988 Houghton Mifflin Company. All rights reserved.

Exercise 3 Choosing the Best Word

Decide which vocabulary word or related form best completes the sentence, and write the letter of your choice on the answer line.

1. The governor spoke __?__ against an increase in taxes. 1. ________
a. restlessly b. vigorously c. sluggishly d. spryly

2. No __?__ is allowed in the school halls. 2. ________
a. dormancy b. spryness c. industriousness d. loitering

3. During the cold winter months, hibernating animals are in a(n) __?__ state. 3. ________
a. dormant b. industrious c. vigorous d. spry

4. Compared with a cheetah, a snail is __?__. 4. ________
a. sluggish b. energetic c. industrious d. vigorous

5. The gentle sound of the waves __?__ the campers to sleep. 5. ________
a. industrialized b. lulled c. loitered d. energized

6. The long training required by medical schools is both expensive and __?__. 6. ________
a. strenuous b. sluggish c. lulling d. restless

7. Mr. Jefferson jumped __?__ over the fence. 7. ________
a. industriously b. spryly c. restlessly d. sluggishly

8. The __?__ of the busy ant is the subject of the fable "The Ant and the Grasshopper." 8. ________
a. restlessness c. strenuousness
b. sluggishness d. industriousness

9. My piano teacher told me to play the march more __?__. 9. ________
a. restlessly b. sluggishly c. energetically d. strenuously

10. Fidgety plane passengers waited __?__ for the fog to lift. 10. ________
a. sluggishly b. vigorously c. energetically d. restlessly

Exercise 4 Using Different Forms of Words

Each sentence contains an italicized vocabulary word in a form that does not fit the sentence. On the answer line, write the form of the word that does fit the sentence.

1. The father *lull* his baby to sleep with a quiet song. 1. ________
2. Marsha worked *strenuous* to clear the sidewalk of snow. 2. ________
3. It is considered bad manners to shake a queen's hand *vigor*. 3. ________
4. Clogged by autumn leaves, the stream moved *sluggish*. 4. ________
5. At present Ted's ambitions are in a state of *dormant*. 5. ________
6. The ragged *loiter* was really an undercover detective. 6. ________

Copyright © 1988 Houghton Mifflin Company. All rights reserved.

Name ______________________________ Date ______________

7. The six-week-old puppies were filled with *energetic*. 7. ______________

8. The art students worked *industrious* on their projects until the bell rang. 8. ______________

9. *Spry* in old age is often the result of good mental and physical health. 9. ______________

10. The tiger paced *restless* in its cage. 10. ______________

Reading Comprehension

Each numbered sentence in the following passage contains an italicized vocabulary word or related form. After you read the passage, you will complete an exercise.

The Oryx: A Study in Survival

If the Arabian oryx has a motto, it might be "Slow and steady wins the race." **(1)** In contrast to its ***sprier*** African cousins, this antelopelike animal seems lazy. **(2)** It runs rarely, spends little time impressing a mate, welcomes strangers into its herd instead of chasing them off, and spends hours ***loitering*** under acacia trees. **(3)** The seeming ***sluggishness*** of the Arabian oryx actually helps it to survive in the desert.

(4) In addition, the body type and habits of the oryx are well suited to the ***strenuousness*** of the desert lifestyle. The oryx is smaller than its African cousins and, unlike them, has a solid, almost pure white coat. Because its coat is light, the oryx attracts a minimum of heat. Because it is small, the oryx fits easily under the branches of low shade trees and needs only a small amount of food. As a result, it can handle constant shortages of food, water, and shade.

Although not all forms of desert life have this slow-and-easy style, all do have ways to combat extreme heat. **(5)** Like the oryx, which will plod miles in the dark to a water hole, many desert animals are more ***energetic*** at night. **(6)** At that time the desert is a picture of ***restlessness.*** **(7)** No longer ***dormant,*** snakes, mice, and other animals pop up from their burrows — to eat or be eaten. **(8)** Most hunt ***industriously*** for food. **(9)** There is barely a ***lull*** in the constant activity.

(10) The patient oryx lazily observes this display of ***vigor.*** Although the oryx's slowness enables it to survive the heat of the desert, this trait also makes it an easy target for hunters. By 1972 hunters had killed almost all of the oryx population. Now, however, as a result of a conservation program called Operation Oryx, large herds of Arabian oryx once again roam the desert.

Please turn to the next page.

Copyright © 1988 Houghton Mifflin Company. All rights reserved.

Reading Comprehension Exercise

Each of the following statements corresponds to a numbered sentence in the passage. Each statement contains a blank and is followed by four answer choices. Decide which choice fits best in the blank. The word or phrase that you choose must express roughly the same meaning as the italicized word in the passage. Write the letter of your choice on the answer line.

1. Many African antelopes are __?__ than the Arabian oryx. 1. ________
   a. livelier b. darker c. heavier d. lighter

2. An oryx likes to __?__ under acacia trees. 2. ________
   a. water b. feed c. idle d. hide

3. The __?__ of the Arabian oryx helps it to survive. 3. ________
   a. inactivity b. strength c. kicking d. stupidity

4. Desert life requires __?__. 4. ________
   a. strong sunlight c. quick growth
   b. lack of water d. great effort

5. Like the oryx, many desert animals are more __?__ at night. 5. ________
   a. sensitive b. thirsty c. conspicuous d. peppy

6. At night there is __?__ in the desert. 6. ________
   a. silence c. little activity
   b. constant motion d. water drinking

7. At this time desert animals are no longer __?__. 7. ________
   a. temporarily inactive c. in danger
   b. thirsty d. in need of food

8. They look __?__ for food. 8. ________
   a. everywhere b. in shifts c. very hard d. casually

9. There is barely a(n) __?__ in the activity. 9. ________
   a. break b. adventure c. difficult moment d. time to hunt

10. The oryx calmly watches the __?__ displayed in this scene. 10. ________
    a. lack of cunning b. physical energy c. beauty d. cleverness

Practice with Analogies

See pages 32, 52, and 86 for some strategies to use with analogies.

DIRECTIONS On the answer line, write the vocabulary word that completes each analogy.

1. Brave is to courageous as hard-working is to __?__. 1. ________
2. Glory is to glorious as __?__ is to vigorous. 2. ________
3. Shy is to timid as nimble is to __?__. 3. ________
4. Ancient is to modern as energetic is to __?__. 4. ________
5. Hurry is to rush as linger is to __?__. 5. ________

Copyright © Houghton Mifflin Company. All rights reserved.

Lesson 17

Agreement and Disagreement

Within any group situation, people have a tendency to agree and disagree, as shown by the following example.

> Members of the Hopkins Junior High School Student Council could not reach a decision about a forthcoming fund-raising project.
>
> "I think we should have a car wash," Roger suggested.
>
> "Good idea," Bob echoed.
>
> "We can't have a car wash in January. We'd be up to our knees in snow!" Anne told Roger. "How about selling magazine subscriptions?"
>
> Her suggestion was met by sighs of disapproval.

Agreement and disagreement are usually part of any discussion, be it a group discussion or just two people talking. The words in this lesson will help you to explain and to describe to what degree people are agreeing or disagreeing.

WORD LIST

conflict
consent
contrary
cooperative
corroborate
friction
negotiate
pact
rapport
rift

DEFINITIONS

After you have studied the definitions and example for each vocabulary word, write the word on the line to the right.

1. **conflict** (kŏn′flĭkt′) *noun* **a.** A clash of opposing ideas or interests: *a personality conflict.* **b.** Prolonged fighting; warfare: *armed conflict.* *verb* (kən-flĭkt′) To be in opposition; differ.

   EXAMPLE Political parties are often in *conflict* over tax policy.

   1. ______________

2. **consent** (kən-sĕnt′) *noun* Agreement; acceptance; permission given. *verb* To give permission; agree.

   EXAMPLE A parent or guardian's written *consent* is required.

   2. ______________

   USAGE NOTE *Assent* is more formal than *consent.* *Dissent* is an antonym.

3. **contrary** (kŏn′trĕr′ē) *adjective* **a.** Opposite in direction, character, or purpose; opposed; completely different: *a contrary opinion.* **b.** (kən-trâr′ē) Stubbornly opposed to others: *a contrary personality.* *noun* (kŏn′trĕr′ē) The opposite.

   RELATED WORD **contrariness** *noun*

   EXAMPLE The jury's verdict was *contrary* to our expectations.

   3. ______________

Copyright © Houghton Mifflin Company. All rights reserved.

4. **cooperative** (kō-ŏp′ər-ə-tĭv) *adjective* **a.** Working willingly with others: *a cooperative patient.* **b.** Done along with others: *a co-operative effort.* **c.** Owned with others: *a cooperative store.* *noun* A business owned by the persons who use its products or services: *a food cooperative.* 4. ___________

RELATED WORDS **cooperate** *verb;* **cooperation** *noun;* **cooperatively** *adverb*

EXAMPLE The *cooperative* students helped their teacher arrange the bulletin board.

5. **corroborate** (kə-rŏb′ə-rāt′) *verb* To support by new facts; show the accuracy or truth of. 5. ___________

RELATED WORDS **corroboration** *noun;* **corroborative** *adjective*

EXAMPLE The witness's testimony *corroborated* Miller's alibi.

6. **friction** (frĭk′shən) *noun* **a.** A disagreement or clash, especially between persons of different opinions or interests. **b.** The rubbing of one surface against another. 6. ___________

EXAMPLE Unkind remarks can cause *friction* between even the best of friends.

7. **negotiate** (nĭ-gō′shē-āt′) *verb* **a.** To confer or discuss (something) in order to come to terms: *to negotiate a peace treaty.* **b.** To transfer ownership of (something) for money: *negotiate a sale.* **c.** To succeed in accomplishing (something): *The car negotiated a difficult turn.* 7. ___________

RELATED WORDS **negotiable** *adjective;* **negotiation** *noun;* **negotiator** *noun*

EXAMPLE The students successfully *negotiated* a bigger choice of lunches in the school cafeteria.

8. **pact** (păkt) *noun* **a.** A formal agreement; treaty. **b.** Any serious agreement. 8. ___________

EXAMPLE The *pact* between the two nations has been in force for ten years.

9. **rapport** (ră-pôr′) *noun* A relationship of shared trust and understanding; harmony. 9. ___________

EXAMPLE As rehearsals progressed, cast members developed a warm *rapport.*

10. **rift** (rĭft) *noun* **a.** A break in friendly relations; split. **b.** A break or crack in a rock. **c.** A narrow opening. *verb* To break or cause to break apart; split. 10. ___________

EXAMPLE In the 1800s the issue of slavery caused a *rift* between the North and the South.

Copyright © 1988 Houghton Mifflin Company. All rights reserved.

Name ______________________________ Date ______________

Exercise 1 Matching Words and Definitions

Match the definition in Column B with the word in Column A. Write the letter of the correct definition on the answer line.

Column A	*Column B*
1. conflict	a. agreement; acceptance; to give permission or agree to
2. rift	b. a relationship of shared trust and understanding
3. negotiate	c. a formal agreement or treaty; any serious agreement
4. rapport	d. disagreement or clash; the rubbing of one surface against another
5. contrary	e. to confer or discuss to reach an agreement; transfer ownership for money
6. friction	f. a clash of opposing ideas; prolonged fighting
7. consent	g. working willingly with others; done along with others; owned with others
8. cooperative	h. opposite; opposed; completely different
9. pact	i. a break in friendly relations; a crack in a rock
10. corroborate	j. to support by new facts; verify the accuracy of

1. ________
2. ________
3. ________
4. ________
5. ________
6. ________
7. ________
8. ________
9. ________
10. ________

Exercise 2 Using Words Correctly

Each of the following statements contains an italicized vocabulary word. Decide whether the sentence is true or false, and write *True* or *False* on the answer line.

1. *Friction* is a category of literature that includes novels. 1. ________
2. If most of your test answers *conflict* with the teacher's, you will get a high grade. 2. ________
3. Close friendship is characterized by deep *rifts*. 3. ________
4. Someone who withholds permission does not give his or her *consent*. 4. ________
5. A front-page news story may also be called a special *rapport*. 5. ________
6. Fruit juice is often sold in *pacts* of six in the market. 6. ________
7. Lawyers need facts to *corroborate* witnesses' stories. 7. ________
8. Believing that the earth is flat is *contrary* to scientific fact. 8. ________
9. It is often difficult for countries that have been at war to *negotiate* peacefully. 9. ________
10. *Cooperative* behavior is necessary on a team. 10. ________

Copyright © 1988 Houghton Mifflin Company. All rights reserved.

Exercise 3 Choosing the Best Definition

For each italicized vocabulary word in the following sentences, write the letter of the best definition on the answer line.

1. The geologist studied the *rift* in the rare rock formation. 1. ________
   a. colors b. crystals c. crack d. leaves
2. A *pact* is not meant to be broken. 2. ________
   a. treaty b. friendship c. vase d. will
3. We were surprised when no *conflict* developed between our two pets. 3. ________
   a. problem b. clash c. growling d. jealousy
4. After two conferences, the lawyers were able to *negotiate.* 4. ________
   a. drop the case c. postpone the case
   b. come to terms d. attend a convention
5. Engines must be properly oiled to prevent damage from *friction.* 5. ________
   a. heat b. leaking c. pressure d. rubbing
6. "I'm for the plan," said the council member, "but will the mayor *consent*?" 6. ________
   a. agree b. disagree c. sign d. give up
7. On the application Mando described himself as "very *cooperative.*" 7. ________
   a. strong b. intelligent c. willing d. mature
8. "Do you always have to take a *contrary* position?" asked my sister. 8. ________
   a. unfriendly b. positive c. opposing d. unexpected
9. "You must *corroborate* these claims," the editor told the reporter. 9. ________
   a. enlarge upon b. verify c. falsify d. alter
10. Frequently there is *rapport* between children and their grandparents. 10. ________
    a. harmony c. distance
    b. respect d. lack of communication

Exercise 4 Using Different Forms of Words

Decide which form of the vocabulary word in parentheses best completes the sentence. The form given may be correct. Write your answer on the answer line.

1. It is the job of diplomats to bridge __?__ between countries. *(rift)* 1. ________
2. Braking causes __?__ between the brake pads and drums. *(friction)* 2. ________
3. Carlos is a natural __?__; he gets what he wants. *(negotiate)* 3. ________
4. The government often made __?__ with Native Americans. *(pact)* 4. ________
5. Because of Lee's __?__, Anne refused to baby-sit again. *(contrary)* 5. ________
6. The two papers printed __?__ reports on the fire. *(conflict)* 6. ________
7. The classes __?__ in raising money for the trip. *(cooperative)* 7. ________
8. "For a report, get __?__ of your facts." Mr. Kim said. *(corroborate)* 8. ________

Copyright © 1988 Houghton Mifflin Company. All rights reserved.

Name ______________________________ Date ______________

9. Mrs. Swanson __?__ to drive the children to a movie. *(consent)* 9. ______________

10. To work with animals, photographers establish __?__. *(rapport)* 10. ______________

Reading Comprehension

Each numbered sentence in the following passage contains an italicized vocabulary word or related form. After you read the passage, you will complete an exercise.

Henry B. Gonzalez: A Dedicated Congressman

Every two years citizens of each state elect men and women to the United States House of Representatives. (1) Some representatives establish outstanding ***rapport*** with those they serve and are elected again and again. Not many, however, can boast over thirty years of service. Henry B. Gonzalez of San Antonio can. (2) His long service is ***corroboration*** of his good record. Why has Gonzalez been able to serve so long? (3) Did an unwritten ***pact*** between Gonzalez and his district enable him to surpass the quarter-century mark?

Today Henry B. Gonzalez is a household name in his district and in his state. (4) He has long had the ***cooperation*** of his party. Gonzalez earned respect by fighting for the rights of minority groups.

Three years after Gonzalez went to Washington, Congress passed the historic Civil Rights Act of 1964. (5) This act said that running a government for the benefit of one group over others was ***contrary*** to the Constitution. (6) Congress would no longer ***consent*** to discrimination.

As a Mexican American, Gonzalez was well aware of the problems of minority groups. He could have tried to ignore the problems, for his engineering and law degrees promised him a good life. Conscience, however, told him to speak out.

Speaking out had its price. (7) For example, Gonzalez once resigned from a county job when he and a judge had ***conflicting*** opinions about equality for a minority employee. (8) In 1957 he risked a serious ***rift*** by telling his fellow members of the Texas Senate: "If we fear long enough, we hate; and if we hate long enough, we fight." Senators listened, and soon eight segregation bills were defeated.

(9) In 1961 Gonzalez's skills at speaking and ***negotiating*** won him a seat in Congress, where he earned a reputation for being outspoken on minority rights. His job has not been easy. (10) There has even been ***friction*** between Gonzalez and those who feel he does not represent his Mexican American voters on every issue. Gonzalez feels otherwise. "I am proud," he has said, "of my ancestry. . . . But it took votes from all . . . to elect me. I should represent them all, and I try to."

Reading Comprehension Exercise

Each of the following statements corresponds to a numbered sentence in the passage. Each statement contains a blank and is followed by four answer choices. Decide which choice fits best in the blank. The word or phrase that you choose must express roughly the same meaning as the italicized word in the passage. Write the letter of your choice on the answer line.

1. A fine __?__ exists between some representatives and their districts. 1. ______________
   a. communication system
   b. voting record
   c. election system
   d. relationship of shared trust

Copyright © Houghton Mifflin Company. All rights reserved.

2. Gonzalez's long service is __?__ of his fine record. 2. ________
a. proof b. one aspect c. the burden d. the result

3. Did a(n) __?__ exist between Gonzalez and his district? 3. ________
a. friendship b. relationship c. agreement d. disagreement

4. For a long time, he has known the __?__ of his party. 4. ________
a. leadership b. admiration c. support d. opposition

5. In 1964 it was decided that the denial of equal rights to all citizens was __?__ the Constitution. 5. ________
a. against b. related to c. supported by d. important in

6. Congress refused to __?__ discrimination. 6. ________
a. permit b. discuss c. oppose d. recognize

7. Gonzalez and a judge had __?__ opinions about an equal-rights question. 7. ________
a. strong b. interesting c. close d. opposing

8. Gonzalez spoke out even when it could result in __?__. 8. ________
a. a series of articles c. a break in friendly relations
b. bad publicity d. uncontrollable anger

9. Gonzalez was good at speaking and __?__. 9. ________
a. acting b. debating c. conferring d. judging

10. His political career has not been free of __?__. 10. ________
a. setbacks b. disagreement c. surprises d. disappointment

Writing Assignment

Select a public figure whom you admire. In a one- or two-paragraph letter to a national news magazine, tell why you think this person should be selected "Man or Woman of the Year." If necessary, ask your librarian to help you find biographical material on this person. Use at least five words from this lesson and underline each one.

Vocabulary Enrichment

The English word *corroborate* comes from the Latin verb *corroborare,* meaning "to strengthen." *Corroborare* breaks down into two parts. The first, *com-*, simply emphasizes the meaning of what follows. *Robur,* the second part, is the word for a very hard type of oak tree. Its wood provides strong support wherever used. Therefore, a statement that is "corroborated" is "made strong."

ACTIVITY Other English words are derived from the Latin names of plants and their parts. Look up the following words in a high school dictionary. Then explain how the meaning of each word is connected with the meaning of the Latin word from which it comes.

1. flourish 2. foliage 3. radical 4. robust 5. rosette

Copyright © 1988 Houghton Mifflin Company. All rights reserved.

The Roots *-man-* and *-ped-*

The roots *-man-* and *-ped-* are both Latin. They come from the words *manus,* meaning "hand," and *pes* or *pedis,* meaning "foot" or "of the foot." The roots often describe how something is done or made. For example, *manufactured* goods, today made by machine or by hand, were once made only by hand. A *pedal* is a foot-operated part of a machine, such as a bicycle. All four-footed animals are classified as *quadrupeds.*

Not all words containing *-man-* or *-ped-* have a "hand" or "foot" meaning. Whenever you run across words with these roots, then, you need to use both common sense and a dictionary to be sure of their meanings.

WORD LIST

emancipate
impede
manacle
maneuver
manipulate
manual
manuscript
pedestal
pedestrian
pedigree

DEFINITIONS

After you have studied the definitions and example for each vocabulary word, write the word on the line to the right.

1. **emancipate** (ĭ-măn′sə-pāt′) *verb* To set free; liberate.

RELATED WORDS **emancipation** *noun;* **emancipator** *noun*

EXAMPLE Roman slaveholders sometimes *emancipated* slaves as a reward for good service.

1. ______________

ETYMOLOGY NOTE When a boy in ancient Rome came of age, his father *emancipated* ("unhanded") him, taking and then freeing his hand.

2. **impede** (ĭm-pēd′) *verb* To slow down the progress of; block.

RELATED WORD **impediment** *noun*

EXAMPLE A stalled car *impeded* the flow of rush-hour traffic.

2. ______________

ETYMOLOGY NOTE The Latin *impedire* means "to shackle a prisoner's feet."

3. **manacle** (măn′ə-kəl) *noun* **a.** A device for locking or shackling the hands; handcuff. **b.** Anything that confines or restrains. *verb* To restrain with manacles.

EXAMPLE In early jails prisoners sometimes wore *manacles.*

3. ______________

USAGE NOTE The noun *manacle* is usually plural: *manacles.*

4. **maneuver** (mə-no͞o′vər) *noun* **a.** A skillful action, move, or plan. **b.** A change in the course or position of a vehicle, as an aircraft. **c.** A movement of troops or naval ships. *verb* **a.** To move about skillfully: *to maneuver through a crowd.* **b.** To bring about by planning or plotting: *to maneuver oneself into favor.* **c.** To carry out a military plan.

EXAMPLE In a daring *maneuver,* the diver escaped the shark.

4. ______________

USAGE NOTE The plural noun *maneuvers* usually refers to military training exercises or war games.

Copyright © Houghton Mifflin Company. All rights reserved.

5. **manipulate** (mə-nĭp′yə-lāt′) *verb* **a.** To arrange or operate with the hands. **b.** To influence or manage cleverly: *to manipulate public opinion.* **c.** To change data dishonestly for personal gain: *to manipulate bank records.* 5. ______

RELATED WORDS **manipulation** *noun;* **manipulative** *adjective;* **manipulator** *noun*

EXAMPLE It takes training to *manipulate* a large movie camera.

6. **manual** (măn′yo͞o-əl) *adjective* **a.** Operated or done by hand: *manual controls.* **b.** Requiring physical rather than mental effort: *manual labor.* *noun* A guidebook; handbook: *a driver's manual.* 6. ______

RELATED WORD **manually** *adverb*

EXAMPLE Does your car have a *manual* or an automatic gearshift?

7. **manuscript** (măn′yə-skrĭpt′) *noun* **a.** A handwritten or typewritten book or document, as distinguished from a printed copy: *to submit a manuscript to a publisher.* **b.** Handwriting as opposed to printing. 7. ______

EXAMPLE The *manuscript* of the famous book is on display at the university library.

8. **pedestal** (pĕd′ĭ-stəl) *noun* A support or base for a column or statue. 8. ______

EXAMPLE On the *pedestal* of the Statue of Liberty is a poem by Emma Lazarus beginning, "Give me your tired, your poor. . . ."

9. **pedestrian** (pə-dĕs′trē-ən) *noun* A person traveling on foot. *adjective* **a.** Of or for pedestrians: *a pedestrian crossing.* **b.** Ordinary; not distinguished: *pedestrian writing.* 9. ______

EXAMPLE *Pedestrians* should always walk on the left side of the road facing traffic.

10. **pedigree** (pĕd′ĭ-grē′) *noun* **a.** A list of ancestors; ancestry; family tree. **b.** A list of ancestors of a purebred animal: *a show dog's pedigree.* 10. ______

RELATED WORD **pedigreed** *adjective*

EXAMPLE Members of royalty have long *pedigrees.*

Copyright © 1988 Houghton Mifflin Company. All rights reserved.

Name ______________________________ Date ____________

Exercise 1 Writing Correct Words

On the answer line, write the word from the vocabulary list that fits each definition.

1. To slow down the progress of; block — 1. ____________
2. A list of ancestors; ancestry; family tree — 2. ____________
3. A support or base for a column or statue — 3. ____________
4. A person traveling on foot — 4. ____________
5. To set free; liberate — 5. ____________
6. A handwritten or typewritten book or document; handwriting — 6. ____________
7. Operated or done by hand — 7. ____________
8. A skillful action, move, or plan — 8. ____________
9. To arrange with the hands; manage cleverly — 9. ____________
10. A metal device for locking or shackling the hands — 10. ____________

Exercise 2 Using Words Correctly

Decide whether the italicized vocabulary word has been used correctly in the sentence. On the answer line, write *Correct* for correct use and *Incorrect* for incorrect use.

1. We can *emancipate* at least two hundred people at the variety show. — 1. ____________
2. Police officers often carry *manacles* on their belts. — 2. ____________
3. Dad doesn't *manipulate* going to the beach soon. — 3. ____________
4. Before the printing press existed, copying a *manuscript* took years. — 4. ____________
5. When their child got sick, the Kings called a *pedestrian.* — 5. ____________
6. Cy *maneuvered* his skateboard around a curb and onto the sidewalk. — 6. ____________
7. A sudden shower *impeded* the progress of the parade. — 7. ____________
8. Always read the owner's *manual* before using a new electric tool. — 8. ____________
9. The sign in the beauty shop read, "*Pedigree* and polish, $15." — 9. ____________
10. Circus elephants are often taught to balance on a *pedestal.* — 10. ____________

Exercise 3 Choosing the Best Definition

For each italicized vocabulary word in the following sentences, write the letter of the best definition on the answer line.

1. When peace came, all prisoners of war were *emancipated.* — 1. ____________
   a. arrested **b.** questioned **c.** freed **d.** handcuffed

Copyright © 1988 Houghton Mifflin Company. All rights reserved.

2. *Manipulate* the center dial until the picture focuses clearly. 2. ______
a. Pull **b.** Operate **c.** Twist **d.** Yank

3. Many childhood games, such as jacks, use skills that are *manual.* 3. ______
a. of the hands **c.** of the mind
b. of the feet **d.** of the eye

4. Those marble columns have simple *pedestals* but fancy caps. 4. ______
a. bases **b.** tops **c.** decorations **d.** statues

5. Some ancient *manuscripts* have beautiful art in the margins. 5. ______
a. typewritten books **c.** handwritten books
b. holy works **d.** printed books

6. *Pedestrians* as well as drivers need to know rules of the road. 6. ______
a. Police **b.** Passengers **c.** Walkers **d.** Tourists

7. To make a point, some women who fought for the right to vote *manacled* themselves to the White House fence! 7. ______
a. roped **b.** handcuffed **c.** tied **d.** strapped

8. Shyness and lack of confidence *impede* success. 8. ______
a. promote **b.** guarantee **c.** block **d.** need

9. Buyers ask how a car *maneuvers* as well as what mileage it gets. 9. ______
a. starts **b.** handles **c.** brakes **d.** stops

10. "My cats," bragged their owner, "have fine *pedigrees.*" 10. ______
a. whiskers **b.** lives **c.** tails **d.** backgrounds

Exercise 4 Using Different Forms of Words

Decide which form of the vocabulary word in parentheses best completes the sentence. The form given may be correct. Write your answer on the answer line.

1. Lincoln's __?__ of the slaves took place in 1863. *(emancipate)* 1. ______
2. On Roman slave ships, men were often __?__ to their oars. *(manacle)* 2. ______
3. Old __?__ should be kept in air-conditioned rooms. *(manuscript)* 3. ______
4. After __?__ the car into a tight space, Mom looked smug. *(maneuver)* 4. ______
5. A crane was used to lower the huge statue onto its __?__. *(pedestal)* 5. ______
6. The __?__ of the Arabian horse goes back centuries. *(pedigree)* 6. ______
7. A Ray Bradbury story tells of a __?__ arrested for taking an evening stroll. *(pedestrian)* 7. ______
8. A swindler is a __?__ of people's trust. *(manipulate)* 8. ______
9. Repairing clocks requires accuracy and __?__ skill. *(manual)* 9. ______
10. Stuttering is a speech __?__. *(impede)* 10. ______

Copyright © 1988 Houghton Mifflin Company. All rights reserved.

Name ______________________ Date ______________

Reading Comprehension

Each numbered sentence in the following passage contains an italicized vocabulary word or related form. After you read the passage, you will complete an exercise.

Slavery in Ancient Rome

(1) ***Pedestrians*** in Rome can find many signs of that city's past glory: a huge arena, emperors' palaces, and a sprawling marketplace. (2) Marble gods and emperors still look from their ***pedestals*** upon an international city. It does not take much imagination to fill these ruins with people again. According to the saying, all roads led to Rome. Over them marched the incredible Roman army carrying prizes of war. Perhaps the most valuable prizes were prisoners of war, who became slaves. (3) Without their labor, ancient ***manuscripts*** suggest, Rome would never have become so great.

(4) Ancient Rome had more slaves and relied more heavily on their ***manual*** labor than has any other civilization. (5) Still, not all of the ***manacled*** Greeks, Britons, Spaniards, Africans, Vikings, and Slavs brought to Rome had grim lives. (6) In Rome slavery was not always an ***impediment*** to a good life. (7) Slaves who knew a craft, were musicians, could read and write, or could ***manipulate*** numbers were highly valued. (8) They might even ***maneuver*** themselves into full citizenship. (9) Indeed, some earned ***emancipation*** as a reward for good service or upon the death of their masters.

As a rule, unskilled slaves were less fortunate. For example, strong but unskilled young men might find themselves assigned to heavy labor or to gladiator school. (10) Like ***pedigreed*** racehorses, gladiators were well fed, exercised, and trained. Their only duty was to perform. They "entertained" the Roman crowds as charioteers or in man-to-man or man-to-lion combat. Most died early. Only a lucky few, mainly the "stars," gained freedom.

Once freed, a slave was accepted into the community. Roman law fully applied to its new citizens, regardless of color or former nationality.

Reading Comprehension Exercise

Each of the following statements corresponds to a numbered sentence in the passage. Each statement contains a blank and is followed by four answer choices. Decide which choice fits best in the blank. The word or phrase that you choose must express roughly the same meaning as the italicized word in the passage. Write the letter of your choice on the answer line.

1. __?__ in Rome see many signs of its past. 1. ________
   a. Travelers **b.** Walkers **c.** Motorists **d.** Photographers

2. From their marble __?__, statues of former rulers gaze at the city. 2. ________
   a. pools **b.** palaces **c.** supports **d.** roofs

3. Old __?__ show that slave labor helped make Rome great. 3. ________
   a. pictures **b.** writings **c.** signs **d.** prisoners

4. The Romans relied heavily on slaves for __?__ labor. 4. ________
   a. hand **b.** mechanical **c.** cheap **d.** quick

Copyright © 1988 Houghton Mifflin Company. All rights reserved.

5. Not all of the slaves brought to Rome __?__ led grim lives. 5. ________
a. by ship **b.** in groups **c.** in handcuffs **d.** from abroad

6. Being a slave was not always a(n) __?__ to the good life. 6. ________
a. threat **b.** end **c.** aid **d.** barrier

7. Slaves who could __?__ numbers were valued. 7. ________
a. fix **b.** handle **c.** invent **d.** read

8. Skilled slaves might __?__ their own citizenship. 8. ________
a. bring about **b.** look into **c.** apply for **d.** give up

9. One reward for good service was __?__. 9. ________
a. punishment **b.** freedom **c.** security **d.** wealth

10. Gladiators, like __?__ racehorses, had to perform. 10. ________
a. purebred **b.** trained **c.** valuable **d.** strong

Writing Assignment

You are an archaeologist camped on the ruins of an ancient Roman general's summer estate. After weeks of nothing but bad weather, you want to give up. Then your spade hits something! That night you write a journal entry describing what you found and how you felt. Use at least four words from this lesson and underline them.

Vocabulary Enrichment

Although rooted in Latin, *pedigree* came into English through Old French. The term came into being along with the growth of a noble class in France. One way for powerful families to maintain their power was to marry one another. Proving ancestry became important, and families kept track of themselves with special charts — what we refer to today as "family trees." The forklike, branching lines on these charts strongly resembled the footprint of a crane, a large heronlike bird. The Old French *pie de grue* meant "crane's footprint" (from Latin: *ped-*, "foot"; *de*, "of"; *grus*, "crane"). In all likelihood the term crossed the English Channel with William the Conqueror in 1066. By 1600 it was spelled as it is today.

ACTIVITY The words below name different parts of the body. Look up and write their meanings and Latin roots. Then tell how each meaning and its root are related.

1. coccyx 2. thyroid 3. muscle 4. capillary 5. vertebra

Copyright © 1988 Houghton Mifflin Company. All rights reserved.

Name ______________________ Date ______________

Reading Skills

READING SKILLS

Dividing Words into Parts

Many words can be divided into parts. These word parts have special names. The part that gives a word its general meaning is called the **root.** Two other word parts are the **prefix** and the **suffix.** The prefix is added to the beginning of the root, and the suffix is added to the end. Here are some examples, which are followed by three facts that you should know about word parts.

PREFIX	ROOT	SUFFIX	WORD
re-	place		replace
pre-	-dict-		predict
	work	-able	workable
	friend	-ly	friendly
un-	friend	-ly	unfriendly

1. *Some roots are words and some are not.* The root *friend* is a word, but the Latin root *-dict-*, which means "say," is not.
2. *Prefixes change the meaning of roots.* The prefix *pre-* means "before." It can be added to the root *-dict-* to form the word *predict,* which means "to say before": that is, "to foretell."
3. *Suffixes can change the part of speech.* The suffix *-ion* can be added to the verb *construct* to form *construction,* a noun.

Exercise Identifying Word Parts

Step 1: Using a dictionary, write a definition of the italicized word in each of the following sentences. Choose the definition that best fits the way the word is used. *Step 2:* Write the parts of the word. *Step 3:* Write a sentence of your own in which you use the word correctly.

1. The farmer had to *replace* the old tractor.

DEFINITION ______________________

WORD PARTS ______________________

SENTENCE ______________________

Please turn to the next page.

Copyright © 1988 Houghton Mifflin Company. All rights reserved.

2. The *shortness* of the movie surprised the audience.

DEFINITION ______________________________

WORD PARTS ______________________________

SENTENCE ______________________________

3. Lost for two days, Melody was at last *reunited* with her parents.

DEFINITION ______________________________

WORD PARTS ______________________________

SENTENCE ______________________________

4. My little sister uses good *judgment* when she crosses a street.

DEFINITION ______________________________

WORD PARTS ______________________________

SENTENCE ______________________________

5. Madeline, a *skillful* athlete, performed difficult dives.

DEFINITION ______________________________

WORD PARTS ______________________________

SENTENCE ______________________________

6. Be careful not to *misspell* anything when you make the sign.

DEFINITION ______________________________

WORD PARTS ______________________________

SENTENCE ______________________________

7. Darnell *politely* introduced Coach Weeden to his aunt.

DEFINITION ______________________________

WORD PARTS ______________________________

SENTENCE ______________________________

8. The actor's face had a *dreamlike* appearance.

DEFINITION ______________________________

WORD PARTS ______________________________

SENTENCE ______________________________

Copyright © 1988 Houghton Mifflin Company. All rights reserved.

Lesson 19

Amount

The words in this lesson describe size and quantity without using numbers. In one way or another, they all measure something. Some words measure size (how large?), and others measure quantity (many? few?). At least one measures skill. Two or three words do double duty, for they can be used to refer to different things or situations. Finally, two pairs of words are close in meaning. In such cases you may have to study the definitions and Usage Notes carefully for differences. Doing so will help you learn to use words carefully and thoughtfully. The precise use of words in speaking and writing is one of the most valuable English skills that you can learn.

WORD LIST

accumulate
adequate
ample
colossal
extensive
meager
partial
sparse
surpass
trifle

DEFINITIONS

After you have studied the definitions and example for each vocabulary word, write the word on the line to the right.

1. **accumulate** (ə-kyo͞om′yə-lāt′) *verb* To pile up; collect; gather: *to accumulate a fortune.* 1. ________

RELATED WORD **accumulation** *noun*

EXAMPLE Old newspapers had *accumulated* for years in the attic.

2. **adequate** (ăd′ĭ-kwĭt) *adjective* **a.** Able to satisfy a requirement; satisfactory; suitable: *an adequate performance.* **b.** Barely satisfactory or enough: *an adequate but not outstanding performance.* 2. ________

RELATED WORDS **adequacy** *noun;* **adequately** *adverb*

EXAMPLE Does your classroom have an *adequate* supply of dictionaries?

3. **ample** (ăm′pəl) *adjective* **a.** More than enough; plenty of: *ample food for everyone.* **b.** Large in size, quantity, area, or capacity: *an ample container.* 3. ________

SEE *extensive.*

RELATED WORDS **ampleness** *noun;* **amply** *adverb*

EXAMPLE "These shoes have *ample* room for growth," said the clerk.

Copyright © 1988 Houghton Mifflin Company. All rights reserved.

4. **colossal** (kə-lŏs′əl) *adjective* Gigantic; enormous in size; tremendous; huge: *of colossal importance.* 4. ____________

RELATED WORD **colossus** *noun*

EXAMPLE Space stations that could exist independently of Earth would have to be of *colossal* size.

ETYMOLOGY NOTE *Colossal* comes from the Greek word for any gigantic statue; the most famous colossus is probably the Colossus of Rhodes.

5. **extensive** (ĭk-stĕn′sĭv) *adjective* **a.** Large or broad in area or range; far-reaching: *an extensive river system.* **b.** Large in quantity: *extensive wealth.* 5. ____________

RELATED WORDS **extend** *verb;* **extensively** *adverb;* **extent** *noun*

EXAMPLE The museum had an *extensive* collection of Hopi pottery.

USAGE NOTE *Ample* usually refers to size. *Extensive* most often refers to range or extent.

6. **meager** (mē′gər) *adjective* Lacking in quantity or quality; less than enough; scanty; skimpy: *meager resources.* 6. ____________

RELATED WORDS **meagerly** *adverb;* **meagerness** *noun*

EXAMPLE Today a dime a week is a rather *meager* allowance!

SEE *sparse.*

7. **partial** (pär′shəl) *adjective* **a.** Not total; incomplete: *only a partial success.* **b.** Favoring one person or side over another; prejudiced: *too partial to judge fairly.* **c.** Liking a particular thing: *partial to Mexican food.* 7. ____________

RELATED WORD **partially** *adverb*

EXAMPLE Mrs. Kwan gives only *partial* credit for late homework.

8. **sparse** (spärs) *adjective* Growing or settled far apart: *a sparse population.* 8. ____________

RELATED WORDS **sparsely** *adverb;* **sparseness** *noun*

EXAMPLE Above ten thousand feet, plant life is quite *sparse.*

USAGE NOTE *Meager* means "not enough." *Sparse* suggests space between items.

9. **surpass** (sər-păs′) *verb* To be better, greater, or stronger than; exceed: *to surpass the previous record.* 9. ____________

RELATED WORDS **surpassing** *adjective;* **surpassingly** *adverb*

EXAMPLE This year's wheat crop *surpassed* last year's by two million bushels.

10. **trifle** (trī′fəl) *noun* **a.** A small amount; bit. **b.** Something of little importance or value. **c.** A rich dessert made of sponge cake. *verb* **a.** To treat with little seriousness: *A rattlesnake is nothing to trifle with.* **b.** To play or toy with: *to trifle with someone's feelings.* 10. ____________

RELATED WORD **trifling** *adjective*

EXAMPLE The salad looks good, but I'm not very hungry; please give me only a *trifle.*

Copyright © Houghton Mifflin Company. All rights reserved.

Name ______________________________ Date ______________

Exercise 1 Writing Correct Words

On the answer line, write the word from the vocabulary list that fits each definition.

1. Growing or settled far apart — 1. ________
2. Lacking in quantity or quality; less than enough — 2. ________
3. Able to satisfy a requirement; suitable — 3. ________
4. Incomplete; favoring one person or side — 4. ________
5. To pile up; collect; gather — 5. ________
6. To be better, greater, or stronger than; exceed — 6. ________
7. More than enough; plenty of; large in size or capacity — 7. ________
8. Large or broad in area or range; far-reaching — 8. ________
9. A small amount; something of little importance or value — 9. ________
10. Gigantic; enormous in size — 10. ________

Exercise 2 Using Words Correctly

Decide whether the italicized vocabulary word has been used correctly in the sentence. On the answer line, write *Correct* for correct use and *Incorrect* for incorrect use.

1. To a wheat farmer, a poor crop is a *trifle.* — 1. ________
2. Junk had *accumulated* halfway to the garage ceiling. — 2. ________
3. A dinosaur might be considered a *colossal* lizard. — 3. ________
4. Because of the *meager* supply of paint, we painted both the house and the garage. — 4. ________
5. The swimmer's success was only *partial;* she crossed the English Channel but did not set a record. — 5. ________
6. Because of many injuries, the Eagles had an *adequate* number of players and called off the game. — 6. ________
7. A seven-foot basketball player has an *extensive* reach. — 7. ________
8. Plant life in a jungle is *sparse.* — 8. ________
9. Five dollars a week is an *ample* starting salary for a teen-ager who works fifteen hours a week bagging groceries. — 9. ________
10. Olympic gold medals are awarded to those who *surpass* their competitors. — 10. ________

Copyright © 1988 Houghton Mifflin Company. All rights reserved.

Exercise 3 Choosing the Best Word

Decide which vocabulary word or related form best expresses the meaning of the italicized word or phrase in the sentence. On the answer line, write the letter of the correct choice.

1. "This paragraph has rather *skimpy* details," noted the teacher. 1. ________
   a. meager **b.** colossal **c.** ample **d.** partial

2. Keeping a general waiting is not an *insignificant* matter. 2. ________
   a. extensive **b.** adequate **c.** trifling **d.** meager

3. What allowance do you think is *just enough* for a sixth grader? 3. ________
   a. sparse **b.** adequate **c.** meager **d.** surpassing

4. The champion runner has had *a great deal of* surgery on her knees. 4. ________
   a. trifling **b.** partial **c.** extensive **d.** adequate

5. The new cook in the school cafeteria serves *generous* portions! 5. ________
   a. adequate **b.** ample **c.** meager **d.** sparse

6. The Mexican and Egyptian pyramids were projects requiring *tremendous* engineering skill. 6. ________
   a. ample **b.** trifling **c.** adequate **d.** colossal

7. How many feet of snow *collect* yearly at the South Pole? 7. ________
   a. accumulate **b.** extend **c.** surpass **d.** trifle

8. How much longer will it take for someone to *go beyond* Bob's 1986 record for the broad jump? 8. ________
   a. extend **b.** trifle **c.** accumulate **d.** surpass

9. That record store allows *incomplete* payments on purchases of over twenty-five dollars. 9. ________
   a. partial **b.** sparse **c.** colossal **d.** ample

10. Because of poor planning, only a *thin* scattering of trees was left in the new development. 10. ________
    a. partial **b.** extensive **c.** trifling **d.** sparse

Exercise 4 Using Different Forms of Words

Decide which form of the vocabulary word in parentheses best completes the sentence. The form given may be correct. Write your answer on the answer line.

1. "The fault is __?__ mine," apologized Jeff. *(partial)* 1. ________

2. __?__ populated areas are shown on the map by dots. *(sparse)* 2. ________

3. The flood left a thick __?__ of mud everywhere. *(accumulate)* 3. ________

4. "Whether we leave at one o'clock or five past is a __?__ matter," said Susan. *(trifle)* 4. ________

5. The inexperienced hiker was __?__ dressed for the mountain weather. *(meager)* 5. ________

Copyright © 1988 Houghton Mifflin Company. All rights reserved.

Name ______________________________ Date ______________

6. Cleopatra, Queen of Egypt from 69–30 B.C., was a woman of __?__ beauty. *(surpass)* 6. ______

7. "Some people go to any __?__ to get attention!" exclaimed Andy. *(extensive)* 7. ______

8. The lunch that Joanie prepared __?__ satisfied our hunger. *(ample)* 8. ______

9. Reaching a height of up to three hundred feet, the redwood is a __?__ tree. *(colossal)* 9. ______

10. "Are you __?__ prepared for the quiz, Teresa?" asked Rafael. *(adequate)* 10. ______

Reading Comprehension

Each numbered sentence in the following passage contains an italicized vocabulary word or related form. After you read the passage, you will complete an exercise.

The Library of Congress

(1) In 1800 Washington, D.C., was a ***sparsely*** settled town rising from the swamps along the Potomac River. That same year President John Adams approved $5000 to start a library in the just-built Capitol. (2) Compared with the collections of some private libraries of the time, the new library's three maps and 740 books seemed ***trifling***. Indeed, members of Congress used the library like a club, relaxing there between meetings.

Before outgrowing its first home, the Library of Congress met disaster twice. (3) In 1812 the British burned Washington, damaging the Library ***extensively***. (4) Concerned about the Library, former President Jefferson soon sold his ***ample*** personal collection of over 6000 books to Congress.

(5) By 1850 the Library had ***accumulated*** 50,000 volumes. (6) On Christmas Eve of 1851, however, the rebuilt collection was ***partially*** ruined by a second fire. (7) Now it was clear that the Capitol was not an ***adequate*** home for the Library. Congress agreed that the Library needed its own building. Eventually, $6 million was approved for a building across the street. This building first welcomed the public on November 1, 1897. (8) Then, as now, visitors marveled at its statues, murals, and ***surpassingly*** beautiful marble halls.

(9) From its ***meager*** beginnings, the Library of Congress has grown tremendously. The three buildings that are now the Library of Congress cover 71 acres. They are named after Presidents Jefferson, Adams, and Madison. By 1985 the Library boasted 77 million items. Among these were books and pamphlets, manuscripts, recordings, films, maps, photographs, art, and special materials for blind and physically handicapped people. The Library is growing by about one million items a year. (10) A ***colossus*** among libraries, it is the largest in the Western world.

Please turn to the next page.

Copyright © 1988 Houghton Mifflin Company. All rights reserved.

Reading Comprehension Exercise

Each of the following statements corresponds to a numbered sentence in the passage. Each statement contains a blank and is followed by four answer choices. Decide which choice fits best in the blank. The word or phrase that you choose must express roughly the same meaning as the italicized word in the passage. Write the letter of your choice on the answer line.

1. When money was approved for the Capitol library, Washington, D.C., was __?__ settled. 1. ________
   a. already **b.** thickly **c.** recently **d.** thinly

2. By comparison, the new library's collection seemed __?__. 2. ________
   a. important **b.** valuable **c.** insignificant **d.** cheap

3. In 1812 fire damaged the Library of Congress __?__. 3. ________
   a. greatly **b.** completely **c.** quickly **d.** enough

4. Thomas Jefferson sold his __?__ collection to Congress. 4. ________
   a. personal **b.** scanty **c.** well-known **d.** large

5. The Library of Congress had __?__ 50,000 books by midcentury. 5. ________
   a. bought **b.** restored **c.** collected **d.** catalogued

6. A second fire __?__ destroyed the Library in 1851. 6. ________
   a. in part **b.** unexpectedly **c.** unfortunately **d.** totally

7. The Capitol was obviously not a(n) __?__ place for the Library. 7. ________
   a. popular **b.** satisfactory **c.** attractive **d.** convenient

8. The marble in the 1897 building is __?__ beautiful. 8. ________
   a. outstandingly **b.** barely **c.** fairly **d.** sufficiently

9. Since its __?__ start, the Library has grown enormously. 9. ________
   a. scanty **b.** early **c.** wealthy **d.** slow

10. Among libraries the Library of Congress is a __?__. 10. ________
    a. model **b.** record **c.** giant **d.** treasury

Practice with Analogies

See pages 32, 52, and 86 for some strategies to use with analogies.

DIRECTIONS On the answer line, write the vocabulary word that completes each analogy.

1. Familiar is to strange as complete is to __?__. 1. ________
2. Keep is to retain as gather is to __?__. 2. ________
3. Expand is to expansive as extend is to __?__. 3. ________
4. Sparkling is to dull as dense is to __?__. 4. ________
5. Speedy is to swift as inadequate is to __?__. 5. ________
6. Hide is to conceal as exceed is to __?__. 6. ________
7. Damp is to soaking as big is to __?__. 7. ________
8. Enough is to plenty as adequate is to __?__. 8. ________

Copyright © Houghton Mifflin Company. All rights reserved.

Lesson 20

Usualness and Unusualness

People's ideas of what is usual and what is unusual change with time. For example, potatoes, tomatoes, and turkeys are now common in many countries. Before the first voyage of Columbus, however, they were unknown to almost everyone except the people of the Americas. Columbus himself is an example of the way in which an action once thought strange can become accepted as familiar. When he first sailed west toward the Orient, many thought Columbus was crazy, but soon other explorers were sailing in the same direction. Ideas, then, do change.

Perhaps because of such changes, we often use words that express degrees and kinds of usualness and unusualness. There are many. As you study the ten words in this lesson, ask yourself in which group — the usual or the unusual — each one belongs.

WORD LIST
absurd
authentic
bizarre
exception
exotic
habitual
norm
novel
superlative
universal

DEFINITIONS

After you have studied the definitions and example for each vocabulary word, write the word on the line to the right.

1. **absurd** (əb-sûrd′) *adjective* Against common sense or reason; ridiculous; extremely silly. 1. ____________

RELATED WORDS **absurdity** *noun;* **absurdly** *adverb*

EXAMPLE Claims like "Dill's Pills Cure All Ills" are *absurd.*

2. **authentic** (ô-thĕn′tĭk) *adjective* **a.** Genuine; not counterfeit or copied: *an authentic antique.* **b.** True; worthy of being believed; reliable: *an authentic story.* 2. ____________

RELATED WORDS **authentically** *adverb;* **authenticate** *verb;* **authenticity** *noun*

EXAMPLE When you apply for a checking account, you will be asked to fill out a card showing your *authentic* signature.

3. **bizarre** (bĭ-zär′) *adjective* Very unusual in manner, style, or appearance; strange; odd: *bizarre behavior.* 3. ____________

USAGE NOTE Do not confuse *bizarre* with *bazaar,* an open market.

RELATED WORDS **bizarrely** *adverb;* **bizarreness** *noun*

EXAMPLE Some of the *bizarre* details in early science-fiction stories have become realities; the laser beam is one example.

Copyright © 1988 Houghton Mifflin Company. All rights reserved.

4. **exception** (ĭk-sĕp′shən) *noun* Something that differs from what is standard or the rule: *to make an exception.* 4. ____________

RELATED WORDS **except** *preposition;* **except** *verb;* **exceptional** *adjective;* **exceptionally** *adverb*

EXAMPLE Buses leave hourly, with the *exception* of Sundays and holidays.

5. **exotic** (ĭg-zŏt′ĭk) *adjective* Unusual or different because of being from another place; foreign; intriguing: *exotic customs.* 5. ____________

RELATED WORD **exotically** *adverb*

EXAMPLE Known to the British as the Princess Pocahontas, Mrs. John Rolfe was considered *exotic* by the court of King James I.

6. **habitual** (hə-bĭch′o͞o-əl) *adjective* **a.** Done by habit; done regularly: *a habitual complainer.* **b.** Established by long use; customary: *her habitual chair.* 6. ____________

RELATED WORDS **habit** *noun;* **habitually** *adverb*

EXAMPLE Most people agree that *habitual* exercise promotes good health.

7. **norm** (nôrm) *noun* **a.** A pattern, standard, or model that is typical for a specific group: *In casual clothing, jeans are the norm.* **b.** In mathematics, an average. 7. ____________

RELATED WORDS **normal** *adjective;* **normally** *adverb*

EXAMPLE The *norm* for letter delivery in the continental United States is three days.

8. **novel** (nŏv′əl) *adjective* Strikingly new, unusual, or different. *noun* A long work of fiction. 8. ____________

RELATED WORD **novelty** *noun*

EXAMPLE At the turn of this century, many people laughed at the *novel* idea of a horseless carriage.

9. **superlative** (so͞o-pûr′lə-tĭv) *adjective* Superior to all others; best; unequaled. *noun* In grammar, the form of an adverb or adjective that indicates the greatest quantity: Most brightly *and* brightest *are superlatives.* 9. ____________

RELATED WORD **superlatively** *adverb*

EXAMPLE The *Guinness Book of World Records* is filled with examples of *superlative* performances and strange events.

10. **universal** (yo͞o′nə-vûr′səl) *adjective* Common to all persons, places, or things; worldwide; general. 10. ____________

RELATED WORDS **universally** *adverb;* **universe** *noun*

EXAMPLE The need to be loved is *universal.*

Copyright © 1988 Houghton Mifflin Company. All rights reserved.

Name ____ Date ______________

Exercise 1 Matching Words and Definitions

Match the definition in Column B with the word in Column A. Write the letter of the correct definition on the answer line.

Column A	*Column B*
1. bizarre	a. against common sense or reason; ridiculous
2. novel	b. unusual because of being from another place; foreign; intriguing
3. absurd	c. done by habit or done regularly; customary
4. universal	d. genuine; true or reliable
5. habitual	e. a typical pattern, standard, or model for a specific group
6. superlative	f. strikingly new, unusual, or different
7. exception	g. something that differs from what is standard or the rule
8. exotic	h. common to all persons, places, or things; worldwide
9. norm	i. superior to all others; best; unequaled
10. authentic	j. very unusual in manner, style, or appearance; strange; odd

1. ______
2. ______
3. ______
4. ______
5. ______
6. ______
7. ______
8. ______
9. ______
10. ______

Exercise 2 Using Words Correctly

Each of the following statements contains an italicized vocabulary word. Decide whether the sentence is true or false, and write *True* or *False* on the answer line.

1. A *novel* idea is one that is borrowed from ancient books. 1. ______
2. When you call something "the real thing," it is *authentic*. 2. ______
3. Backyard weeds are *exotic* plants. 3. ______
4. It is *absurd* to think that our moon is green cheese. 4. ______
5. A rosebush with red flowers is a *bizarre* sight. 5. ______
6. Anyone who takes care of a building does *superlative* work. 6. ______
7. A smile is a nearly *universal* way of expressing pleasure. 7. ______
8. A height of about six feet is the *norm* for an American woman. 8. ______
9. An example of *habitual* behavior is always putting the same shoe on first. 9. ______
10. The word *sieve* is an *exception* to the "*i* before *e*" spelling rule. 10. ______

Copyright © 1988 Houghton Mifflin Company. All rights reserved.

Exercise 3 Choosing the Best Definition

For each italicized vocabulary word or related form in the following sentences, write the letter of the best definition on the answer line.

1. An adventurous eater, Julie likes *exotic* foods. 1. ________
   a. well-done **b.** spicy **c.** garden **d.** unusual

2. Redheads are an *exception* in most populations. 2. ________
   a. rule **b.** problem **c.** rarity **d.** beauty

3. Laboratory tests showed that the painting was *authentic.* 3. ________
   a. fake **b.** stolen **c.** genuine **d.** valuable

4. Carol often has a *novel* way to solve problems. 4. ________
   a. new **b.** humorous **c.** better **d.** hard

5. Wally is *habitually* early for work. 5. ________
   a. regularly **b.** never **c.** sometimes **d.** extremely

6. Don't be *absurd,* Martin; flying carpets aren't real! 6. ________
   a. funny **b.** tiresome **c.** sensible **d.** ridiculous

7. The team's playing tonight was *superlative.* 7. ________
   a. so-so **b.** unequaled **c.** disappointing **d.** unusual

8. Curiosity among babies is *universal.* 8. ________
   a. healthy **b.** psychological **c.** common **d.** weird

9. In a *bizarre* twist of events, Phoenix had 18 inches of snow. 9. ________
   a. freezing **b.** strange **c.** unpredicted **d.** annual

10. Owning a television set has become the *norm* for most Americans. 10. ________
    a. goal **b.** problem **c.** rule **d.** average

Exercise 4 Using Different Forms of Words

Decide which form of the vocabulary word in parentheses best completes the sentence. The form given may be correct. Write your answer on the answer line.

1. He is a __?__ admired athlete. *(universal)* 1. ________
2. In the nineteenth century, female doctors were a __?__. *(novel)* 2. ________
3. Don't let eating junk food become a __?__. *(habitual)* 3. ________
4. The prize-winning hat was __?__ decorated. *(bizarre)* 4. ________
5. The lawyer was asked to __?__ Mr. Todd's will. *(authentic)* 5. ________
6. "These paintings are __?__, not art!" sneered the critic. *(absurd)* 6. ________
7. Ms. Jones, who was __?__ qualified, got the job. *(superlative)* 7. ________
8. Is snow in October the __?__ for your area of the country? *(norm)* 8. ________
9. The platypus and the spiny anteater are __?__ mammals. *(exception)* 9. ________
10. On the island we ate many __?__ prepared seafood dishes. *(exotic)* 10. ________

 Copyright © 1988 Houghton Mifflin Company. All rights reserved.

Name ______________________________ Date __________

Reading Comprehension

Each numbered sentence in the following passage contains an italicized vocabulary word or related form. After you read the passage, you will complete an exercise.

Zoos, Old and New

(1) As long as there have been travelers, there have been stories about ***exotic*** animals. (2) That many of these tales were ***bizarre*** is clear from maps drawn when people still believed in a flat world. Fantastic creatures rimmed these maps, helping to create a desire to see them. The growth of exploration and the natural sciences fed this desire.

Explorers and scientists of the 1700s and 1800s — and even before — collected many birds and animals. (3) In time, public demand for these ***novelties*** resulted in zoos. Conditions in these first zoos were unhealthful. (4) Small, isolated cages were the ***norm,*** even for large animals. (5) Neither the captors nor the public were critical of the lack of ***authenticity*** in the animals' natural settings. (6) For example, the ***absurdity*** of a long-legged flamingo standing in a tiny puddle went unnoticed.

Today, in the 1990s, animals are seen in more natural settings. (7) Animals that are ***habitually*** active at night, such as bats, are displayed in the dark. At night cages are lighted and the animals sleep.

Now some zoos avoid cages altogether. At the San Diego Zoo, rhinos, lions, elephants, and antelopes live as in the wild. Only fences separate them from visitors. In Toronto and in a few other cities, several kinds of birds live together in a huge area. They fly about freely, cut off from onlookers by only a few nets.

Fortunately, zoos like San Diego's and Toronto's are becoming more common. Most modern zoos understand the need to keep animals healthy and to preserve rare species. (8) A few zoos have done their jobs ***superlatively*** well. For example, an English zoo saved the Hawaiian goose. Several zoos helped save the European bison.

(9) Today most zoos show deep concern for their animals, although excellent zoos are still not ***universal.*** (10) Public pressure, however, is making up-to-date zoos less and less of an ***exception.***

Reading Comprehension Exercise

Each of the following statements corresponds to a numbered sentence in the passage. Each statement contains a blank and is followed by four answer choices. Decide which choice fits best in the blank. The word or phrase that you choose must express roughly the same meaning as the italicized word in the passage. Write the letter of your choice on the answer line.

1. For ages there have been stories about __?__ animals. 1. __________
   a. furry **b.** wild **c.** foreign **d.** traveling

2. Old maps make it obvious that many such tales were __?__. 2. __________
   a. strange **b.** ancient **c.** true **d.** illustrated

3. People wanted to see these __?__. 3. __________
   a. foreign products **c.** rare books
   b. new things **d.** old maps

Copyright © Houghton Mifflin Company. All rights reserved.

4. At first, unhealthful cages were the __?__ . 4. ______
a. standard **b.** problem **c.** rage **d.** law

5. People did not criticize the lack of __?__ in the natural surroundings. 5. ______
a. beauty **b.** quality **c.** wholesomeness **d.** genuineness

6. Flamingos in small puddles were a(n) __?__ . 6. ______
a. popular attraction **c.** unhealthy situation
b. unexpected event **d.** ridiculous sight

7. Viewers at today's zoos can see animals that are __?__ active at night. 7. ______
a. seldom **b.** regularly **c.** nervously **d.** never

8. Some zoos take care of animals __?__ well. 8. ______
a. rather **b.** equally **c.** exceedingly **d.** usually

9. Very good zoos are not __?__ . 9. ______
a. everywhere **b.** in space **c.** famous **d.** rich

10. However, excellent zoos are less and less of a __?__ . 10. ______
a. problem **b.** rarity **c.** rule **d.** possibility

Writing Assignment

Write a riddle about something unusual or special that you have seen, heard about, or tasted. Write your riddle on a note card, ending it with "What am I?" On the back of the card, write the answer. As an editing step, try out your riddle on a classmate before passing it in. Use at least three words from this lesson and underline them.

Vocabulary Enrichment

The word *universe* comes from the Latin word *universum,* a form of *universus,* meaning "whole." That word in turn comes from the two words *unus,* "one," and *versus,* a form of the word for "to turn." The meaning of *universe* has changed a bit since it came into English. Through the 1500s most Europeans believed that the sun, stars, and planets "turned as one" around Earth. Nicolaus Copernicus (1473–1543), a Polish astronomer, insisted otherwise. He said that Earth and the other planets revolved around the sun. Some people were very shocked by this claim, but now it is accepted almost universally as true.

ACTIVITY To many people the universe means space. Look up and record the histories and present meanings of these space words. Use each word in a sentence.

1. asteroid 2. galaxy 3. stellar 4. quasar 5. zodiac

Copyright © Houghton Mifflin Company. All rights reserved.

Lesson 21

Government

When a group of people live together, they must form a political unit to protect and to govern themselves. When you study history, you learn about the rise and fall of different governments around the world throughout time. Compared with governments in European countries, the United States government is quite new. It has three branches, which you will learn about in this lesson. It also has three levels: national, state, and local. In this lesson you will learn words that describe how Americans and others govern themselves.

WORD LIST
Congress
democratic
economy
endorse
forum
judicial
legislation
monarchy
municipal
veto

DEFINITIONS

After you have studied the definitions and example for each vocabulary word, write the word on the line to the right.

1. **Congress** (kŏng′grĭs) *noun* **a.** The national lawmaking body of the United States, made up of the Senate and the House of Representatives. **b. congress.** A formal meeting, as of nations or professional groups, to discuss problems; assembly; gathering. 1. ____________

   RELATED WORDS **congressional** *adjective;* **congressman** *noun;* **congresswoman** *noun*

   EXAMPLE Members of *Congress* must be United States citizens.

2. **democratic** (dĕm′ə-krăt′ĭk) *adjective* **a.** Run by the people, either directly or through their elected representatives: *a democratic government.* **b.** Based on the principle of equal rights for all: *a democratic election.* **c. Democratic.** Belonging to the Democratic Party. 2. ____________

   RELATED WORDS **democracy** *noun;* **democrat, Democrat** *noun;* **democratically** *adverb*

   EXAMPLE Not every *democratic* country is headed by a president.

Copyright © 1988 Houghton Mifflin Company. All rights reserved.

3. **economy** (ĭ-kŏn′ə-mē) *noun* **a.** The management of money or other resources; system for managing wealth: *the remarkable growth of the Japanese economy.* **b.** Thrifty use of resources, such as materials or labor: *hints for fuel economy.* 3. ______

RELATED WORDS **economic** *adjective;* **economical** *adjective;* **economically** *adverb;* **economics** *noun;* **economize** *verb*

EXAMPLE In 1850 cotton was king of the South's *economy.*

4. **endorse** (ĕn-dôrs′) *verb* **a.** To approve; support: *a plan endorsed by the President.* **b.** To sign, especially the back of a check. 4. ______

RELATED WORD **endorsement** *noun*

EXAMPLE The Senate must *endorse* a bill before it can go on to the President.

USAGE NOTE Since *endorse* comes from a Latin word meaning "upon the back," say "endorse this check" rather than "endorse this check on the back."

5. **forum** (fôr′əm) *noun* **a.** A place for public discussions. **b.** Often **Forum.** The Forum of ancient Rome. 5. ______

EXAMPLE Congress is a national *forum.*

6. **judicial** (jo͞o-dĭsh′əl) *adjective* Related to courts, judges, or the carrying out of justice. 6. ______

RELATED WORDS **judicially** *adverb;* **judiciary** *noun*

EXAMPLE The highest court in the United States *judicial* system is the Supreme Court.

7. **legislation** (lĕj′ĭ-slā′shən) *noun* **a.** The process of making or enacting laws. **b.** A planned or passed law or group of laws. 7. ______

RELATED WORDS **legislate** *verb;* **legislative** *adjective;* **legislator** *noun;* **legislature** *noun*

EXAMPLE The Constitution sets forth rules for *legislation.*

8. **monarchy** (mŏn′ər-kē) *noun* **a.** Government by a king or queen. **b.** A country headed by a king or queen. 8. ______

RELATED WORD **monarch** *noun*

EXAMPLE *Monarchy* was thoroughly disliked by most of the framers of the Constitution of the United States.

9. **municipal** (myo͞o-nĭs′ə-pəl) *adjective* Related to the running of a town or city; local: *municipal government.* 9. ______

RELATED WORD **municipality** *noun*

EXAMPLE The police department is a *municipal* service.

10. **veto** (vē′tō) *verb* To refuse to approve; prevent officially: *to veto a bill.* *noun* The right to reject or the act of rejecting: *a presidential veto.* 10. ______

EXAMPLE Mrs. Craig *vetoed* two field trips in the same week.

Copyright © Houghton Mifflin Company. All rights reserved.

Name ______________________ Date ______________

Exercise 1 Matching Words and Definitions

Match the definition in Column B with the word in Column A. Write the letter of the correct definition on the answer line.

Column A	*Column B*
1. legislation	a. run by the people, either directly or through elected representatives
2. Congress	b. the national lawmaking body of the United States
3. democratic	c. to approve; support
4. economy	d. related to the running of a town or city
5. forum	e. the process of making or enacting laws
6. veto	f. to refuse to approve; prevent officially
7. endorse	g. a place for public discussions
8. monarchy	h. government by a king or queen
9. judicial	i. the management of money or other resources; a system for managing wealth
10. municipal	j. related to courts, judges, or the carrying out of justice

1. ______
2. ______
3. ______
4. ______
5. ______
6. ______
7. ______
8. ______
9. ______
10. ______

Exercise 2 Using Words Correctly

Each of the following questions contains an italicized vocabulary word. Choose the correct answer to the question, and write *Yes* or *No* on the answer line.

1. Is a *monarchy* headed by a king or queen? 1. ______
2. Are you against a plan if you *veto* it? 2. ______
3. Is a *democratic* nation governed by just one person? 3. ______
4. Are courts of law a part of the *judicial* branch of government? 4. ______
5. Does the term *municipal* refer to state governments? 5. ______
6. Is the *economy* a branch of the United States government? 6. ______
7. Do the Senate and the House of Representatives make up the United States *Congress?* 7. ______
8. When you *endorse* a product or plan, are you against it? 8. ______
9. Is *legislation* the making of laws? 9. ______
10. Is a *forum* the same as a yes vote? 10. ______

Copyright © 1988 Houghton Mifflin Company. All rights reserved.

Exercise 3 Choosing the Best Word

Decide which vocabulary word or related form best expresses the meaning of the italicized word or phrase in the sentence. On the answer line, write the letter of the correct choice.

1. A *government by citizens* existed two thousand years ago in Athens. 1. ________
   a. legislature **b.** monarchy **c.** democracy **d.** judiciary
2. The city chose a bridge plan that was *not too costly.* 2. ________
   a. judicial **b.** economical **c.** legislative **d.** municipal
3. We can't start a school newspaper without the principal's *approval.* 3. ________
   a. endorsement **b.** veto **c.** forum **d.** legislation
4. The biggest news in the paper was the *local* election. 4. ________
   a. democratic **b.** legislative **c.** municipal **d.** judicial
5. The size of *lawmaking bodies* varies from state to state. 5. ________
   a. judiciaries **b.** forums **c.** municipalities **d.** legislatures
6. In the United States, the President has *disapproval* power. 6. ________
   a. endorsement **b.** veto **c.** economic **d.** judicial
7. A *formal gathering* was held to discuss saving the rain forests. 7. ________
   a. congress **b.** municipality **c.** economy **d.** democracy
8. Courts are found in the government branch that is *concerned with judging.* 8. ________
   a. legislative **b.** judicial **c.** democratic **d.** municipal
9. The texts of some speeches made in the Roman *discussion center* still exist. 9. ________
   a. Monarchy **b.** Forum **c.** Municipality **d.** Judiciary
10. England's *king or queen* reigns but does not rule; true power lies in Parliament and the prime minister. 10. ________
    a. legislator **b.** democrat **c.** judiciary **d.** monarch

Exercise 4 Using Different Forms of Words

Decide which form of the vocabulary word in parentheses best completes the sentence. The form given may be correct. Write your answer on the answer line.

1. The New England town meeting is an example of a __?__. *(forum)* 1. ________
2. How many schools are there in your __?__? *(municipal)* 2. ________
3. The top official in the United States __?__ is the Attorney General. *(judicial)* 3. ________
4. Because Josh is __?__, he has a savings account in a bank. *(economy)* 4. ________
5. Declarations of war require __?__ approval. *(Congress)* 5. ________
6. Dad __?__ our plans to watch the late movie. *(veto)* 6. ________
7. Which English __?__ was nicknamed Good Queen Bess? *(monarchy)* 7. ________

Copyright © 1988 Houghton Mifflin Company. All rights reserved.

Name ____ Date ______________

8. The Canadian __?__ is called Parliament, not Congress. *(legislation)* 8. ______________

9. Presidential __?__ of a bill often helps its passage. *(endorse)* 9. ______________

10. Coaches cannot run their teams __?__; they must tell their players what to do. *(democratic)* 10. ______________

Reading Comprehension

Each numbered sentence in the following passage contains an italicized vocabulary word or related form. After you read the passage, you will complete an exercise.

Rome's Gift to American Democracy

When colonial lawmakers gathered in a Continental Congress to write rules for governing the United States, they drew some of their ideas from other countries. They inherited many laws, written and unwritten, from Great Britain. France, as well as Britain, contributed ideas on basic human rights. Some of these ideas can be traced to ancient Greece or to Rome.

The debt to Rome was especially significant. (1) From Rome came not only basic ideas about the ***legislative*** part of a government but also the concept of a government in which the use of power is carefully controlled.

The framers of our Constitution knew their history well. Some of it they did not care to repeat. Above all, they did not want a government that abused power. They admired the Roman senate but knew that it lost its ability to control its rulers. (2) They did not want what eventually replaced elected officials, an all-powerful ***monarch.***

After long debate the planners of the Constitution rejected a strong central ruler in favor of strong states and a President with limited power. (3) One of the few powers to be given the President was the ***veto.*** (4) By rejecting a bill, the chief executive could check ***congressional*** actions. (5) On the other hand, if two thirds of the members of both houses of Congress voted for a bill, it could become law without the President's ***endorsement.***

Other checks were built in to balance the distribution of power. For example, citizens could challenge an unfair law in court. (6) This meant that the ***judiciary*** could act as a check on the legislative and executive branches.

The careful timing of elections also limited powers, for a completely new government could never be elected all at once. (7) ***Municipalities*** could elect national representatives every two years. Senators were to be chosen every six years. The President's term was four years. All could be re-elected.

(8) Some delegates to the Continental Congress felt that a four-year presidential term was not an ***economical*** use of power. They argued that it was too little time in which to accomplish what needed to be done. (9) Public ***forums*** still debate the ideal term. If a majority of citizens decides to alter the rules for presidential elections, however, the Constitution provides a tool for doing so. This tool is called an "amendment."

The idea that laws can be changed is Roman. (10) This principle is perhaps Rome's greatest gift to ***democracy.*** It helps ensure a government that is, in the words of Abraham Lincoln, "of the people, by the people, for the people."

Please turn to the next page.

Copyright © 1988 Houghton Mifflin Company. All rights reserved.

Reading Comprehension Exercise

Each of the following statements corresponds to a numbered sentence in the passage. Each statement contains a blank and is followed by four answer choices. Decide which choice fits best in the blank. The word or phrase that you choose must express roughly the same meaning as the italicized word in the passage. Write the letter of your choice on the answer line.

1. Rome gave the framers of the United States Constitution some ideas about __?__ structure. 1. ________
   a. lawmaking b. government c. ruling d. financial
2. American lawmakers did not want a __?__. 2. ________
   a. timid ruler c. member of the nobility
   b. central government d. king or queen
3. The Constitution gave the President the power to __?__. 3. ________
   a. say no b. approve c. appoint d. declare war
4. By using the veto, the President could stop __?__ actions. 4. ________
   a. important b. unwise c. national d. lawmakers'
5. If enough legislators voted for a bill, however, it could become law without the __?__ of the President. 5. ________
   a. influence b. power c. approval d. advice
6. The __?__ could check the other two branches. 6. ________
   a. courts b. juries c. newspapers d. Vice President
7. __?__ could elect representatives every two years. 7. ________
   a. Local districts b. Counties c. Grand juries d. Committees
8. Some people thought that a four-year term would not be __?__. 8. ________
   a. correct b. essential c. effective d. perfect
9. The length of the President's term is sometimes a topic in __?__. 9. ________
   a. colleges b. the press c. open meetings d. the Capitol
10. The Roman idea that laws can be changed is important in a __?__. 10. ________
    a. court of law c. lawmaking body
    b. people-run government d. political party

Writing Assignment

Interview someone who has immigrated to the United States. Find out (1) why the person immigrated to this country, (2) what he or she thinks of its system of government, and (3) what he or she likes best about the United States. Use either a tape recorder or note cards for the interview, and write it up for your classmates to read. In your final paper, use at least three words from this lesson and underline them.

If it is not possible to interview an immigrant, imagine that you yourself have immigrated to the United States. Answer the questions from the point of view of the person whom you are imagining.

Copyright © 1988 Houghton Mifflin Company. All rights reserved.

Name ________________________________ Date ________________

Reading Skills

READING SKILLS

The Prefixes *non-* and *un-*

You can add to your vocabulary if you know the meanings of common prefixes. To figure out the meaning of a new word, add the definition of a prefix to the definition of the root to which it is attached. Two common prefixes are *non-* and *un-*. Both mean "not." Here are some examples of words formed with these two prefixes.

PREFIX/MEANING	WORD	DEFINITION
1. *non:* not	nonfiction	not fiction
	nonmember	not a member
2. *un:* not	untrue	not true
	unavoidable	not avoidable

Exercise **Using the Prefixes *non-* and *un-***

Step 1: Write your own definition of the italicized word in each of the following sentences. *Step 2:* Write the dictionary definition of the word. Choose the definition that best fits the way the word is used in the sentence. *Step 3:* Write a sentence of your own in which you use the word correctly.

1. The *nonprofit* group is supported by public contributions.

YOUR DEFINITION ________________________________

DICTIONARY DEFINITION ________________________________

SENTENCE ________________________________

2. The deck around the pool has a *nonskid* surface.

YOUR DEFINITION ________________________________

DICTIONARY DEFINITION ________________________________

SENTENCE ________________________________

3. The location of the treasure was *unknown.*

YOUR DEFINITION ________________________________

DICTIONARY DEFINITION ________________________________

SENTENCE ________________________________

Please turn to the next page.

Copyright © Houghton Mifflin Company. All rights reserved.

4. The performer used *nonverbal* means to tell the story.

YOUR DEFINITION ______________________________

DICTIONARY DEFINITION ______________________________

SENTENCE ______________________________

5. I'm afraid your statement is *unclear.*

YOUR DEFINITION ______________________________

DICTIONARY DEFINITION ______________________________

SENTENCE ______________________________

6. The injury forced the coach to put in an *untried* player.

YOUR DEFINITION ______________________________

DICTIONARY DEFINITION ______________________________

SENTENCE ______________________________

7. Thanks to Lila's *nonstop* work, we finished the project on time.

YOUR DEFINITION ______________________________

DICTIONARY DEFINITION ______________________________

SENTENCE ______________________________

8. In the mountains the winds are often *unpredictable.*

YOUR DEFINITION ______________________________

DICTIONARY DEFINITION ______________________________

SENTENCE ______________________________

9. In our town *nonresidents* cannot run for mayor.

YOUR DEFINITION ______________________________

DICTIONARY DEFINITION ______________________________

SENTENCE ______________________________

10. A *nonstandard* replacement part caused the machine to break down.

YOUR DEFINITION ______________________________

DICTIONARY DEFINITION ______________________________

SENTENCE ______________________________

Copyright © 1988 Houghton Mifflin Company. All rights reserved.

Lesson 22

Limiting and Releasing

The words in this lesson express various kinds of limits and various forms of release. A limit is a kind of maximum or minimum beyond which a person or thing cannot or may not go. The idea of limiting covers a wide range: the limit of endurance, age limits, and city limits. You are born with some limits, accept some, ignore others, and test still others. Release, on the other hand, suggests a letting go. A few kinds of letting go are releasing the brakes of a car, releasing a person or animal from confinement, and releasing someone from responsibility. After studying the definitions that follow, try putting each vocabulary word into the category of limit or release.

WORD LIST
compress
concise
eject
exclusion
expulsion
liberate
propel
regulate
restrain
restriction

DEFINITIONS

After you have studied the definitions and example for each vocabulary word, write the word on the line to the right.

1. **compress** (kəm-prĕs′) *verb* **a.** To force into a smaller place by pressing or squeezing together; to compact: *to compress trash into blocks.* **b.** To shorten or condense: *wisdom compressed into a clever saying.* *noun* (kŏm′prĕs′) A pad applied to a wound or injury.

   RELATED WORD **compression** *noun*

   EXAMPLE Bus riders were *compressed* like canned sardines.

   1. ______________

2. **concise** (kən-sīs′) *adjective* Clearly stated in a few words; brief; compact: *a concise paragraph.*

   RELATED WORDS **concisely** *adverb;* **conciseness** *noun*

   EXAMPLE Kurt was chosen club secretary because he was a good speller and a *concise* writer.

   2. ______________

3. **eject** (ĭ-jĕkt′) *verb* **a.** To throw out by force. **b.** To force to leave. **c.** To make an emergency exit from a disabled aircraft in flight: *The pilot ejected over water.*

   RELATED WORD **ejection** *noun*

   EXAMPLE During the eruption the volcano *ejected* rivers of lava.

   3. ______________

   USAGE NOTE *Eject* refers mainly to the hurling out of things or to the forcible physical removal of people. SEE *expulsion.*

Copyright © Houghton Mifflin Company. All rights reserved.

4. **exclusion** (ĭk-skloo͞′zhən) *noun* **a.** The act or state of keeping or shutting out: *the exclusion of all but the top-rated players.* **b.** The state of being left out or disregarded: *Becky's exclusion from the class list was due to a programming error.*

RELATED WORDS **exclude** *verb;* **exclusive** *adjective*

EXAMPLE The *exclusion* of people from jobs because of race, religion, or sex is illegal.

4. ______

5. **expulsion** (ĭk-spŭl′shən) *noun* **a.** The act of forcing or driving out. **b.** The state of being forced or driven out.

RELATED WORD **expel** *verb*

EXAMPLE At the hospital clinic, the patient was given an examination that tested the *expulsion* of air from her lungs.

5. ______

USAGE NOTE *Expel* applies mainly to the permanent removal of a person from membership in a group. SEE *eject.*

6. **liberate** (lĭb′ə-rāt′) *verb* To set free; release.

RELATED WORDS **liberation** *noun;* **liberator** *noun*

EXAMPLE The class poster for Library Week said, "Reading *liberates* the mind."

6. ______

7. **propel** (prə-pĕl′) *verb* To cause to move or keep in motion.

RELATED WORDS **propellant** *noun;* **propeller** *noun*

EXAMPLE Sailboats are *propelled* by wind.

7. ______

USAGE NOTE A *propeller* is a bladed engine part that helps move a craft. A *propellant* is fuel.

8. **regulate** (rĕg′yə-lāt′) *verb* **a.** To direct; control according to certain rules. **b.** To adjust for accuracy or certain requirements: *to regulate engine speed.*

RELATED WORDS **regulation** *noun;* **regulator** *noun*

EXAMPLE The Food and Drug Administration *regulates* the availability of foods and medicines.

8. ______

9. **restrain** (rĭ-strān′) *verb* To check; control by holding back: *to restrain one's temper.*

RELATED WORDS **restrained** *adjective;* **restraint** *noun*

EXAMPLE A good rider knows when to *restrain* a horse and when to let it gallop.

9. ______

SEE *restriction.*

10. **restriction** (rĭ-strĭk′shən) *noun* The act or state of limiting; limitation: *dietary restrictions.*

RELATED WORDS **restrict** *verb;* **restrictive** *adjective*

EXAMPLE Because of drought, our town put *restrictions* on water use.

10. ______

USAGE NOTE To *restrain* is to limit by force. To *restrict* is to limit by setting boundaries.

Copyright © Houghton Mifflin Company. All rights reserved.

Name ______________________________ Date ____________

Exercise 1 **Matching Words and Definitions**

Match the definition in Column B with the word in Column A. Write the letter of the correct definition on the answer line.

Column A	*Column B*
1. liberate	a. clearly stated in a few words; brief
2. exclusion	b. the act of forcing or driving out; the state of being forced out
3. compress	c. to throw out by force; force to leave
4. restriction	d. the act or state of limiting; a limitation
5. propel	e. to force together by pressing; shorten or condense
6. eject	f. to direct or control according to rules; adjust for accuracy
7. restrain	g. to set free; release
8. concise	h. to check; control by holding back
9. regulate	i. to cause to move or keep in motion
10. expulsion	j. the act of keeping out; the state of being left out

1. ________
2. ________
3. ________
4. ________
5. ________
6. ________
7. ________
8. ________
9. ________
10. ________

Exercise 2 **Using Words Correctly**

Each of the following questions contains an italicized vocabulary word. Choose the correct answer to the question, and write *Yes* or *No* on the answer line.

1. Is a fifty-five-page book report *concise?* 1. ________
2. Is *expulsion* from school an honor? 2. ________
3. Is the speed limit of fifty-five miles per hour a driving *restriction?* 3. ________
4. Is a wet sponge easy to *compress?* 4. ________
5. When you get a polio shot, are you *ejected?* 5. ________
6. If you *liberate* a trapped animal, are you helping it? 6. ________
7. Are dams used to *regulate* water flow? 7. ________
8. When you are disgusted by something, are you *propelled* by it? 8. ________
9. Is to *restrain* the same as to "reteach"? 9. ________
10. Is *exclusion* the opposite of "conclusion"? 10. ________

Copyright © 1988 Houghton Mifflin Company. All rights reserved.

Exercise 3 Choosing the Best Word

Decide which vocabulary word or related form best expresses the meaning of the italicized word or phrase in the sentence. On the answer line, write the letter of the correct choice.

1. Horses are sometimes *confined* by fences. 1. ________
   a. propelled b. liberated c. restricted d. ejected
2. Is being *forcefully thrown* from the end of a water slide fun? 2. ________
   a. restrained b. ejected c. excluded d. liberated
3. It is hard to show self-*control* when faced with delicious food. 3. ________
   a. compression b. ejection c. restraint d. conciseness
4. Trash compactors *squeeze* rubbish into smaller packs for handy disposal. 4. ________
   a. compress b. restrain c. regulate d. restrict
5. Kim's report was a model of *clear and brief expression.* 5. ________
   a. regulation b. conciseness c. liberation d. restraint
6. People who enter the country illegally are sometimes *deported* by the authorities. 6. ________
   a. propelled b. restrained c. liberated d. expelled
7. "Pay your dues or be *left out of* the club party," announced the treasurer. 7. ________
   a. compressed by c. restricted to
   b. regulated by d. excluded from
8. That family has a *rule* that no one does chores on his or her birthday. 8. ________
   a. regulation b. ejection c. exclusion d. compress
9. Students nicknamed the last day of school *Setting Free* Day. 9. ________
   a. Expulsion b. Ejection c. Exclusion d. Liberation
10. A small but powerful engine *moves* the boat. 10. ________
    a. propels b. expels c. ejects d. liberates

Exercise 4 Using Different Forms of Words

Each sentence contains an italicized vocabulary word in a form that does not fit the sentence. On the answer line, write the form of the word that does fit the sentence.

1. An internal-combustion engine works by means of the *compress* of the vapor mixture in the cylinders. 1. ________
2. The high point of the circus was the *eject* of a man from a cannon. 2. ________
3. Do you have any idea how many gallons of water a whale can *expulsion* in one blow? 3. ________
4. A boat with a *propel* should steer clear of fishing nets. 4. ________
5. No one who wants a part will be *exclusion* from the class play. 5. ________

Copyright © 1988 Houghton Mifflin Company. All rights reserved.

Name ________________________________ Date ____________

6. Silence at meals calls for a great deal of *restrain.* 6. ____________

7. "This device," explained the mechanic, "is a heat *regulate.*" 7. ____________

8. Simón Bolívar (1783–1830), a hero in South America's struggles for independence, earned the name of *Liberate.* 8. ____________

9. In writing, aim for *concise.* 9. ____________

10. "I must *restriction* you to bed rest for a week," ordered the doctor. 10. ____________

Reading Comprehension

Each numbered sentence in the following passage contains an italicized vocabulary word or related form. After you read the passage, you will complete an exercise.

The Challenge of White-Water Rafting

A small raft glides down a calm river for a scenic ride. **(1)** Suddenly the raft begins to spin and its passengers are nearly ***ejected.*** Shooting headlong into rapids, these adventurers are experiencing the challenge of white-water rafting.

(2) White-water rafters use inflatable rafts made of tough, coated fabric that can be ***compressed*** for storage. **(3)** Rafters use oars or paddles to ***propel*** their craft through the water. White-water rafting equipment also includes rope, a bail bucket, extra oars, a repair kit, and a first-aid kit.

Skill is essential for white-water rafting. Rafters must be able to steer, ride rapids, make turns, and avoid hitting obstacles. Although some rivers are flat and still, others have dangerous rapids. As it flows over large rocks on the river bottom, the water churns and turns white. A rafter must have the ability to "read" a river and watch for changes in the current. The International Scale of River Difficulty helps rafters decide which rivers they can safely travel. **(4)** This ***concise*** list rates each river in the United States from very easy to extremely difficult.

(5) Because white-water rafting is dangerous, rafters must abide by safety ***regulations.*** **(6)** In most states authorities impose ***restrictions*** on people who take part in the sport. **(7)** Those who cannot swim, for example, are ***excluded.*** People who are accepted for rafting trips must wear life jackets at all times. Those who direct rafting trips must obtain necessary permits and follow safety rules. **(8)** If they do not, they risk being ***expelled*** from the rafting organization to which they belong. Rafters must routinely check equipment, consult maps and guidebooks, and be on the alert for changing weather conditions. They must learn and practice special safety techniques.

(9) Despite the necessary ***restraints,*** rafting is a thrilling sport for all those who like adventure. Rafters travel along stretches of clear, still water that quickly become boiling rapids. **(10)** Meeting the exhilarating challenge of white water gives rafters a feeling of ***liberation*** from everyday duties and routines. Just as exciting is the feeling of adventure that white-water rafters experience as they navigate the larger and smaller rivers of our vast country.

Please turn to the next page.

Copyright © 1988 Houghton Mifflin Company. All rights reserved.

Reading Comprehension Exercise

Each of the following statements corresponds to a numbered sentence in the passage. Each statement contains a blank and is followed by four answer choices. Decide which choice fits best in the blank. The word or phrase that you choose must express roughly the same meaning as the italicized word in the passage. Write the letter of your choice on the answer line.

1. As the raft begins to spin, its passengers are almost __?__. 1. ________
   a. injured **b.** made dizzy **c.** thrown out **d.** depressed
2. Rafts are made of a strong fabric that can be __?__ for storage. 2. ________
   a. made smaller **b.** made bulkier **c.** made lighter **d.** rinsed
3. Rafters __?__ their craft with oars or paddles. 3. ________
   a. repair **b.** balance **c.** stop **d.** move
4. Rivers are rated for difficulty in a list that is __?__. 4. ________
   a. readily available **c.** expressed briefly
   b. published yearly **d.** expressed in many words
5. Because their sport is dangerous, rafters must be familiar with safety __?__. 5. ________
   a. lectures **b.** procedures **c.** handbooks **d.** rules
6. Authorities set __?__ for rafters in most states. 6. ________
   a. fees **b.** limits **c.** goals **d.** penalties
7. For safety reasons nonswimmers are __?__. 7. ________
   a. barred **b.** welcomed **c.** tested **d.** given lessons
8. Members of rafting organizations can be __?__ if they do not follow the rules of safety. 8. ________
   a. blamed **b.** forced out **c.** criticized **d.** made to pay fines
9. Rafting is an exciting sport despite the safety __?__. 9. ________
   a. techniques **b.** equipment **c.** problems **d.** controls
10. The exhilaration of their sport gives white-water rafters a feeling of __?__. 10. ________
   a. release **b.** challenge **c.** letdown **d.** satisfaction

Practice with Analogies

DIRECTIONS On the answer line, write the vocabulary word that completes each analogy.

See pages 32, 52, and 86 for some strategies to use with analogies.

1. Inside is to outside as inclusion is to __?__. 1. ________
2. Lengthy is to brief as wordy is to __?__. 2. ________
3. Repel is to repulsion as expel is to __?__. 3. ________
4. Tighten is to loosen as enslave is to __?__. 4. ________
5. Microphone is to amplify as shackles is to __?__. 5. ________

Copyright © Houghton Mifflin Company. All rights reserved.

Lesson 23

Necessities and Extras

Dictionaries tell us that a necessity is an absolute requirement, while an extra goes beyond the usual or the expected. A necessity, then, is a basic, and an extra is something additional. It is not always possible to make clear-cut distinctions between the two categories, however. Food, clothing, and shelter are obvious necessities, but beyond that, people's needs and choices vary. The question of necessities and extras is an interesting one, and it has no definite answers. You may like to think about the idea as you study the vocabulary words in this lesson.

WORD LIST

accessory
appropriate
auxiliary
entail
essence
excess
frivolous
imperative
pertinent
significant

Lesson 23 WORD LIST

DEFINITIONS

After you have studied the definitions and example for each vocabulary word, write the word on the line to the right.

1. **accessory** (ăk-sĕs'ə-rē) *noun* **a.** An extra that goes with and adds to the overall effect or usefulness of something: *earrings and other accessories.* **b.** Someone who aids a lawbreaker but is not present at the crime. **c.** Something that accompanies or assists. *adjective* **a.** Not main; secondary. **b.** Additional.

   EXAMPLE A basket was the only *accessory* on the new bicycle.

   1. ______________

2. **appropriate** (ə-prō'prē-ĭt) *adjective* Suitable for a particular person, situation, or place; proper; fitting: *appropriate remarks.* *verb* (ə-prō'prē-āt') **a.** To take, often without permission: *Tom's sister appropriated his hockey jacket.* **b.** To set apart for a particular use: *Congress appropriated money for education.*

   RELATED WORDS **appropriately** *adverb;* **appropriateness** *noun*

   EXAMPLE Blue jeans are not the *appropriate* dress for a wedding.

   2. ______________

3. **auxiliary** (ŏg-zĭl'yə-rē) *adjective* **a.** Giving assistance or support; helping: Have, can, *and* will *are auxiliary verbs.* **b.** Held in reserve; additional; *auxiliary troops.* *noun* **a.** A helper. **b.** An organization that helps a larger one.

   EXAMPLE Some trucks have *auxiliary* gas tanks.

   3. ______________

Copyright © 1988 Houghton Mifflin Company. All rights reserved.

4. **entail** (ĕn-tāl′) *verb* To have as a necessary part; involve; require: *an assignment that entails library research.* 4. ______

EXAMPLE The plan to build a new school *entailed* raising taxes.

5. **essence** (ĕs′əns) *noun* **a.** Basic nature; identifying quality; absolutely necessary part; what is at the heart of something: *The essence of friendship is trust.* **b.** An extract: *essence of vanilla.* **c.** Perfume; scent. 5. ______

RELATED WORDS **essential** *adjective;* **essential** *noun;* **essentially** *adverb*

EXAMPLE Freedom of choice is the *essence* of democracy.

6. **excess** (ĭk-sĕs′) *noun* **a.** Something that is more than the normal, necessary, or desirable amount or quantity: *an excess of carbohydrates.* **b.** An amount or quantity by which something exceeds another: *an excess of two gallons over capacity.* *adjective* Over what is required or normal: *excess fat.* 6. ______

RELATED WORDS **excessive** *adjective;* **excessively** *adverb*

EXAMPLE An *excess* of sun is unwise for redheads.

7. **frivolous** (frĭv′ə-ləs) *adjective* **a.** Not significant or worth attention; trivial: *wasting time on frivolous things.* **b.** Silly: *a frivolous person.* 7. ______

RELATED WORDS **frivolity** *noun;* **frivolously** *adverb*

EXAMPLE The Puritans considered holiday celebrations *frivolous.*

8. **imperative** (ĭm-pĕr′ə-tĭv) *adjective* **a.** Absolutely required; necessary: *A change in the rules is imperative.* **b.** Expressing a command: *an imperative tone of voice.* 8. ______

RELATED WORD **imperatively** *adverb*

EXAMPLE The loudspeaker announced, "It is *imperative* that all field-trip students bring in signed permission slips."

9. **pertinent** (pŭr′tn-ənt) *adjective* Related in some specific way; relevant: *pertinent data.* 9. ______

RELATED WORDS **pertain** *verb;* **pertinence** *noun*

EXAMPLE An outline should contain only *pertinent* details.

10. **significant** (sĭg-nĭf′ĭ-kənt) *adjective* **a.** Having meaning; meaningful: *a significant clue.* **b.** Valuable; worthy of note: *a significant contribution.* 10. ______

RELATED WORDS **significance** *noun;* **significantly** *adverb;* **signify** *verb*

EXAMPLE The newspaper story contained all *significant* details of the election.

Copyright © 1988 Houghton Mifflin Company. All rights reserved.

Name ______________________________ Date ______________

Exercise 1 Completing Definitions

On the answer line, write the word from the vocabulary list that best completes each definition.

1. Behavior that is fitting for a certain occasion is __?__ to it. 1. ________
2. To have as a necessary part is to __?__. 2. ________
3. The basic nature of something is its __?__. 3. ________
4. Something that is related (for example, to a topic) is __?__. 4. ________
5. Something or someone that serves as a helper or as an addition is a(n) __?__. 5. ________
6. Something that is absolutely necessary is said to be __?__. 6. ________
7. Something that is meaningful or valuable in some way is __?__. 7. ________
8. A paperweight is a common desk __?__. 8. ________
9. A(n) __?__ of something is more than enough of it. 9. ________
10. Silly, unimportant, or trivial matters could all be termed __?__. 10. ________

Exercise 2 Using Words Correctly

Decide whether the italicized vocabulary word has been used correctly in the sentence. On the answer line, write *Correct* for correct use and *Incorrect* for incorrect use.

1. Because of fire it was *imperative* for students to leave the building immediately. 1. ________
2. Elena, Nick, and George are *pertinent;* they are cousins. 2. ________
3. Although born with long tails, lambs are *entailed* when still young. 3. ________
4. In winter wood stoves are a common *auxiliary* source of heat. 4. ________
5. A person who is indirectly involved in a crime is an *accessory.* 5. ________
6. It is *appropriate* to use a vase as a hammer. 6. ________
7. Abdul had to pay *excess* postage for the overweight letter. 7. ________
8. The *essence* of Faye's long explanation for not turning in her homework was that she had forgotten to do it. 8. ________
9. Every once in a while, *frivolous* conversation is fun. 9. ________
10. A penny raise in an hourly wage is a *significant* increase. 10. ________

Copyright © 1988 Houghton Mifflin Company. All rights reserved.

Exercise 3 Choosing the Best Word

Decide which vocabulary word or related form best completes the sentence, and write the letter of your choice on the answer line.

1. Absolute honesty was the __?__ of his character. 1. ________
   a. excess b. accessory c. auxiliary d. essence

2. Fashion magazines are full of advice on using __?__ to give a new look to last year's clothes. 2. ________
   a. accessories b. frivolities c. auxiliaries d. pertinence

3. Computer programming jobs often __?__ a lot of overtime work. 3. ________
   a. appropriate b. entail c. pertain d. signify

4. Most application forms have room for work experience __?__ to the job. 4. ________
   a. excessive b. pertinent c. frivolous d. auxiliary

5. __?__ forces were called in to fight the six-alarm blaze. 5. ________
   a. Significant b. Pertinent c. Frivolous d. Auxiliary

6. "If you go grocery shopping when you're hungry," warned Mom, "you may end up buying a(n) __?__ amount of food." 6. ________
   a. essential b. appropriate c. significant d. excessive

7. "Is it really __?__ for us to hand in our reports by April 1?" asked Ginger. 7. ________
   a. pertinent b. excessive c. imperative d. significant

8. "Is there any __?__ to rumors that the President will veto the new tax bill?" the reporter asked the press secretary. 8. ________
   a. appropriateness b. excess c. significance d. auxiliary

9. Under certain conditions, the state has the right to __?__ and to use privately owned land. 9. ________
   a. signify b. entail c. pertain d. appropriate

10. Unprepared for the quiz, Lou gave up and wrote witty but __?__ answers. 10. ________
    a. frivolous b. accessory c. auxiliary d. imperative

Exercise 4 Using Different Forms of Words

Each sentence contains an italicized vocabulary word in a form that does not fit the sentence. On the answer line, write the form of the word that does fit the sentence.

1. Our teacher says that birthday parties are a necessary *frivolous.* 1. ________
2. Joan used her charge cards *excess.* 2. ________
3. When in doubt about a movie's *appropriate,* check its rating. 3. ________
4. The witness squirmed *significant* under the lawyer's stare. 4. ________
5. "Which *accessory* come with the car and which are extra?" asked the buyer. 5. ________

Copyright © 1988 Houghton Mifflin Company. All rights reserved.

Name ______________________________ Date ____________

6. Food, shelter, and clothing are the three *essence* of life. 6. ____________

7. When revising a composition, cross out all details that do not *pertinent* to your topic. 7. ____________

8. Today, a college education often *entail* loans and part-time work. 8. ____________

9. The sentry spoke *imperative* as he said, "Give the password!" 9. ____________

10. Women are no longer mere *auxiliary* in politics; today they hold offices at all levels of government. 10. ____________

Reading Comprehension

Each numbered sentence in the following passage contains an italicized vocabulary word or related form. After you read the passage, you will complete an exercise.

Ole: A Medical Robot

The automatic mechanical workers known as robots are increasingly a part of everyday life. (1) In some situations robots work alone, and in others they are the ***accessories*** of human workers. Few robots have the human appearance of creatures in science fiction. Indeed, most are simply armlike structures that can handle a tool skillfully. (2) Robots work on such ***frivolous*** (but delicious) products as fruit bars and on such complicated products as electronic circuits.

(3) One field in which robots have made a ***significant*** contribution is medicine. (4) In particular an ***auxiliary*** arm called "Ole" is helping brain surgeons. Ole, which looks like an arm hooked to a long pencil, was named for Svend C. Olson. Olson paid for the robot's development, but Dr. Yik San Kwoh created Ole.

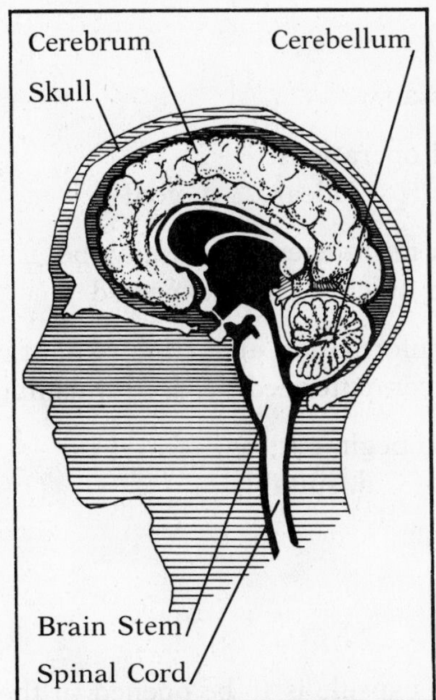

(5) All surgery ***entails*** risk, but brain surgery has perhaps the most of all. (6) Obviously, it is ***imperative*** that a brain surgeon be highly trained and greatly experienced. (7) Precision is the ***essence*** of successful operations for brain tumors, or growths. (8) Even an extra millimeter or two may make the length of a surgical incision ***excessive,*** inviting complications. Ole helps to provide the crucial precision.

(9) Into Ole's control center is fed ***pertinent*** information about the patient's brain and the tumor. (10) In seconds Ole's pencil indicates the exact spot and ***appropriate*** angle for the first surgical cut. Even if the patient's head is moved, Ole's pencil will return to the correct place.

Ole's performance gets high marks from both surgeon and patient. Now operations are faster and thus less tiring to the patient. As a result patients have less pain and walk sooner after the operation. Thanks to Ole, the road to recovery is both shorter and safer.

Please turn to the next page.

Copyright © 1988 Houghton Mifflin Company. All rights reserved.

Reading Comprehension Exercise

Each of the following statements corresponds to a numbered sentence in the passage. Each statement contains a blank and is followed by four answer choices. Decide which choice fits best in the blank. The word or phrase that you choose must express roughly the same meaning as the italicized word in the passage. Write the letter of your choice on the answer line.

1. In some situations robots are the __?__ of human workers. 1. ________
   a. slaves **b.** assistants **c.** operators **d.** bosses

2. Robots work on both __?__ products and sophisticated products. 2. ________
   a. trivial **b.** expensive **c.** useful **d.** simple

3. Robots have made a __?__ contribution to the field of medicine. 3. ________
   a. small **b.** limited **c.** little-known **d.** valuable

4. Ole is the name of a(n) __?__ robot arm. 4. ________
   a. computerized **b.** life-giving **c.** helpful **d.** extra

5. Brain surgery __?__ great risks. 5. ________
   a. adds **b.** involves **c.** reduces **d.** removes

6. It is __?__ for a brain surgeon to have years of training and experience. 6. ________
   a. helpful **c.** highly desirable
   b. customary **d.** absolutely necessary

7. Exactness is the __?__ of successful operations. 7. ________
   a. starting place **b.** basic quality **c.** ideal **d.** goal

8. In a surgical incision, even an extra millimeter or two may be __?__. 8. ________
   a. acceptable **b.** precise **c.** too much **d.** unexpected

9. Ole's control center receives __?__ information about the patient. 9. ________
   a. relevant **b.** complicated **c.** computerized **d.** astonishing

10. Ole tells surgeons the __?__ place to begin cutting. 10. ________
    a. easiest **b.** deepest **c.** fastest **d.** suitable

Writing Assignment

Write a letter for a time capsule. The capsule is to be opened in the year 2020, when your letter will be read to a class of sixth graders. Describe the role of robots now and ask questions about their role in 2020. Use at least five words from this lesson and underline each one.

Copyright © 1988 Houghton Mifflin Company. All rights reserved.

Lesson 24

-*sta*- and Related Roots

The root -*sta*- and such related forms as -*sist*- come from Latin words that mean "to stand" and "to cause to stand." Words derived from these roots often suggest strength, support, control, or purpose. For example, have you ever *taken a firm stand* or *stood up for* something? If so, you may have had to *withstand* pressure from friends who were not *understanding.* You *insisted* your position was right, didn't you? Little wonder, then, that *stand* is another word for "strong opinion." As you study the vocabulary words, look for a connection with the root meanings.

WORD LIST
circumstance
consistent
constitution
destination
destiny
destitute
institution
stately
stationary
statistic

Lesson 24 WORD LIST

DEFINITIONS

After you have studied the definitions and example for each vocabulary word, write the word on the line to the right.

1. **circumstance** (sûr′kəm-stăns′) *noun* **a.** A condition, fact, or event affecting someone or something; factor: *an unusual circumstance.* **b.** Conditions beyond one's control: *a victim of circumstance.* **c. circumstances.** Financial state: *in comfortable circumstances.*

   RELATED WORD **circumstantial** *adjective*

   EXAMPLE What would you do in such a *circumstance?*

   1. ______________

2. **consistent** (kən-sĭs′tənt) *adjective* **a.** In agreement; not contradictory: *a statement consistent with earlier claims.* **b.** Sticking to the same principles or course of action; not varying: *a consistent supporter of school teams.*

   RELATED WORDS **consistency** *noun;* **consistently** *adverb*

   EXAMPLE Your actions should be *consistent* with your words.

   2. ______________

3. **constitution** (kŏn′stĭ-tōō′shən) *noun* **a.** The basic laws or principles of a nation or organization. **b. the Constitution.** The document that sets forth the structure and laws of the United States government. **c.** The structure or make-up of something, especially a person's physical make-up: *a nervous constitution.*

   RELATED WORDS **constitute** *verb;* **constitutional** *adjective*

   EXAMPLE Many national *constitutions* are modeled after that of the United States.

   3. ______________

Copyright © 1988 Houghton Mifflin Company. All rights reserved.

4. **destination** (dĕs'tə-nā'-shən) *noun* A place or point set out for; end point; goal: *Rome was the destination of the package.* 4. ______

EXAMPLE In 1492 what was Columbus's *destination?*

5. **destiny** (dĕs'tə-nē) *noun* Fate; fortune; one's lot in life, regarded as determined in advance: *Her destiny was to be a courtroom lawyer.* 5. ______

RELATED WORD **destine** *verb*

EXAMPLE Is *destiny* birth, character, chance, or all three?

6. **destitute** (dĕs'tĭ-to͞ot') *adjective* **a.** Very poor; penniless: *a town made destitute by the flood.* **b.** Totally lacking something necessary or desirable: *destitute of experience.* 6. ______

RELATED WORD **destitution** *noun*

EXAMPLE Dust storms left many farmers *destitute* in the 1930s.

7. **institution** (ĭn'stĭ-to͞o'shən) *noun* **a.** An established organization and its buildings, such as a school, church, or prison. **b.** A custom or long-standing social practice: *the institution of marriage.* **c.** The act or process of beginning something: *the institution of a sales tax.* 7. ______

RELATED WORDS **institute** *verb;* **institutional** *adjective*

EXAMPLE Most museums in Washington, D.C., are part of the Smithsonian *Institution.*

8. **stately** (stāt'lē) *adjective* Dignified; impressive; majestic: *a stately mansion.* 8. ______

RELATED WORD **stateliness** *noun*

EXAMPLE A *stately* swan glided silently past some noisy ducks.

9. **stationary** (stā'shə-nĕr'ē) *adjective* **a.** Not moving; fixed; at rest: *a stationary target.* **b.** Not increasing or decreasing; unchanging: *stationary prices.* 9. ______

USAGE NOTE Do not confuse *stationary* with *stationery,* which means "writing paper."

RELATED WORDS **station** *noun;* **station** *verb*

EXAMPLE Birds hide by freezing in a *stationary* position.

10. **statistic** (stə-tĭs'tĭk) *noun* A numerical item; datum: *an unchecked statistic.* **statistics. a.** A collection of numerical items, or data: *How recent are those population statistics?* **b.** The branch of mathematics dealing with collecting and analyzing data: *a course in statistics.* 10. ______

USAGE NOTE *Statistics* takes a plural verb when it means "data" and a singular verb when it names a course of study.

RELATED WORDS **statistical** *adjective;* **statistically** *adverb*

EXAMPLE Joanne found the *statistic* in her almanac.

Copyright © 1988 Houghton Mifflin Company. All rights reserved.

Name ______________________ Date ______________

Exercise 1 **Writing Correct Words**

On the answer line, write the word from the vocabulary list that fits each definition.

1. The basic laws or principles of a nation or organization 1. ______
2. Fate; fortune 2. ______
3. Dignified; impressive; majestic 3. ______
4. In agreement; sticking to the same principles or action; not varying 4. ______
5. A place or point set out for; end point; goal 5. ______
6. A numerical item; datum 6. ______
7. An established organization; a custom or social practice 7. ______
8. Not moving; fixed; at rest 8. ______
9. A condition, fact, or event affecting someone or something 9. ______
10. Very poor; totally lacking something necessary or desirable 10. ______

Exercise 2 **Using Words Correctly**

Decide whether the italicized vocabulary word has been used correctly in the sentence. On the answer line, write *Correct* for correct use and *Incorrect* for incorrect use.

1. The radio announcement urged, "Use your seat belt. Don't become a *statistic.*" 1. ______
2. Strange *circumstances* surrounded the actor's disappearance. 2. ______
3. Oh no! That's our train pulling out of the *stationary!* 3. ______
4. Tim got his healthy *institution* from his mother. 4. ______
5. The judge's ruling is *consistent* with others on similar cases. 5. ______
6. Flight 503's final *destination* was Hong Kong. 6. ______
7. Do you believe in *destiny?* 7. ______
8. John D. Rockefeller's great wealth made his children *destitute.* 8. ______
9. Dressed only in a diaper, the royal baby looked *stately.* 9. ______
10. Do you know which state was the first to approve the *Constitution?* 10. ______

Copyright © 1988 Houghton Mifflin Company. All rights reserved.

Exercise 3 Choosing the Best Word

Decide which vocabulary word or related form best expresses the meaning of the italicized word or phrase in the sentence. On the answer line, write the letter of the correct choice.

1. The athlete's performance was *very nearly the same* from day to day. 1. ______
   a. destitute b. consistent c. circumstantial d. stately
2. On its last voyage, the old ocean liner looked as *impressive* as ever. 2. ______
   a. stately b. stationary c. destitute d. institutional
3. It seemed as if *fate* had decreed a conflict between the two nations. 3. ______
   a. destination b. consistency c. destitution d. destiny
4. Orpheus was told that under no *condition* should he look at Eurydice. 4. ______
   a. statistic b. destiny c. circumstance d. destitution
5. Many organizations have a written *set of rules* to guide them. 5. ______
   a. stationary b. institution c. constitution d. statistic
6. "Keep one foot *still* when you stop dribbling!" yelled the coach. 6. ______
   a. stationary b. stately c. destitute d. consistent
7. Many charitable *organizations* are run mainly by volunteers. 7. ______
   a. destinations b. circumstances c. statistics d. institutions
8. A good coach studies *numerical data* on the team after each game. 8. ______
   a. destitutions b. destinations c. statistics d. destinies
9. Have you decided on a *place to set out for?* 9. ______
   a. institution b. destination c. destiny d. destitution
10. *Extreme poverty* may be the result of a natural disaster or a war. 10. ______
   a. Circumstances b. Destination c. Destiny d. Destitution

Exercise 4 Using Different Forms of Words

Each sentence contains an italicized vocabulary word in a form that does not fit the sentence. On the answer line, write the form of the word that does fit the sentence.

1. We will *stationary* ourselves behind that door and surprise them! 1. ______
2. Even without his crown, the aging king had an air of *stately.* 2. ______
3. Our two *destination* were Calgary and Dawson Creek. 3. ______
4. Is it *statistic* true that female babies are stronger than males? 4. ______
5. "We have only *circumstance* evidence," said the lawyer. 5. ______
6. The singer is famous for his lack of *consistent.* 6. ______
7. How many *Constitution* amendments are there? 7. ______
8. Banks do not lend money to businesses they feel are *destiny* to fail. 8. ______
9. Rather than face a life of *destitute,* the family emigrated. 9. ______
10. The library *institution* a new set of rules about returning books. 10. ______

Copyright © 1988 Houghton Mifflin Company. All rights reserved.

Name ______________________________ Date ______________

Reading Comprehension

Each numbered sentence in the following passage contains an italicized vocabulary word or related form. After you read the passage, you will complete an exercise.

A Chapter in Hawaii's History

The last monarch to rule what is now part of the United States died in 1917. If this fact does not fit your idea of American history, perhaps it is time for you to rediscover Hawaii.

(1) At her death in 1917, Queen Liliuokalani lived in the ***stately*** Iolani Palace. (2) In comfortable ***circumstances,*** she was respected but crownless. (3) Indeed, her short reign (1891–1893) had been ***destined*** to fail.

(4) The Hawaii into which Lydia Kamekeha Paki was born in 1838 was not ***stationary,*** but changing very fast. Although over two thousand years old, Hawaii was united politically only in the late 1700s, by Kamehameha I. (5) When his line died out, in 1874, the ***institution*** of monarchy was all but dead. Opposing forces were too strong.

Education, technology, and social and political unrest combined to bring change to Hawaii. First, American missionaries came. Their schools paved the way for English as the official language. Clipper ships and then steamboats made fast transport possible. Unrest in China created a flood of labor.

(6) As Yankee money poured into plantations in the nineteenth century, Hawaii became the ***destination*** of waves of cheap labor. After the Chinese came Polynesians, Japanese, and Portuguese. Later, Filipinos, Koreans, Puerto Ricans, and others would arrive.

By 1842 the United States had formally recognized the kingdom of Hawaii. (7) As the years passed, the sugar industry ***consistently*** thrived, and a special trade agreement was drawn up between Hawaii and the United States. American influence increased. (8) By 1887 the king was forced to sign a ***constitution*** handing over most of his powers to cabinet members.

This was what Liliuokalani inherited. The situation grew worse when a law made in Washington, D.C., took away American protection of Hawaiian sugar. Much money was lost. (9) Trade ***statistics*** showed a severe depression. (10) As Hawaii threatened to become ***destitute,*** Americans who lived in the islands pushed for annexation. They overthrew the queen. Hawaii became a territory of the United States; many years later, in 1959, it became a state.

The brave Queen Liliuokalani, who had actually been arrested during the conflict, was never forgotten. Her voice is still heard, in her well-loved song "Aloha-Oe" and through Hawaiians' pride in their past.

Please turn to the next page.

Copyright © Houghton Mifflin Company. All rights reserved.

Reading Comprehension Exercise

Each of the following statements corresponds to a numbered sentence in the passage. Each statement contains a blank and is followed by four answer choices. Decide which choice fits best in the blank. The word or phrase that you choose must express roughly the same meaning as the italicized word in the passage. Write the letter of your choice on the answer line.

1. Queen Liliuokalani lived in a(n) __?__ home. 1. ________
   a. impressive b. decaying c. political d. official
2. She lived in comfortable __?__. 2. ________
   a. places b. conditions c. apartments d. clothes
3. However, her reign had been __?__ to fail. 3. ________
   a. expected b. fated c. forced d. known
4. In 1838 Hawaii was certainly not __?__. 4. ________
   a. well known b. discovered c. forgotten d. unchanging
5. As a(n) __?__ the Hawaiian monarchy was almost dead by 1874. 5. ________
   a. strength b. influence c. establishment d. result
6. From 1854 to 1872, Hawaii was the __?__ of waves of workers. 6. ________
   a. homeland b. boss c. goal d. port
7. The sugar plantations were __?__ successful. 7. ________
   a. always b. seldom c. sometimes d. never
8. The 1887 __?__ handed over most royal power to advisers. 8. ________
   a. letter b. guidelines c. ruler d. organization
9. When sugar was no longer protected, trade __?__ worsened. 9. ________
   a. figures b. importance c. exports d. imports
10. Some thought that Hawaii might become a __?__ land. 10. ________
    a. rich b. forgotten c. politically troubled d. very poor

Practice with Analogies

DIRECTIONS On the answer line, write the vocabulary word that completes each analogy.

See pages 32, 52, and 86 for some strategies to use with analogies.

1. Consequence is to consequential as __?__ is to circumstantial. 1. ________
2. Erratic is to steady as contradictory is to __?__. 2. ________
3. Enormous is to tiny as wealthy is to __?__. 3. ________
4. Game is to rules as nation is to __?__. 4. ________
5. Campaign is to objective as journey is to __?__. 5. ________
6. Inappropriate is to proper as undignified is to __?__. 6. ________
7. Word is to fact as number is to __?__. 7. ________
8. Window is to movable as wall is to __?__. 8. ________

Copyright © Houghton Mifflin Company. All rights reserved.

Name ______________________ Date ______________________

Reading Skills

The Prefix *trans-*

The prefix *trans-* is part of such familiar words as *transportation, transfer,* and *transmit.* The prefix *trans-* has one common meaning: "across."

PREFIX MEANING	WORD	DEFINITION
across	transcontinental	across the continent
	transform	to change in form or appearance
	transfer	to move or shift

Transfer is formed from *trans-* and the Latin root *-fer-*, which means "to bear" or "to carry." Many of the words that begin with *trans-* have a Latin root. When you cannot define such a word, be sure to look it up in a dictionary.

Exercise **Using the Prefix *trans-***

Step 1: Write your own definition of the italicized word in each of the following sentences. *Step 2:* In your own words, restate each sentence without using the italicized word. *Step 3:* Check your definition in a dictionary. Then write a sentence of your own in which you use the word correctly.

1. The *transatlantic* cruise ended at Lisbon, Portugal.

DEFINITION ______________________

RESTATEMENT ______________________

SENTENCE ______________________

2. Large trees are difficult to *transplant.*

DEFINITION ______________________

RESTATEMENT ______________________

SENTENCE ______________________

Please turn to the next page.

Copyright © 1988 Houghton Mifflin Company. All rights reserved.

3. The television signal was *transmitted* from Chicago to Dallas. (Clue: *-mit-* is a Latin root meaning "to send.")

DEFINITION ______________________________

RESTATEMENT ______________________________

SENTENCE ______________________________

4. Maria *transports* her books to school in a backpack. (Clue: *-port-* is a Latin root meaning "to carry.")

DEFINITION ______________________________

RESTATEMENT ______________________________

SENTENCE ______________________________

5. They made the *transoceanic* crossing in a balloon.

DEFINITION ______________________________

RESTATEMENT ______________________________

SENTENCE ______________________________

6. Bo and Jim took public *transit* to the museum. (Clue: *-it-* is a Latin root meaning "to go.")

DEFINITION ______________________________

RESTATEMENT ______________________________

SENTENCE ______________________________

7. Villagers *transacted* business in the outdoor market.

DEFINITION ______________________________

RESTATEMENT ______________________________

SENTENCE ______________________________

8. By mistake I *transposed* two drawers in the bureau. (Clue: *-pos-* is a Latin root meaning "to place.")

DEFINITION ______________________________

RESTATEMENT ______________________________

SENTENCE ______________________________

Copyright © 1988 Houghton Mifflin Company. All rights reserved.

Lesson 25

Attack and Defense

The vocabulary words in this lesson are "fighting words." Their basic meanings have to do with war: attacking or defending, striking at or striking back. However, words that express the idea of striking at or striking back can often apply to peacetime situations that in some way suggest war. We can attack a problem as well as an enemy, for example. We can also defend our rights or our point of view as well as our country. As you learn the words, be aware of both types of meanings.

WORD LIST
battalion
camouflage
casualty
corps
encampment
garrison
infiltrate
parry
provoke
siege

DEFINITIONS

After you have studied the definitions and example for each vocabulary word, write the word on the line to the right.

1. **battalion** (bə-tăl′yən) *noun* **a.** A large unit of soldiers made up of a headquarters company and four fighting companies. **b.** A great number, usually of people: *a battalion of tourists.* 1. ______

   EXAMPLE A regiment usually has three *battalions* and is led by a colonel.

2. **camouflage** (kăm′ə-fläzh′) *noun* **a.** The hiding of people, buildings, or equipment from an enemy by covering them with coloring and patterns to make them blend into the background. **b.** A disguise or concealment based on colors or patterns: *a camouflage of leaves and twigs.* *verb* To hide or conceal by using camouflage. 2. ______

   EXAMPLE Colonial soldiers learned *camouflage* from the Native Americans.

3. **casualty** (kăzh′o͞o-əl-tē) *noun* **a.** Someone injured, killed, or captured, as in battle: *a casualty of war.* **b.** An unfortunate accident involving loss of life: *a highway casualty.* 3. ______

   EXAMPLE Lieutenant Todd had the sad duty of reporting *casualties.*

Copyright © 1988 Houghton Mifflin Company. All rights reserved.

4. **corps** (kôr) *noun* **a.** A branch or department of the armed forces with a certain job: *Marine Corps, Medical Corps.* **b.** A military body made up of two divisions and support groups commanded by a lieutenant general. **c.** Persons acting together or sharing a purpose: *diplomatic corps.*

4. ________

USAGE NOTE The *s* and the *p* in *corps* are silent.

EXAMPLE A *corps* of army engineers built a bridge almost overnight.

5. **encampment** (ĕn-kămp′mənt) *noun* A camp or camping place.

5. ________

RELATED WORD **encamp** *verb*

EXAMPLE The snow began to fall on General Washington's *encampment* at Valley Forge.

6. **garrison** (găr′ĭ-sən) *noun* A military post, especially a permanent one, or the soldiers at that post. *verb* **a.** To supply a post with troops. **b.** To take over or occupy as a garrison.

6. ________

EXAMPLE The army of King George III used colonists' homes as *garrisons.*

7. **infiltrate** (ĭn-fĭl′trāt′) *verb* **a.** To enter gradually or secretly: *to infiltrate enemy territory.* **b.** To leak into or through, as a liquid or gas: *Water infiltrated the cellar wall.*

7. ________

MEMORY CUE *Infiltrate* contains part of the verb *filter* and means simply "to filter in."

RELATED WORD **infiltration** *noun*

EXAMPLE Spies *infiltrated* the general's headquarters.

8. **parry** (păr′ē) *verb* **a.** To turn aside, as in self-defense: *to parry a blow.* **b.** To avoid skillfully: *to parry someone's questions.* *noun* **a.** The action of turning aside a blow. **b.** An action or answer that escapes or avoids something.

8. ________

EXAMPLE The fencer *parried* the thrust of her opponent's weapon.

9. **provoke** (prə-vōk′) *verb* To cause an action or an emotion by stirring up, exciting, or upsetting: *to provoke a fight; to provoke anger.*

9. ________

RELATED WORDS **provocation** *noun;* **provoking** *adjective*

EXAMPLE The early wake-up call *provoked* much grumbling.

10. **siege** (sēj) *noun* **a.** The act of trying to capture a place by surrounding it and cutting off supplies. **b.** A repeated attempt to gain control or overcome opposition. **c.** A long period, as of illness: *a siege of flu.*

10. ________

MEMORY CUE The spelling of *siege* follows the rule *"i* before *e* except after *c."*

EXAMPLE Expecting a *siege,* the soldiers at the fort had piled up supplies.

Copyright © Houghton Mifflin Company. All rights reserved.

Name ______________________________ Date __________

Exercise 1 **Matching Words and Definitions**

Match the definition in Column B with the word in Column A. Write the letter of the correct definition on the answer line.

Column A	Column B
1. garrison	a. someone injured, killed, or captured
2. provoke	b. a military post; to supply a post with troops
3. casualty	c. a branch of the armed forces with a certain job; persons with a common purpose
4. siege	d. to cause an action or an emotion by stirring up, exciting, or upsetting
5. infiltrate	e. the act of trying to capture a place by surrounding it and cutting off supplies
6. battalion	f. a large unit of soldiers
7. parry	g. the use of coloring and patterns to conceal
8. encampment	h. to turn aside; avoid skillfully
9. corps	i. a camp or camping place
10. camouflage	j. to enter gradually or secretly

1. ________
2. ________
3. ________
4. ________
5. ________
6. ________
7. ________
8. ________
9. ________
10. ________

Exercise 2 **Using Words Correctly**

Each of the following questions contains an italicized vocabulary word. Choose the correct answer to the question, and write *Yes* or *No* on the answer line.

1. Can a spy *infiltrate* an organization? 1. ________
2. Are you *provoked* if someone praises you? 2. ________
3. Could you call a circle of tents an *encampment?* 3. ________
4. Would you find soldiers in a *battalion?* 4. ________
5. Is bright orange usually a good color for *camouflage?* 5. ________
6. When you peel a potato, do you *parry* it? 6. ________
7. Is the center of an apple also called a *corps?* 7. ________
8. Could a fort be used as a *garrison* for soldiers? 8. ________
9. In a battle does the loser usually suffer more *casualties?* 9. ________
10. In a city under *siege,* might people run out of food? 10. ________

Exercise 3 **Choosing the Best Word**

Decide which vocabulary word or related form best completes the sentence, and write the letter of your choice on the answer line.

1. Footprints and warm ashes signaled a recent __?__. 1. ________
   a. casualty **b.** encampment **c.** camouflage **d.** siege

Copyright © 1988 Houghton Mifflin Company. All rights reserved.

2. In 1836 the Mexican army laid __?__ to a fort named the Alamo. 2. ________
a. garrison b. parry c. siege d. corps

3. The President __?__ reporters' questions with more questions. 3. ________
a. parried b. camouflaged c. provoked d. encamped

4. Michelle's sloppiness __?__ a scolding from her father. 4. ________
a. camouflaged b. provoked c. infiltrated d. parried

5. Dust __?__ the supposedly spotless laboratory. 5. ________
a. infiltrated b. camouflaged c. encamped d. garrisoned

6. Factory roofs were painted to provide __?__ from enemy bombs. 6. ________
a. encampment b. casualties c. corps d. camouflage

7. The earthquake caused few __?__. 7. ________
a. encampments b. casualties c. sieges d. camouflages

8. Most towns with names containing *Fort* or *-chester* were once army __?__. 8. ________
a. garrisons b. corps c. battalions d. infiltrations

9. Members of the press __?__ receive special license plates. 9. ________
a. siege b. camouflage c. infiltration d. corps

10. The nickname "Seabee" stands for Construction __?__, one group in a navy corps founded in 1941 to build naval air bases. 10. ________
a. Infiltration b. Battalion c. Casualty d. Encampment

Exercise 4 Using Different Forms of Words

Decide which form of the vocabulary word in parentheses best completes the sentence. The form given may be correct. Write your answer on the answer line.

1. Watchdogs will attack at the least __?__. *(provoke)* 1. ________
2. The mother cat __?__ her kittens in the barn. *(garrison)* 2. ________
3. A family of raccoons had __?__ under the porch. *(encampment)* 3. ________
4. The mascot of the Drum __?__ is a duck named Drumstick. *(corps)* 4. ________
5. Cattle are among the first __?__ of a blizzard. *(casualty)* 5. ________
6. Some animals' coats turn white in winter as __?__. *(camouflage)* 6. ________
7. The two toddlers punched and __?__ like prizefighters. *(parry)* 7. ________
8. During World War II, Leningrad withstood a long __?__. *(siege)* 8. ________
9. __?__ of army ants attacked anything in their way. *(battalion)* 9. ________
10. Viruses are experts at __?__ of the body's defenses. *(infiltrate)* 10. ________

Copyright © 1988 Houghton Mifflin Company. All rights reserved.

Name ______________________________ Date ______________

Reading Comprehension

Each numbered sentence in the following passage contains an italicized vocabulary word. After you read the passage, you will complete an exercise.

The Minutemen: Early Heroes of the American Revolution

The year was 1774, and the place was the British colony of Massachusetts. Tensions were growing between the colonists and their British rulers. (1) Acts of the British government had ***provoked*** the colonists to the point of open rebellion. At the Boston Tea Party, a group of colonists protested by dumping tea into the city's harbor.

Britain struck back. (2) The port of Boston was shut down, and ***battalions*** of highly trained soldiers were sent to the city. (3) There they were ***garrisoned*** in people's homes. (4) Citizens began to feel that their city was under ***siege.*** In September patriots gathered at the First Continental Congress in Philadelphia. (5) In October, Massachusetts officials organized a ***corps*** of volunteer soldiers in various towns of the colony.

These soldiers were the "minutemen." They were ordinary citizens who had been instructed to be ready for duty at the "shortest notice." The minutemen wore no special uniforms. (6) They lived in their own homes, not in formal ***encampments.*** They carried their own weapons and trained on the open land of their farms. As the political situation grew worse, defiant minutemen began to store arms to fight the British.

Britain was quick to act. In April of 1775, the commanding general in Boston ordered troops to capture a supply of arms in the town of Concord. Minutemen stopped the troops at the nearby town of Lexington. Before the battle their commander, Captain John Parker, gave a famous order: "Don't fire unless fired upon. But if they want a war, let it begin here." (7) The minutemen stood their ground, attempting to ***parry*** the British attack. (8) In the end they had eighteen ***casualties,*** eight dead and ten wounded.

The overwhelming force of British soldiers pressed on toward Concord. (9) A local doctor ***infiltrated*** British lines to warn the town of the soldiers' approach. (10) Partially ***camouflaged*** by the trees and shrubs of the wooded country, more minutemen poured into Concord, where they met the British at North Bridge. Against odds the minutemen won the day, and British troops straggled back to Boston. The American Revolution had begun.

Years later, the Concord writer Ralph Waldo Emerson recorded the minutemen's achievement in these famous lines: "Here once the embattled farmers stood / And fired the shot heard round the world."

Reading Comprehension Exercise

Each of the following statements corresponds to a numbered sentence in the passage. Each statement contains a blank and is followed by four answer choices. Decide which choice fits best in the blank. The word or phrase that you choose must express roughly the same meaning as the italicized word in the passage. Write the letter of your choice on the answer line.

1. Acts of the British government had __?__ Massachusetts colonists. 1. ________
   a. angered **b.** puzzled **c.** divided **d.** pleased

Copyright © 1988 Houghton Mifflin Company. All rights reserved.

2. Many __?__ British soldiers arrived in Boston. 2. ______
a. wives of **b.** supplies for **c.** weapons for **d.** units of

3. The troops were __?__ in citizens' homes. 3. ______
a. fed **b.** placed **c.** imprisoned **d.** spied on

4. The people of Boston felt that they were in a state of __?__. 4. ______
a. ruin **b.** threatened capture **c.** imprisonment **d.** starvation

5. The colony organized a __?__ of part-time soldiers. 5. ______
a. drill group **b.** ruling group **c.** military group **d.** spy group

6. The minutemen did not live in military __?__. 6. ______
a. camps **b.** forts **c.** barracks **d.** headquarters

7. At Lexington the minutemen tried to __?__ the British assault. 7. ______
a. reverse **b.** defeat **c.** stand up under **d.** turn aside

8. Eighteen men were __?__ in the battle. 8. ______
a. decorated **c.** killed or injured
b. not accounted for **d.** missing

9. To warn the people of Concord, a Lexington man __?__ enemy lines. 9. ______
a. walked through **b.** secretly entered **c.** spied on **d.** attacked

10. Moving through the wooded country, minutemen were __?__ to some degree. 10. ______
a. concealed **b.** reorganized **c.** nervous **d.** excited

Writing Assignment

Think of something you have battled with, such as a problem, homework, or feelings. Using battle terms, write a letter of advice telling a friend how to handle a similar situation. Use at least four words from this lesson and underline them.

Vocabulary Enrichment

The word *camouflage* is both English and French. It comes from the French verb *camoufler,* which means "to disguise." In time the noun form *camouflet,* "a whiff of smoke," came to have a military meaning, referring to a smoke bomb that could be used to cover up troop movement. The idea of disguising or concealing is the heart of today's word *camouflage.*

ACTIVITY English has a number of words that began as French military terms. Using a dictionary, write the origins and definitions of the following words.

1. barricade 2. espionage 3. reconnaissance 4. sabotage 5. sortie

Copyright © 1988 Houghton Mifflin Company. All rights reserved.

Lesson 26

Certainty and Uncertainty

Have you ever been sure of a situation and then suddenly found yourself in doubt about what really did happen? Suppose, for example, that you witness an automobile accident. You are certain that the car that sped away was light blue. Then you overhear another witness telling a police officer that the car was gray. Your certainty about the car's color quickly disappears. Was it blue or was it gray?

Some of the words in this lesson express this sort of uncertainty. Other words in the lesson express certainty. As you read the definitions, study the sample phrases and sentences carefully to see the kinds of situations that best fit each word.

WORD LIST

approximate
assumption
attentive
certify
distinguish
emphasize
essential
illusion
probable
vague

DEFINITIONS

After you have studied the definitions and example for each vocabulary word, write the word on the line to the right.

1. **approximate** (ə-prŏk′sə-mĭt) *adjective* Close to in amount or number; almost exact or accurate: *approximate height.* *verb* (ə-prŏk′sə-māt′) To come close to; be nearly the same as: *to approximate the cry of an owl.* 1. ____________

RELATED WORDS **approximately** *adverb;* **approximation** *noun*

EXAMPLE What is the *approximate* size of your bedroom?

2. **assumption** (ə-sŭmp′shən) *noun* **a.** A statement, fact, or idea that is accepted as true (without proof) or taken for granted: *a false assumption about what she is really like.* **b.** The act of taking on or taking over: *assumption of power.* 2. ____________

RELATED WORD **assume** *verb*

EXAMPLE The *assumption* that toads cause warts is false.

USAGE NOTE *Assume,* in the sense of "to take for granted," is almost synonymous with *presume,* but *presume* implies more doubt and is often used in a questioning tone.

3. **attentive** (ə-tĕn′tĭv) *adjective* **a.** Paying attention; listening; observant: *attentive during class.* **b.** Considerate; thoughtful; devoted: *an attentive aunt.* 3. ____________

RELATED WORDS **attentively** *adverb;* **attentiveness** *noun*

EXAMPLE A good carpenter is *attentive* to detail.

Copyright © Houghton Mifflin Company. All rights reserved.

4. certify (sûr′tə-fī′) *verb* **a.** To declare to be true or genuine, especially in writing: *to certify a document.* **b.** To guarantee as meeting a standard: *to certify a teacher.* 4. ______

RELATED WORD **certification** *noun*

EXAMPLE Someone at the bank will *certify* that check.

5. distinguish (dĭ-stĭng′gwĭsh) *verb* **a.** To see or hear clearly: *to distinguish forms in the fog.* **b.** To recognize as different or distinct: *to distinguish fact from opinion.* **c.** To make (oneself) well known: *to distinguish oneself in politics.* 5. ______

USAGE NOTE The adjective *distinguished* means "well known."

RELATED WORD **distinguished** *adjective*

EXAMPLE Using binoculars, they were barely able to *distinguish* the comet in the southern sky.

6. emphasize (ĕm′fə-sīz′) *verb* To state boldly or forcefully; stress: *to emphasize a point.* 6. ______

RELATED WORDS **emphasis** *noun;* **emphatic** *adjective;* **emphatically** *adverb*

EXAMPLE Italic type is used to *emphasize* important words.

7. essential (ĭ-sĕn′shəl) *adjective* Basic; necessary: *Water is essential to life.* *noun* Something that is necessary: *the essentials of democracy.* 7. ______

RELATED WORD **essentially** *adverb*

EXAMPLE A motor is an *essential* part of a car; a radio is not.

8. illusion (ĭ-lo͞o′zhən) *noun* A misleading or mistaken impression or idea: *a picture with the illusion of depth.* 8. ______

USAGE NOTE Do not confuse *illusion* with *allusion*, a reference to something.

RELATED WORD **illusory** *adjective*

EXAMPLE Is that puddle in the road ahead real or just an *illusion?*

9. probable (prŏb′ə-bəl) *adjective* **a.** Likely to happen or be true: *the probable cost of the trip.* **b.** Likely but not certain: *the probable cause.* 9. ______

RELATED WORDS **probability** *noun;* **probably** *adverb*

EXAMPLE Judging from that dark sky, I would say that rain is *probable.*

10. vague (vāg) *adjective* **a.** Not clearly expressed or thought out; unclear: *vague plans.* **b.** Not able to be seen clearly: *a vague shape in the fog.* **c.** Not able to be felt or remembered clearly: *vague memories.* 10. ______

RELATED WORDS **vaguely** *adverb;* **vagueness** *noun*

EXAMPLE Because of Cal's *vague* directions, we got lost.

Copyright © 1988 Houghton Mifflin Company. All rights reserved.

Name ______________________________ Date ______________

Exercise 1 Matching Words and Definitions

Match the definition in Column B with the word in Column A. Write the letter of the correct definition on the answer line.

1. ________
2. ________
3. ________
4. ________
5. ________
6. ________
7. ________
8. ________
9. ________
10. ________

Column A

1. approximate
2. certify
3. illusion
4. emphasize
5. vague
6. assumption
7. distinguish
8. attentive
9. essential
10. probable

Column B

a. an idea that is accepted as true (without proof) or taken for granted
b. to see or hear clearly; recognize as distinct
c. likely to happen or be true; likely but not certain
d. not clearly expressed, seen, or felt
e. basic; necessary; something that is necessary
f. to state boldly or forcefully; stress
g. a misleading or mistaken impression or idea
h. paying attention; considerate
i. close to in amount or number
j. to declare to be true or genuine, especially in writing

Exercise 2 Using Words Correctly

Decide whether the italicized vocabulary word has been used correctly in the sentence. On the answer line, write *Correct* for correct use and *Incorrect* for incorrect use.

1. The police worked on the *assumption* that the fire had been set. 1. ________
2. A detective must be *attentive* to details. 2. ________
3. Before you leave, *distinguish* the campfire. 3. ________
4. Water is *essential* to fish. 4. ________
5. The victim remembered only *vague* details of the accident. 5. ________
6. Behind by twenty points, the Whales were the *probable* winners. 6. ________
7. I am *certified* that you are mistaken. 7. ________
8. The astronomer made an *illusion* to his famous book on comets. 8. ________
9. The *approximate* age of that huge pine is exactly eighty-three years. 9. ________
10. Speakers often *emphasize* main points by repeating them. 10. ________

Exercise 3 Choosing the Best Definition

For each italicized vocabulary word or related form in the following sentences, write the letter of the best definition on the answer line.

1. The child watched *attentively* while her grandmother painted. 1. ________
   a. quietly **b.** observantly **c.** cautiously **d.** occasionally

Copyright © 1988 Houghton Mifflin Company. All rights reserved.

2. Mockingbirds are experts at creating *illusions.* 2. ______
a. false impressions **b.** loud noises **c.** melodies **d.** trouble

3. Poison ivy is the *probable* cause of that itchy rash. 3. ______
a. certain **b.** impossible **c.** unfortunate **d.** likely

4. Carmen had a *vague* feeling of uneasiness. 4. ______
a. strong **b.** not reasonable **c.** clear **d.** not defined

5. Juries accept the *assumption* "innocent until proven guilty." 5. ______
a. case **b.** quotation **c.** idea **d.** verdict

6. In your opinion, which is more *essential,* television or radio? 6. ______
a. necessary **b.** expensive **c.** accurate **d.** definite

7. What is the *approximate* population of your state? 7. ______
a. official **c.** close to the actual number
b. exact **d.** most recently counted

8. Which two syllables are *emphasized* in the verb in this sentence? 8. ______
a. silent **b.** stressed **c.** clearest **d.** longest

9. Mrs. Chung was *certified* to teach high school mathematics. 9. ______
a. approved **b.** anxious **c.** certain **d.** asked

10. Many animals can *distinguish* sounds that humans cannot hear. 10. ______
a. imitate **b.** utter **c.** recognize **d.** repeat

Exercise 4 Using Different Forms of Words

Decide which form of the vocabulary word in parentheses best completes the sentence. The form given may be correct. Write your answer on the answer line.

1. What is the __?__ that we can land on Mars? *(probable)* 1. ______
2. The painter's work is generally considered to be __?__. *(distinguish)* 2. ______
3. The monster that the special-effects artist created was __?__. *(illusion)* 3. ______
4. The guest spoke __?__, punctuating his words with gestures. *(emphasize)* 4. ______
5. A teacher must receive state __?__ to work in a school system. *(certify)* 5. ______
6. This question is __?__ a matter of individual choice. *(essential)* 6. ______
7. Jo, your map is a better __?__ of Kenya than mine. *(approximate)* 7. ______
8. Tess remembered only __?__ the first house she lived in. *(vague)* 8. ______
9. When you drive, __?__ can save your life. *(attentive)* 9. ______
10. It is wrong to __?__ that all smart people are good spellers. *(assumption)* 10. ______

Copyright © 1988 Houghton Mifflin Company. All rights reserved.

Name ______________________________ Date ______________

Reading Comprehension

Each numbered sentence in the following passage contains an italicized vocabulary word or related form. After you read the passage, you will complete an exercise.

Dactyloscopy: The Science of Fingerprints

The worst enemy of a criminal is not police questioning, a surprise witness, or a clever lawyer. (1) It is ***probable*** that the number one enemy is *dactyloscopy,* the identification of the criminal's own fingerprints. (2) Today fingerprinting may be the single most ***essential*** crime-fighting tool. (3) When a crime is committed, witnesses may give only a ***vague*** description of the criminal. (4) They may have had no reason to be watching the scene of the crime with particular ***attentiveness.*** (5) Witnesses may even make false ***assumptions*** about what happened and who the guilty person is. (6) The identification of fingerprints, on the other hand, is never ***approximate.*** (7) The fingerprints of one person can be ***distinguished*** from those of anyone else in the world. When photographs of a set of fingerprints are sent to a crime laboratory for identification, the general pattern of prints is established first. There are three distinct types, based on the shape of the ridges on a person's fingertips. The prints are checked to see if their unique combination of whorls, arches, or loops matches those in any set of prints on file with the authorities.

Loop

Arch

Whorl

Then there must be further matching. (8) Experts ***emphasize*** the importance of examining the one-of-a-kind spacing and number of tiny holes along the ridges in the prints. These tiny holes are the final proof. (9) They are what makes it possible for a fingerprint expert to ***certify*** a set of prints as an exact match with another set. In this way the identity of a criminal can be established with absolute certainty.

(10) Today a criminal whose fingerprints are on file can have few ***illusions*** about remaining unidentified if he or she has left even traces of prints at the scene of a crime. Modern technology, including computers and lasers, can build whole prints from mere traces. It can even help to lift fingerprints from the inside of a glove. Using all the tools of dactyloscopy, an expert can quickly match a new pair of prints with a single set drawn from the millions on file.

Reading Comprehension Exercise

Each of the following statements corresponds to a numbered sentence in the passage. Each statement contains a blank and is followed by four answer choices. Decide which choice fits best in the blank. The word or phrase that you choose must express roughly the same meaning as the italicized word in the passage. Write the letter of your choice on the answer line.

1. It is __?__ that dactyloscopy is the chief enemy of the criminal. 1. 
   a. certain **b.** absolutely untrue **c.** possible **d.** very likely

Copyright © 1988 Houghton Mifflin Company. All rights reserved.

2. Fingerprinting may be the most ___?___ weapon against crime. 2. ________
a. common **b.** unusual **c.** important **d.** obvious

3. Some witnesses give a(n) ___?___ description of the guilty person. 3. ________
a. clear **b.** unclear **c.** definite **d.** false

4. Witnesses may not have been watching with ___?___. 4. ________
a. concentration **b.** doubt **c.** experience **d.** sympathy

5. They may even have incorrect ___?___ about what happened. 5. ________
a. proofs **b.** ideas **c.** prejudices **d.** information

6. Identifying fingerprints is *not* a matter of being ___?___. 6. ________
a. definite **c.** only partially accurate
b. exact **d.** certain

7. The fingerprints of one person can be ___?___. 7. ________
a. shown to be common **c.** proved to be false
b. recognized as distinct **d.** found to be faulty

8. Professionals ___?___ the examination of the spacing and number of tiny holes along the ridges of the fingertips. 8. ________
a. ignore **b.** consider unimportant **c.** perform **d.** stress

9. Professionals can ___?___ a set of prints to be an exact match with another set. 9. ________
a. consider **b.** guarantee **c.** report **d.** test

10. Those whose fingerprints are on file with the authorities can have few ___?___ about remaining unknown. 10. ________
a. mistaken ideas **c.** correct impressions
b. clear ideas **d.** strong wishes

Practice with Analogies

See pages 32, 52, and 86 for some strategies to use with analogies.

DIRECTIONS On the answer line, write the letter of the phrase that best completes the analogy.

1. Essential is to necessary as 1. ________
(A) must is to may (B) water is to live (C) keys is to car
(D) reliable is to dependable

2. Likely is to probable as 2. ________
(A) cheap is to inexpensive (B) cheerful is to anxious
(C) know is to guess (D) inexpensive is to costly

3. Exact is to approximate as 3. ________
(A) house is to dwelling (B) sharp is to fuzzy
(C) clear is to distinct (D) pen is to pencil

4. Awake is to attentive as 4. ________
(A) asleep is to night (B) asleep is to unobservant
(C) asleep is to careful (D) asleep is to dream

5. Illusion is to reality as 5. ________
(A) dog is to leash (B) fact is to dreamy (C) falsehood is to truth
(D) teacher is to subject

Copyright © Houghton Mifflin Company. All rights reserved.

Lesson 27

The Suffix *-logy*

A **suffix** is a word element added to the end of a root to form a complete word. The suffix *-logy* comes from the Greek word *logos*, which means "word" or "speech." Nouns ending in *-logy* refer to the "science, theory, or study" of something. Usually they contain a root that also comes from the Greek language. *Genealogy*, for example, comes from the Greek word *genea*, which means "family." The word *genealogy* means "study of family histories," and a *genealogist* is a person whose special field is family histories. The names of many subjects studied in schools, colleges, and universities end in *-logy*. You will consider ten such words in this lesson. Probably you can think of additional *-logy* words.

WORD LIST
anthropology
archaeology
biology
geology
mythology
physiology
psychology
sociology
technology
theology

DEFINITIONS

After you have studied the definitions and example for each vocabulary word, write the word on the line to the right.

1. **anthropology** (ăn'thrə-pŏl'ə-jē) *noun* The study of human beings, especially the arts, customs, and beliefs of different societies of the past and present.

   RELATED WORDS **anthropological** *adjective;* **anthropologist** *noun*

   EXAMPLE Myths are of great interest to someone who is studying *anthropology*.

   1. ______________

2. **archaeology** (är'kē-ŏl'ə-jē) *noun* The study of the remains of past civilizations, including graves, buildings, tools, and pottery.

   RELATED WORDS **archaeological** *adjective;* **archaeologist** *noun*

   EXAMPLE If you like solving puzzles and sifting sand, *archaeology* might interest you.

   2. ______________

   USAGE NOTE The word *archaeology* is often spelled *archeology*. Either spelling is correct.

3. **biology** (bī-ŏl'ə-jē) *noun* The study of plant and animal life.

   RELATED WORDS **biological** *adjective;* **biologically** *adverb;* **biologist** *noun*

   EXAMPLE Marine *biology* is the study of sea animals and plants.

   3. ______________

Copyright © 1988 Houghton Mifflin Company. All rights reserved.

4. **geology** (jē-ŏl′ə-jē) *noun* **a.** The study of the history and structure of the earth. **b.** The structure of a specific region: *the geology of the Great Lakes.* 4. ______

RELATED WORDS **geological** *adjective;* **geologist** *noun*

EXAMPLE Petroleum engineers need to study *geology.*

5. **mythology** (mĭ-thŏl′ə-jē) *noun* **a.** The study of old-time stories about gods, heroes, and natural events. **b.** A collection of such stories: *Aztec mythology.* 5. ______

RELATED WORD **mythological** *adjective*

EXAMPLE In West African *mythology,* a spider called Anansi created the world and then enjoyed playing tricks on everyone.

6. **physiology** (fĭz′ē-ŏl′ə-jē) *noun* **a.** The study of life processes, activities, and functions (such as breathing, feeding, motion, and growth). **b.** The life processes of a particular living thing: *cell physiology.* 6. ______

RELATED WORDS **physiological** *adjective;* **physiologist** *noun*

EXAMPLE Students of *physiology* learn how animals take in oxygen.

7. **psychology** (sī-kŏl′ə-jē) *noun* **a.** The study of the mind and resulting behavior. **b.** The emotions and behavior associated with a being, group, or activity: *child psychology.* 7. ______

RELATED WORDS **psychological** *adjective;* **psychologically** *adverb;* **psychologist** *noun*

EXAMPLE Students of *psychology* learn about mental health.

8. **sociology** (sō′sē-ŏl′ə-jē) *noun* The study of human behavior as part of social and community living. 8. ______

RELATED WORDS **sociological** *adjective;* **sociologist** *noun*

EXAMPLE Such institutions as schools are a part of *sociology.*

9. **technology** (tĕk-nŏl′ə-jē) *noun* **a.** The application of scientific knowledge and skills, especially to industry and business: *the growth of technology.* **b.** The methods and machines used to apply knowledge and skills: *space technology.* 9. ______

RELATED WORDS **technician** *noun;* **technological** *adjective;* **technologically** *adverb*

EXAMPLE Our level of *technology* would amaze ancient peoples.

10. **theology** (thē-ŏl′ə-jē) *noun* The study of God and religious truths: *Buddhist theology.* 10. ______

RELATED WORDS **theologian** *noun;* **theological** *adjective*

EXAMPLE *Theology* considers questions like "Why are we here?"

Copyright © 1988 Houghton Mifflin Company. All rights reserved.

Name ______________________________ Date ______________

Exercise 1 Matching Words and Definitions

Match the definition in Column B with the word in Column A. Write the letter of the correct definition on the answer line.

Column A	Column B
1. technology	a. the study of the mind and resulting behavior
2. anthropology	b. the study of human behavior as part of social and community living
3. theology	c. the study of the remains of past civilizations
4. physiology	d. the study of plant and animal life
5. biology	e. the study of life processes, activities, and functions
6. sociology	f. the study of God and religious truths
7. mythology	g. the study of human beings, especially the arts, customs, and beliefs of past and present societies
8. psychology	h. the study of the history and structure of the earth
9. archaeology	i. the study of old-time stories about gods, heroes, and natural events
10. geology	j. the application of scientific knowledge and skills, especially to industry and business

1. ________
2. ________
3. ________
4. ________
5. ________
6. ________
7. ________
8. ________
9. ________
10. ________

Exercise 2 Using Words Correctly

Each of the following questions contains an italicized vocabulary word. Choose the correct answer to the question, and write *Yes* or *No* on the answer line.

1. Would you study the religions of the world in *geology?* 1. ________
2. Might you use a shovel during a field trip in *archaeology?* 2. ________
3. Might *mythology* explain why winter comes? 3. ________
4. Is a computer chip an example of modern *technology?* 4. ________
5. Would a *biology* course explain how valleys are formed? 5. ________
6. Does a secretary need to study *physiology?* 6. ________
7. Do the people who plan advertisements use *psychology?* 7. ________
8. In *sociology* might you study city neighborhoods? 8. ________
9. Would *theology* answer the question "Is the koala a bear?" 9. ________
10. Would Stone Age customs and tools interest a student of *anthropology?* 10. ________

Copyright © 1988 Houghton Mifflin Company. All rights reserved.

Exercise 3 Choosing the Best Word

Decide which vocabulary word or related form best completes the sentence, and write the letter of your choice on the answer line.

1. The Rocky Mountains were formed at a time of great __?__ change. 1. ______
   a. technological b. biological c. geological d. psychological
2. Chapter 6 of your __?__ textbook is about the life cycle of a tree. 2. ______
   a. mythology b. sociology c. anthropology d. biology
3. Muslim __?__ is explained in the Koran, the sacred book of Islam. 3. ______
   a. theology b. archaeology c. technology d. geology
4. The word *cereal* comes from Ceres, a goddess of Roman __?__ . 4. ______
   a. technology b. sociology c. biology d. mythology
5. Finding arrowheads interested Pat in __?__. 5. ______
   a. archaeology b. psychology c. physiology d. theology
6. Dr. Payne spoke on the __?__ of human muscles. 6. ______
   a. technology b. geology c. physiology d. sociology
7. Today's __?__ class was on teen-age clubs. 7. ______
   a. mythology b. sociology c. geology d. technology
8. Plows were a huge step forward in farm __?__ . 8. ______
   a. theology b. technology c. archaeology d. psychology
9. The __?__ Pavlov studied ways to control animal behavior. 9. ______
   a. anthropologist b. theologian c. geologist d. psychologist
10. The __?__ Margaret Mead studied peoples of the Pacific islands. 10. ______
    a. technician b. theologian c. anthropologist d. geologist

Exercise 4 Using Different Forms of Words

Each sentence contains an italicized vocabulary word in a form that does not fit the sentence. On the answer line, write the form of the word that does fit the sentence.

1. Since I am adopted, I am not *biology* related to my parents. 1. ______
2. Some *geology* say that all continents came from a single land mass. 2. ______
3. One *physiology* sign of fear or stress is sweating. 3. ______
4. In 1000 B.C., China was *technology* far ahead of the West. 4. ______
5. Edith Hamilton and Thomas Bulfinch wrote fascinating accounts of *mythology* characters. 5. ______
6. Ishi, the last member of his tribe, was studied by Theodora and Alfred Kroeber, two California *anthropology*. 6. ______
7. The Bible and the Talmud are great *theology* works. 7. ______

Copyright © 1988 Houghton Mifflin Company. All rights reserved.

Name ______________________________ Date ______________

8. If I become a *sociology,* what jobs can I look forward to? 8. ______________

9. Jan is *psychology* tough; nothing seems to upset her. 9. ______________

10. The Rosetta Stone helped *archaeology* decode ancient symbols. 10. ______________

Reading Comprehension

Each numbered sentence in the following passage contains an italicized vocabulary word. After you read the passage, you will complete an exercise.

Beyond the Three R's

The words in this lesson name courses that you may meet in higher education. Every one of the courses has something to do with human beings — how they act, how the life processes of their bodies work, what they know, and what they think about.

Some college courses consider human beings in familiar settings. (1) ***Psychology*** courses investigate human behavior: why people feel and act as they do. If you are interested in what makes people "tick," you might study psychology. (2) ***Sociology*** courses, on the other hand, investigate how people behave in groups. Such courses consider why people vote as they do, how people divide into social classes, and why communities have such problems as crime and poverty.

Other college courses focus on human societies that are distant from our own in both space and time. (3) In ***anthropology*** courses the subject matter might range from fossil remains of early humans at Olduvai Gorge to marriage customs of primitive peoples in New Guinea. (4) A good accompaniment to anthropology is the reading of ***mythology.*** The myths and legends of a group are a key to its character. Already you are probably learning something about the Greeks and the Romans from reading the legends of these peoples.

(5) ***Archaeology*** forms another approach to exploring older civilizations. Courses in this subject might cover the Anasazi of the Southwest or the many levels of the excavated city of Troy, in Asia Minor. (6) Courses in ***geology*** would form a starting place for an archaeologist, for people in this field must understand different kinds of terrain. The two fields share some of the same terms and research methods.

Perhaps, on the other hand, you would prefer courses that investigate the miracle of human and animal life. (7) ***Biology,*** which you can take in high school, is a basic science course. It covers plants as well as animals, including human beings. (8) ***Physiology*** is an advanced form of biology. Courses in this subject are available only in college and in graduate school. They are part of the education of all doctors. A physiology course might involve detailed studies of the mysteries of sleep and dreaming, or the way in which bone marrow produces red blood cells. (9) The advanced ***technology*** of medicine today is of immense help in studying life processes and diagnosing illness. You may have read about laser technology and CAT scans, for example.

(10) Just as physiology is taught in medical school, ***theology*** is taught in theological school. Ideas about religion have been a subject of study for thousands of years. The subject is part of the education of anyone who wants to be a member of the clergy or has a religious vocation of any kind.

Your career plans, then, to some extent determine the courses that you will take as you go through school and beyond. Your interests, too, are important. Never be afraid to study a subject that is not directly related to a career goal. A single course could change your goals. It is important to be open to new ideas and new interests. Whatever your interests and ambitions are, high school and college will help you to pursue them.

Please turn to the next page.

Copyright © 1988 Houghton Mifflin Company. All rights reserved.

Reading Comprehension Exercise

Each of the following statements corresponds to a numbered sentence in the passage. Each statement contains a blank and is followed by four answer choices. Decide which choice fits best in the blank. The phrase that you choose must express roughly the same meaning as the italicized word in the passage. Write the letter of your choice on the answer line.

1. Human behavior is the subject of courses in the science of __?__. 1. _____
   a. the human mind c. animals and plants
   b. the human body d. the earth

2. Group behavior is the subject of courses in the science of __?__. 2. _____
   a. religious ideas c. animal behavior
   b. life processes d. social behavior

3. Marriage customs might be studied in courses in the science of __?__. 3. _____
   a. the family b. the Pacific c. human societies d. city life

4. The study of __?__ might accompany courses in anthropology. 4. _____
   a. old-time stories c. religious figures
   b. musical instruments d. natural disasters

5. The study of their __?__ is another approach to cultures of the past. 5. _____
   a. rock formations c. life processes
   b. buried remains d. religious ideas

6. Courses in the science of __?__ are useful to archaeologists. 6. _____
   a. animals and plants c. the earth
   b. the human mind d. life processes

7. __?__ is a basic course that can be studied in high school. 7. _____
   a. The science of animals and plants c. The science of cells
   b. The study of dreams d. The study of machinery

8. The study of __?__ is an advanced form of biology. 8. _____
   a. mental health c. life processes
   b. rock formations d. social systems

9. Medicine today uses advanced __?__. 9. _____
   a. blood studies c. life processes
   b. sleep studies d. machines and methods

10. __?__ has been a subject of study for thousands of years. 10. _____
    a. Earth theory c. Applied science
    b. Religious truth d. Education

Writing Assignment

Use an encyclopedia and other library materials to investigate several courses of study covered in this lesson. Choose the three courses that interest you the most. Then write a short composition in which you explain to an older friend or relative why you would like to study these courses. Underline the course names and any related words.

Copyright © 1988 Houghton Mifflin Company. All rights reserved.

Name ______________________ Date ______________

Reading Skills

READING SKILLS

The Prefix *de-*

Like all prefixes, *de-* alters the meaning of the root to which it is added. This prefix has two different meanings. One meaning is "the reverse of" or "the opposite of." The second meaning is "down" or "away from." Here are examples of words formed with *de-*.

PREFIX MEANING	WORD	DEFINITION
1. the reverse of; the opposite of	decode	to convert from code
	decompress	to release from pressure
2. down, away from	depress	to press down
	descend	to move down

The root of the last word in the list, *descend,* is *-scend-*. The root is from Latin and means "to climb." Many words formed with *de-* have Latin roots. Whenever you are uncertain of the meaning of a root, be sure to consult a dictionary.

Exercise **Using the Prefix *de-***

Step 1: Write your own definition of the italicized word in each of the following sentences. *Step 2:* In your own words, restate each sentence without using the italicized word. *Step 3:* Check your definition in a dictionary. Then write a sentence of your own in which you use the word correctly.

1. Terri was sorry she had to *decline* the invitation. (Clue: *-cline-* is a Latin root meaning "to bend.")

DEFINITION ______________________

RESTATEMENT ______________________

SENTENCE ______________________

2. The people wanted to *dethrone* the unjust king.

DEFINITION ______________________

RESTATEMENT ______________________

SENTENCE ______________________

Please turn to the next page.

Copyright © 1988 Houghton Mifflin Company. All rights reserved.

3. The judges *deducted* one point from the gymnast's score.

DEFINITION ______

RESTATEMENT ______

SENTENCE ______

4. You should *defrost* the refrigerator.

DEFINITION ______

RESTATEMENT ______

SENTENCE ______

5. The ticket agent said we will *depart* from Gate 12.

DEFINITION ______

RESTATEMENT ______

SENTENCE ______

6. Rex used a rag to *defog* the windshield.

DEFINITION ______

RESTATEMENT ______

SENTENCE ______

7. *Deposit* the trash in the litter can, please. (Clue: *-posit-* is a Latin root meaning "to put.")

DEFINITION ______

RESTATEMENT ______

SENTENCE ______

8. The long cold spell *deformed* the pumpkins.

DEFINITION ______

RESTATEMENT ______

SENTENCE ______

Copyright © 1988 Houghton Mifflin Company. All rights reserved.

Lesson 28

The Family

The words in this lesson concern one of society's oldest units, the family. The term *family* can mean few or many people. We usually use the word to describe a group of people who are related and who live in the same home. Sometimes we speak of a "nuclear" family — one or two parents and their child or children. We also speak of the "extended" family — a larger unit that includes grandparents, aunts, uncles, and cousins. We even speak of larger family groups, such as clans.

Family relationships span many generations, from early ancestors to the newly born. In this lesson you will explore some of the varied kinds of family ties, distant and close, that link human beings together.

WORD LIST
ancestor
clan
compatible
domestic
filial
hereditary
kin
matrimony
spouse
tradition

DEFINITIONS

After you have studied the definitions and example for each vocabulary word, write the word on the line to the right.

1. **ancestor** (ăn′sĕs′tər) *noun* **a.** A person from whom someone is descended, especially a person several generations back; forebear: *ancestors from Poland.* **b.** A forerunner of a person, thing, or idea: *A peach basket was the ancestor of the basketball hoop.*

   RELATED WORDS **ancestral** *adjective;* **ancestry** *noun*

   EXAMPLE The *ancestors* of the Incas came from Asia.

1. ______________

USAGE NOTE An *ancestor* is a person. *Ancestry* is one's line of descent.

2. **clan** (klăn) *noun* **a.** A division of a tribe whose members are all descended from the same person. **b.** A group of related families from the Scottish Highlands: *the MacGregor clan.* **c.** A large group of relatives, friends, or associates.

   RELATED WORD **clannish** *adjective*

   EXAMPLE This *clan* is part of the Navajo nation.

2. ______________

3. **compatible** (kəm-păt′ə-bəl) *adjective* Getting along or working well together; harmonious: *compatible neighbors, machine parts, colors.*

   RELATED WORDS **compatibility** *noun;* **compatibly** *adverb*

   EXAMPLE The two toddlers were *compatible.*

3. ______________

Copyright © 1988 Houghton Mifflin Company. All rights reserved.

4. **domestic** (də-mĕs′tĭk) *adjective* **a.** Relating to the family or household: *domestic chores.* **b.** Not wild; tame: *domestic animals.* **c.** Not foreign: *domestic oil.* *noun* A household servant; a hired helper. 4. ____________

RELATED WORDS **domestically** *adverb;* **domesticate** *verb*

EXAMPLE Larry's *domestic* duties included feeding the cat.

5. **filial** (fĭl′ē-əl) *adjective* Appropriate to or describing a son or daughter. 5. ____________

RELATED WORD **filially** *adverb*

EXAMPLE In some cultures, not looking a parent in the eye is a sign of *filial* respect.

6. **hereditary** (hə-rĕd′ĭ-tĕr′ē) *noun* **a.** Passed down biologically from parents to offspring; inborn: *hereditary characteristics.* **b.** Passed down through inheritance: *a hereditary title.* 6. ____________

RELATED WORD **heredity** *noun*

EXAMPLE The shape of one's nose is *hereditary;* a cold in the nose is not.

7. **kin** (kĭn) *noun* One's blood relatives. 7. ____________

RELATED WORD **kinship** *noun*

EXAMPLE Aunts, uncles, cousins, and grandparents count as *kin.*

8. **matrimony** (măt′rə-mō′nē) *noun* The state of being married; marriage. 8. ____________

RELATED WORDS **matrimonial** *adjective;* **matrimonially** *adverb*

EXAMPLE She did not consider *matrimony* until she had finished college.

9. **spouse** (spous) *noun* A marriage partner; a wife or husband. 9. ____________

EXAMPLE If you are a widow or widower, your *spouse* is no longer living.

10. **tradition** (trə-dĭsh′ən) *noun* **a.** The passing down of customs and beliefs, especially orally; **b.** a custom or usage: *Hispanic tradition, wedding traditions.* 10. ____________

RELATED WORDS **traditional** *adjective;* **traditionally** *adverb*

EXAMPLE Thanksgiving Day is a *tradition* in both the United States and Canada.

Copyright © Houghton Mifflin Company. All rights reserved.

Name ______________________________ Date __________

Exercise 1 Completing Definitions

On the answer line, write the word from the vocabulary list that best completes each definition.

1. The state of marriage is __?__. 1. ________
2. Blood relatives are one's __?__. 2. ________
3. __?__ things are related to the family or household. 3. ________
4. People or things that work well together are __?__. 4. ________
5. Inborn characteristics are __?__. 5. ________
6. The passing down of customs or beliefs is called __?__. 6. ________
7. Behavior appropriate to a son or daughter may be called __?__. 7. ________
8. A tribal group whose members are all descended from the same person is called a __?__. 8. ________
9. A person from whom one is descended is one's __?__. 9. ________
10. The person to whom one is married is one's __?__. 10. ________

Exercise 2 Using Words Correctly

Each of the following statements contains an italicized vocabulary word. Decide whether the sentence is true or false, and write *True* or *False* on the answer line.

1. *Matrimony* is money that a bride saves for her marriage. 1. ________
2. Enemies are people who are *compatible*. 2. ________
3. Your second cousin is your *kin*. 3. ________
4. A *spouse* is a tiny blood-drinking insect. 4. ________
5. Your *ancestors* are older than you are. 5. ________
6. Your taste in clothes and music is *hereditary*. 6. ________
7. A *clan* lives in a shell and can be eaten. 7. ________
8. Obeying parents' wishes is appropriate *filial* behavior. 8. ________
9. The eagle, the rhinoceros, and the whale are *domestic* animals. 9. ________
10. According to *tradition* an engagement ring is likely to have a diamond. 10. ________

Copyright © 1988 Houghton Mifflin Company. All rights reserved.

Exercise 3 Choosing the Best Definition

For each italicized vocabulary word in the following sentences, write the letter of the best definition on the answer line.

1. In more than half of American families, both *spouses* work. 1. ______
   a. men and women **c.** parents and children
   b. grandparents **d.** marriage partners
2. All members of the *clan* lived in a community north of the Arctic Circle. 2. ______
   a. nation **b.** tribe **c.** group within a tribe **d.** nuclear family
3. My dog's white paws are *hereditary.* 3. ______
   a. unusual **c.** extremely dirty
   b. attractive **d.** inherited biologically
4. That telephone is not *compatible* with this computer hookup. 4. ______
   a. usable **b.** supplied **c.** cheap **d.** allowed
5. After the birth of triplets, Mrs. Clark needed *domestic* help. 5. ______
   a. medical **b.** parental **c.** household **d.** additional
6. Some people enjoy doing library research on their *ancestors.* 6. ______
   a. place of birth **c.** neighbors
   b. parents' lives **d.** forebears
7. Arranged *matrimony* is still common in many countries. 7. ______
   a. dating **b.** marriage **c.** employment **d.** burial
8. According to *tradition* our flag should never touch the ground. 8. ______
   a. the President **b.** custom **c.** law **d.** experts
9. Jan glowed with *filial* pride when her father received an award. 9. ______
   a. appropriate to a son or daughter
   b. appropriate to a sister or brother
   c. appropriate to a wife or husband
   d. appropriate to a grandparent
10. Only close *kin* were present at the small wedding ceremony. 10. ______
    a. friends **b.** reporters **c.** relatives **d.** contacts

Exercise 4 Using Different Forms of Words

Each sentence contains an italicized vocabulary word in a form that does not fit the sentence. On the answer line, write the form of the word that does fit the sentence.

1. *Compatible* of interests is important for married couples. 1. ______
2. Because Alex has always been *domestic* inclined, he plans a career as an interior designer. 2. ______
3. *Hereditary* determines such traits as the color of one's eyes. 3. ______
4. The bridegroom had a bad case of *matrimony* nervousness. 4. ______
5. Don's *clan* family made his friend feel like an outsider. 5. ______

Copyright © 1988 Houghton Mifflin Company. All rights reserved.

Name ______________________________ Date ____________

6. On his birthday Mr. Suarez's children embraced him *filial*. 6. ____________

7. There is a close *kin* between wolves and dogs. 7. ____________

8. Does that health plan cover employees' children and *spouse?* 8. ____________

9. Kara's *ancestor* is Dutch, Carib, and West African. 9. ____________

10. In our society wedding guests *tradition* throw rice. 10. ____________

Reading Comprehension

Each numbered sentence in the following passage contains an italicized vocabulary word or related form. After you read the passage, you will complete an exercise.

Traditions of the Hopi

In the language of the Hopi Indian nation, the word *Hopi* means "good, peaceful, and right-living people." The Hopi live in Arizona, in an area of small villages and high mesas. Many continue to live by farming and herding sheep, and most consider the land as a sacred source of spiritual strength. (1) The Hopi feel that goodness and peacefulness come from preserving the land and respecting their ***traditions.***

(2) An important custom is the way in which the Hopi regard their ***ancestry.*** (3) They trace their ***hereditary*** descent through the mother's line only. (4) Women are the center of ***domestic*** life. The Hopi consider the oldest woman in a family group to be the head of the family. Nevertheless, the woman's brother may hold the real authority.

(5) Hopi customs of ***kinship*** are complicated. (6) ***Matrimonial*** customs are changing, but when a couple marry, it is still usual for the husband to move into his wife's household. Couples generally do not go visiting together. (7) Husbands may leave their ***spouses*** at home when they attend ceremonies at the homes of their sisters or their mothers. (8) ***Filial*** ties are strong, but children are taught and disciplined not so much by their father as by their uncles on their mother's side.

By custom every Hopi also belongs to a group even larger than the family at home. (9) This large group is a ***clan.*** There are hundreds of them in the Hopi nation. Members of a clan have religious duties and take part in special ceremonies that may be secret. (10) For the most part, the Hopi find these ceremonies to be ***compatible*** with life in the twentieth century. Indeed, the religious rites renew people's spirits and give reassurance that the crops of the sacred land will continue to grow.

Reading Comprehension Exercise

Each of the following statements corresponds to a numbered sentence in the passage. Each statement contains a blank and is followed by four answer choices. Decide which choice fits best in the blank. The word or phrase that you choose must express roughly the same meaning as the italicized word in the passage. Write the letter of your choice on the answer line.

1. The Hopi believe in respecting their __?__. 1. ____________
   a. harvest **b.** good name **c.** customs **d.** lands

Copyright © 1988 Houghton Mifflin Company. All rights reserved.

2. An important Hopi tradition is the way in which people regard their ___?___. 2. ________

a. arts and crafts c. possessions
b. line of descent d. relatives

3. A Hopi values his or her ___?___ standing through the mother's line. 3. ________

a. inherited b. financial c. legal d. community

4. Women are the most important figures in ___?___ life. 4. ________

a. agricultural b. religious c. artistic d. household

5. Among the Hopi, customs of ___?___ are complicated. 5. ________

a. religious festivals c. holiday observances
b. family relationships d. obedience to authorities

6. The customs of ___?___ are beginning to change. 6. ________

a. education b. agriculture c. arts and crafts d. marriage

7. A Hopi man often leaves his ___?___ at home when he goes visiting. 7. ________

a. sister b. mother c. marriage partner d. aunt

8. The Hopi value ___?___ ties. 8. ________

a. child-parent c. child-grandparent
b. sister-brother d. child-uncle

9. There are many ___?___ in the Hopi nation. 9. ________

a. kinship groups c. high mesas
b. marriage customs d. religious households

10. Most Hopi find their religious customs and present-day life to be ___?___. 10. ________

a. interesting b. valuable c. in harmony d. in conflict

Writing Assignment

Imagine that you are able to travel back in time. Visit an ancestor (real or imaginary) and then describe your visit in a journal entry. Use at least four vocabulary words and underline them.

Vocabulary Enrichment

In Latin, the language of the ancient Romans, the words for "daughter" and "son" are similar. *Filia* means "daughter," and *filius* means "son." The English word *filial* is a close relative of these words. *Filial* is correctly used to describe actions and attitudes appropriate to both daughters and sons.

ACTIVITY Like *filial,* the following words come from root words that describe specific family relationships. Look up the words in a high school dictionary and write their origins and definitions. Include an example sentence with each definition.

1. avuncular 2. fraternal 3. germane 4. nepotism 5. sorority

Copyright © Houghton Mifflin Company. All rights reserved.

Lesson 29

The Roots *-mit-* and *-mis-*

The roots *-mit-* and *-mis-* come from the Latin word *mittere,* meaning "to send." Many words formed from these roots begin with a prefix. These prefixes help to describe a specific kind of sending: out, in, into, back, across, and for. For example, the prefix in the word *remit* is *re-,* which often means "back." *Remit,* then, means "to send back." Other words formed from *-mit-* and *-mis-* end with a suffix, such as *-ion* or *-ible.* The suffix *-ion* is used for nouns, and *-ible* is used for adjectives. Some *-mit-* and *-mis-* words have both a prefix and a suffix. Be aware of these word elements when you study the vocabulary words and their related forms.

WORD LIST

admit
compromise
emit
mission
omit
permissible
premise
remit
submit
transmit

DEFINITIONS

After you have studied the definitions and example for each vocabulary word, write the word on the line to the right.

1. **admit** (ăd-mĭt′) *verb* **a.** To allow to enter; let in: *a ticket to admit the whole group.* **b.** To recognize as true; confess: *to admit guilt.* — 1. ____________

   RELATED WORDS **admission** *noun;* **admittedly** *adverb*

   EXAMPLE The bus driver *admitted* only people with exact change.

2. **compromise** (kŏm′prə-mīz′) *verb* **a.** To settle differences in such a way that both sides give in a little or give up something. **b.** To act in a way that invites danger, suspicion, or loss of reputation: *to compromise safety.* *noun* An agreement reached by compromise: *a fair compromise.* — 2. ____________

   EXAMPLE Workers and managers *compromised* in a salary dispute.

3. **emit** (ĭ-mĭt′) *verb* **a.** To give off or send out: *to emit heat.* **b.** To let out a sound; utter: *to emit a giggle.* — 3. ____________

   RELATED WORD **emission** *noun*

   EXAMPLE The old bus *emitted* dark smoke from its tail pipe.

Copyright © 1988 Houghton Mifflin Company. All rights reserved.

4. **mission** (mĭsh′ən) *noun* **a.** A special duty or task that a person or group is sent to do: *a secret mission.* **b.** A permanent diplomatic office in a foreign land. **c.** Religious work, often abroad, or the buildings from which that work is carried out. 4. ____________

RELATED WORD **missionary** *noun*

EXAMPLE The diplomat did not discuss the details of her *mission.*

5. **omit** (ō-mĭt′) *verb* **a.** To remove; not include: *to omit the unnecessary words.* **b.** To fail to include; neglect: *to omit an important detail.* 5. ____________

RELATED WORD **omission** *noun*

EXAMPLE *Omit* periods in Postal Service state abbreviations.

6. **permissible** (pər-mĭs′ə-bəl) *adjective* Allowable; permitted: *permissible behavior.* 6. ____________

RELATED WORDS **permission** *noun;* **permit** *verb*

EXAMPLE Two teaspoonfuls is the maximum *permissible* dose.

7. **premise** (prĕm′ĭs) *noun* A statement or idea that is the basis of an argument or conclusion: *a sound premise, a faulty premise.* 7. ____________

EXAMPLE What is the error in the *premise* "If you're not for me, you're against me"?

8. **remit** (rĭ-mĭt′) *verb* **a.** To send money. **b.** To cancel (a penalty): *to remit a fine.* **c.** To allow to slow down; lessen in power or intensity: *The symptoms of the disease remitted.* 8. ____________

USAGE NOTE A *remittance* is a payment. A *remission* is a period of less activity.

RELATED WORDS **remission** *noun;* **remittance** *noun*

EXAMPLE I promptly *remitted* the amount I owed.

9. **submit** (səb-mĭt′) *verb* **a.** To offer for consideration or review: *to submit a job application.* **b.** To give in to control by another; be under someone's power: *to submit to orders.* 9. ____________

RELATED WORD **submission** *noun*

EXAMPLE All contest entries must be *submitted* by May 1.

10. **transmit** (trănz-mĭt′) *verb* To send from one person or place to another: *to transmit a message.* 10. ____________

RELATED WORDS **transmission** *noun;* **transmitter** *noun*

EXAMPLE Rodents and insects can *transmit* disease.

Copyright © Houghton Mifflin Company. All rights reserved.

Name ______________________________ Date __________

Exercise 1 Writing Correct Words

On the answer line, write the word from the vocabulary list that fits each definition.

1. To give off or send out 1. __________
2. To send from one person or place to another 2. __________
3. To allow to enter; confess 3. __________
4. To offer for consideration or review; give in to control by another 4. __________
5. To send money; cancel; allow to slow down; lessen in power 5. __________
6. Allowable 6. __________
7. To remove; fail to include; neglect 7. __________
8. To settle differences in such a way that both sides give up something 8. __________
9. A statement or idea that is the basis of an argument or conclusion 9. __________
10. A special duty or task that a person or group is sent to do 10. __________

Exercise 2 Using Words Correctly

Each of the following questions contains an italicized vocabulary word. Choose the correct answer to the question, and write *Yes* or *No* on the answer line.

1. If your name is missing from a class list, has it been *emitted?* 1. __________
2. Does a telegraph machine *transmit* messages? 2. __________
3. Do open curtains *submit* light? 3. __________
4. In a *compromise* do both sides give up something? 4. __________
5. When a store bills you, does it *remit* money? 5. __________
6. If you fail to keep your word, do you break a *premise?* 6. __________
7. Is politeness in class *permissible?* 7. __________
8. Is a *mission* a very large house owned by a rich person? 8. __________
9. If you *omit* the zero from 201, do you get 21? 9. __________
10. When you apply for camp, do you *admit* an application? 10. __________

Exercise 3 Choosing the Best Definition

For each italicized vocabulary word in the following sentences, write the letter of the best definition on the answer line.

1. Kozar's *mission* was to break the Razokian code. 1. __________
   a. plan **b.** assignment **c.** hope **d.** punishment

Copyright © 1988 Houghton Mifflin Company. All rights reserved.

2. The judge *remitted* the sentence because the defendant had already spent six months in jail while awaiting trial. 2. ______
a. subtracted from **b.** added to **c.** canceled **d.** appealed

3. Olympic athletes must *submit to* long and difficult training. 3. ______
a. give up **b.** undergo **c.** apply for **d.** pay for

4. Claire questioned the *premise* of Harry's editorial. 4. ______
a. basic idea **b.** choice of topic **c.** intelligence **d.** honesty

5. Some deep-sea fish *emit* light. 5. ______
a. attract **b.** follow **c.** swallow **d.** produce

6. When writing your name, do not *omit* your middle initial. 6. ______
a. remember **b.** drop **c.** print **d.** include

7. During World War II, Dutch freedom fighters *transmitted* secret messages by arranging the vanes of windmills in certain ways. 7. ______
a. sent **b.** received **c.** decoded **d.** scrambled

8. Are jeans *permissible* clothing in your school? 8. ______
a. fashionable **b.** recommended **c.** allowable **d.** forbidden

9. My stubborn brother rarely *compromises.* 9. ______
a. gives in **b.** is sensible **c.** keeps promises **d.** tells lies

10. The sign on Mike's door said, "No one over 12 *admitted.*" 10. ______
a. entered **b.** refused **c.** confessed **d.** allowed

Exercise 4 Using Different Forms of Words

Decide which form of the vocabulary word in parentheses best completes the sentence. The form given may be correct. Write your answer on the answer line.

1. The __?__ of toxic gases by automobiles causes air pollution. *(emit)* 1. ______
2. Nerves are __?__ of messages to and from the brain. *(transmit)* 2. ______
3. "Where is your letter of __?__?" asked Mr. Ray. *(permissible)* 3. ______
4. In every family one person usually __?__ more than the others. *(compromise)* 4. ______
5. What is the main __?__ of the Declaration of Independence? *(premise)* 5. ______
6. All __?__ become the property of Bonus Bonanza and cannot be returned. *(submit)* 6. ______
7. Forgetting lines onstage is __?__ very embarrassing. *(admit)* 7. ______
8. A one-letter __?__ can ruin a computer program. *(omit)* 8. ______
9. Mother enclosed a letter of complaint with her __?__. *(remit)* 9. ______
10. Some western cities with names starting with *San* began as __?__. *(mission)* 10. ______

Copyright © 1988 Houghton Mifflin Company. All rights reserved.

Name ______________________________ Date ______________

Reading Comprehension

Each numbered sentence in the following passage contains an italicized vocabulary word or related form. After you read the passage, you will complete an exercise.

Grace Hopper, Computer Pioneer

(1) Any history of computer science that *omits* mention of Grace Hopper (1906–1992) is incomplete. She was a pioneer and inventor and was called the "conscience of the computer industry." She was also a retired rear admiral in the United States Naval Reserve.

Hopper was not always in the navy. For nearly ten years she was a mathematics professor. After World War II began, Hopper joined the navy and was trained as an officer. Within a year she was working on Mark I, the first large-scale digital computer. **(2)** From then on she worked without ***remission*** on computers — on Mark II, Mark III, UNIVAC I, and other models up to those of the present day.

Hopper invented COBOL, the first widely used computer language. She also invented the first practical compiler, a computer program that converts the input language into machine language. She even helped to coin the word *debug,* meaning "to get rid of the problems in something," when she was working on the Mark I. **(3)** The machine stalled, ***emitting*** a strange noise. A technician spotted the problem: a moth was trapped in the great machine. The Mark I was debugged — and the word has been in the language ever since.

In a way Grace Hopper is the Henry Ford of the computer industry. Both were inventors, and both wanted standardized machinery. **(4)** His invention carried people; her computers ***transmit*** information. **(5)** Henry Ford's ***premise*** that the United States was ready for a mass-produced car was correct. Overnight his Model T became a success. Hopper sees a lesson in his story. **(6)** "Microcomputers," she ***submitted,*** "are Model T's — people can *own* them."

After retiring, Hopper spent much time speaking to audiences of people working in the computer field. **(7)** So strong was her sense of ***mission*** that she toured the nation, preaching common sense, cooperation, and efficiency. **(8)** By her own admission, the ways in which we use computers are already outdated. **(9)** Hopper felt that we must stop ***compromising*** and begin to solve problems in new ways.

With a twinkle she told youth to go ahead with ideas. **(10)** It is "easier to apologize later than to get ***permission.***" She may have rocked the boat, but she did very little apologizing! Even in retirement Rear Admiral Grace Hopper was still very much the captain of her ship.

Please turn to the next page.

Copyright © Houghton Mifflin Company. All rights reserved.

Reading Comprehension Exercise

Each of the following statements corresponds to a numbered sentence in the passage. Each statement contains a blank and is followed by four answer choices. Decide which choice fits best in the blank. The word or phrase that you choose must express roughly the same meaning as the italicized word in the passage. Write the letter of your choice on the answer line.

1. Computer-science historians should not ___?___ Grace Hopper. 1. ________
   a. neglect b. discuss c. remember d. honor
2. For more than forty years, she has worked on computers without ___?___. 2. ________
   a. complaining c. being appreciated
   b. recognition d. slowing down
3. The Mark I stalled, ___?___ a certain sound. 3. ________
   a. suggesting b. echoing c. giving off d. failing to make
4. Ford's cars carried people, and Hopper's computers ___?___ data. 4. ________
   a. receive b. send along c. store d. safely protect
5. Henry Ford's ___?___ proved to be correct. 5. ________
   a. design b. timing c. basic idea d. manufacturing methods
6. Hopper ___?___ that microcomputers are today's Model T's. 6. ________
   a. writes b. forgets c. hopes d. suggests
7. She has a strong sense of ___?___. 7. ________
   a. patriotism b. history c. anger d. duty
8. According to her own ___?___, computers can be made even more useful. 8. ________
   a. research b. confession c. guess d. reading
9. When handling problems, Hopper says, we must stop ___?___. 9. ________
   a. giving in c. thinking independently
   b. delaying d. failing to keep promises
10. She feels that ___?___ going ahead should not be needed. 10. ________
    a. approval for b. success in c. preparation for d. skill in

Practice with Analogies

See pages 32, 52, and 86 for some strategies to use with analogies.

DIRECTIONS On the answer line, write the vocabulary word that completes each analogy.

1. Enter is to exit as ___?___ is to deny. 1. ________
2. Add is to subtract as include is to ___?___. 2. ________
3. Antenna is to receive as telegraph is to ___?___. 3. ________
4. Worker is to job as agent is to ___?___. 4. ________
5. Discuss is to agreement as negotiate is to ___?___. 5. ________

Copyright © Houghton Mifflin Company. All rights reserved.

Lesson 30

Literature

Why have people through the centuries continued to read literature? There are several important reasons. Reading fills our need to have experiences that carry us beyond the boundaries of where we live and what we know. Reading makes us wiser because it presents us with facts that we did not know before. Reading makes us less lonely because it satisfies our need to share the confidences of others. Finally, because it acquaints us with courage and gives us new insights, reading helps us to grow.

The ten words in this lesson will help you to understand and discuss literature. Later in the lesson, you will learn more about the nature of literature and its history.

WORD LIST

autobiography
biography
folklore
metaphor
narrate
prose
proverb
stanza
symbol
theme

DEFINITIONS

After you have studied the definitions and example for each vocabulary word, write the word on the line to the right.

1. **autobiography** (ô′tō-bī-ŏg′rə-fē) *noun* The story of a person's life, written by that person. 1. ______________

RELATED WORD **autobiographical** *adjective*

EXAMPLE *What Little I Remember* is the *autobiography* of Otto Frisch, a famous scientist.

2. **biography** (bī-ŏg′rə-fē) *noun* The story of a person's life, written by someone else. 2. ______________

RELATED WORDS **biographer** *noun;* **biographical** *adjective*

EXAMPLE Tanya reported on a *biography* of Catherine the Great.

3. **folklore** (fōk′lôr′) *noun* The traditional customs, legends, and tales of a people. 3. ______________

RELATED WORD **folklorist** *noun*

EXAMPLE The Appalachians are a region rich in *folklore.*

4. **metaphor** (mĕt′ə-fôr) *noun* A comparison between two things that are not usually thought to be similar: *"The road was a ribbon of moonlight. . . ."* 4. ______________

RELATED WORDS **metaphoric** *adjective;* **metaphorically** *adverb*

EXAMPLE "The ship of state" is a *metaphor* for government.

USAGE NOTE When a comparison contains the word *like* or *as,* it may be called a *simile,* not a metaphor.

Copyright © 1988 Houghton Mifflin Company. All rights reserved.

5. **narrate** (năr′āt′) *verb* To tell a story orally or in writing: *to narrate one's adventures.* 5. ____________

RELATED WORDS **narrative** *adjective;* **narrative** *noun;* **narrator** *noun*

EXAMPLE From whose point of view is that story *narrated?*

6. **prose** (prōz) *noun* Speech or writing that is not poetry: *newspaper prose.* 6. ____________

EXAMPLE Novels, short stories, and many plays are written in prose.

7. **proverb** (prŏv′ûrb′) *noun* A short, common saying that expresses a truth. 7. ____________

RELATED WORDS **proverbial** *adjective;* **proverbially** *adverb*

EXAMPLE Dad answered with the *proverb* "Better safe than sorry."

USAGE NOTE A *proverb* (or an adage) expresses mainly folk wisdom, often in a metaphor: "A stitch in time saves nine."

8. **stanza** (stăn′zə) *noun* Two or more lines in a poem that are grouped together and printed as a unit. 8. ____________

EXAMPLE Some *stanzas* contain rhyming words at the ends of lines.

USAGE NOTE *Stanza* can also refer to the verses of a song or a hymn.

9. **symbol** (sĭm′bəl) *noun* An object that stands for something greater than itself: *a national symbol.* 9. ____________

RELATED WORDS **symbolic** *adjective;* **symbolically** *adverb;* **symbolize** *verb*

EXAMPLE A heart is one *symbol* for love.

10. **theme** (thēm) *noun* **a.** The main thought or meaning of a literary work or speech. **b.** A short composition, often an essay. **c.** In music, the main melody. 10. ____________

RELATED WORDS **thematic** *adjective;* **thematically** *adverb*

EXAMPLE The healing power of love is the *theme* of the story.

Copyright © Houghton Mifflin Company. All rights reserved.

Name ______________________________ Date ______________

Exercise 1 Matching Words and Definitions

Match the definition in Column B with the word in Column A. Write the letter of the correct definition on the answer line.

Column A	Column B
1. biography	a. the main thought of a literary work or speech
2. symbol	b. the traditional customs, legends, and tales of a people
3. metaphor	c. an object that stands for something greater
4. theme	d. to tell a story orally or in writing
5. narrate	e. story of a person's life, written by another
6. autobiography	f. story of a person's life, written by him or her
7. folklore	g. speech or writing that is not poetry
8. stanza	h. a comparison between two things that are not usually thought to be similar
9. prose	i. a short, common saying that expresses a truth
10. proverb	j. two or more lines in a poem that are grouped together and printed as a unit

1. ________
2. ________
3. ________
4. ________
5. ________
6. ________
7. ________
8. ________
9. ________
10. ________

Exercise 2 Using Words Correctly

Decide whether the italicized vocabulary word has been used correctly in the sentence. On the answer line, write *Correct* for correct use and *Incorrect* for incorrect use.

1. Bigfoot is part of American *folklore.* 1. ________
2. Novels are made up of sections called *stanzas.* 2. ________
3. Cal was chosen to *narrate* the story in the class show. 3. ________
4. My mother is always quoting *proverbs* like "Waste not, want not." 4. ________
5. That writer is known for her witty *prose.* 5. ________
6. Our guide gave us an *autobiography* of the Empire State Building. 6. ________
7. Which political party has the elephant as its *symbol?* 7. ________
8. The stories in that unit share a common *theme.* 8. ________
9. In *biography* we studied plants. 9. ________
10. Signal flags are called *metaphors.* 10. ________

Exercise 3 Choosing the Best Word

Decide which vocabulary word or related form best completes the sentence, and write the letter of your choice on the answer line.

1. Paul Bunyan is a character from American __?__. 1. ________
   a. folklore **b.** metaphor **c.** proverbs **d.** autobiography

Copyright © 1988 Houghton Mifflin Company. All rights reserved.

2. The book's rambling __?__ lulled Lois to sleep. 2. ________
a. theme **b.** stanza **c.** symbol **d.** prose

3. Each star in the American flag is the __?__ of a state. 3. ________
a. narrative **b.** theme **c.** symbol **d.** metaphor

4. "When I'm famous," said T.J., "who will write my __?__?" 4. ________
a. proverb **b.** folklore **c.** autobiography **d.** biography

5. We read a __?__ by a blind woman who became a successful lawyer. 5. ________
a. narrative **b.** symbol **c.** metaphor **d.** proverb

6. The story's __?__ is the experience of growing up. 6. ________
a. autobiography **b.** stanza **c.** proverb **d.** theme

7. The rhyme pattern of that __?__ could be charted as *a-b-a-b*. 7. ________
a. stanza **b.** theme **c.** metaphor **d.** narrative

8. In his __?__ Benjamin Franklin tells about his experiment with a kite. 8. ________
a. proverb **b.** autobiography **c.** stanza **d.** symbol

9. Jill's story illustrated the __?__ "Haste makes waste." 9. ________
a. proverb **b.** prose **c.** folklore **d.** symbol

10. A journey is a common __?__ for the course of a person's life. 10. ________
a. stanza **b.** prose **c.** metaphor **d.** proverb

Exercise 4 Using Different Forms of Words

Decide which form of the vocabulary word in parentheses best completes the sentence. The form given may be correct. Write your answer on the answer line.

1. Is the __?__ of that novel the main character? *(narrate)* 1. ________
2. The poet Gwendolyn Brooks has also written works of __?__. *(prose)* 2. ________
3. The author's account of a skiing accident is clearly __?__. *(autobiography)* 3. ________
4. The __?__ Iona and Peter Opie collected children's rhymes. *(folklore)* 4. ________
5. Some __?__ trot along in a singsong, predictable way. *(stanza)* 5. ________
6. Tim let the __?__ cat out of the bag when he told Jan about the surprise party. *(proverb)* 6. ________
7. Dreaming is a way of expressing feelings and ideas __?__. *(symbol)* 7. ________
8. Agnes Dooley was the __?__ of Dr. Thomas Dooley, her son. *(biography)* 8. ________
9. "I'm up the creek without a paddle," Julie said __?__. *(metaphor)* 9. ________
10. Songwriters sometimes use __?__ from orchestral pieces. *(theme)* 10. ________

Copyright © 1988 Houghton Mifflin Company. All rights reserved.

Name ______________________________ Date ______________

Reading Comprehension

Each numbered sentence in the following passage contains an italicized vocabulary word or related form. After you read the passage, you will complete an exercise.

Literature as Storytelling

Those who read and study literature define it in different ways. Nearly everyone, however, agrees on one aspect of literature: it is writing that tells a story. **(1)** Almost all literature has some kind of ***narrative,*** if only of the briefest kind. The narrative element has been part of literature since it began.

(2) The first literature of a people always grows out of ***folklore.*** It is story in the form of poetry. **(3)** In the beginning the stories that are told in poetic ***stanzas*** are oral. Among the ancient Greek people, for example, Homer's *Odyssey* was one of the many storytelling poems that passed from generation to generation before being written down. The *Odyssey* told of the long voyage of Greek sailors returning from war. **(4)** A striking feature of works like the *Odyssey* is the use of ***metaphors.*** Metaphors provided vivid pictures for the audience to remember.

(5) In time the folk stories of a people begin to be told in the form of ***prose*** as well as poetry. **(6)** Among the Greeks, for example, the prose fables of the slave Aesop were told to illustrate ***proverbs.***

Most early tales in any literature, however, are myths and legends. Myths are stories of gods and goddesses, told to explain some mystery of life or nature. **(7)** One Greek myth, for example, is about the sun, the ***symbol*** of life itself. The myth explains why the sun rises and sets each day. Legends, on the other hand, are stories of human heroes, who are often aided by gods and goddesses. **(8)** Because they are about humans and their adventures, ancient legends might be thought of as an early kind of ***biography.***

Biography and autobiography are modern classifications for stories that recount the lives of actual people. **(9)** Among the ancient Greeks and Romans, diaries and journals were the only kinds of ***autobiographical*** writing. For example, a seventeen-year-old Roman named Pliny the Younger saw the eruption of the great volcano Vesuvius and wrote about his escape from the disaster.

Through the centuries since Greek and Roman times, people have continued to tell and write stories. Today readers enjoy short stories and book-length novels, as well as biographical and autobiographical narratives, poems, and plays. What makes these various kinds of storytelling hold our attention?

The answer is quite simple. **(10)** Literature appeals to us because of the ***themes*** that appear in it again and again — themes that we recognize as part of the experience of living. People may lose those they love, for example. They may grow through loving. On the other hand, they may become victims of their own excessive pride or ambition, or of some other fault of character. Nevertheless, people may also triumph in the face of difficulty. The themes of literature are as numerous as human experience is broad.

Please turn to the next page.

Copyright © 1988 Houghton Mifflin Company. All rights reserved.

Reading Comprehension Exercise

Each of the following statements corresponds to a numbered sentence in the passage. Each statement contains a blank and is followed by four answer choices. Decide which choice fits best in the blank. The word or phrase that you choose must express roughly the same meaning as the italicized word in the passage. Write the letter of your choice on the answer line.

1. Some kind of ___?___ exists in most literature. 1. ________
   a. definition b. rhyme c. story d. rhythm

2. Early literature grows out of ___?___. 2. ________
   a. people's traditions c. people's interests
   b. picture writing d. written history

3. Divided into ___?___, early storytelling poems are oral. 3. ________
   a. pictures b. rhymes c. many chapters d. line groups

4. These poems are filled with ___?___. 4. ________
   a. animal characters c. striking ideas
   b. forceful comparisons d. rhyming lines

5. In time some folk stories begin to be told in ___?___. 5. ________
   a. old sayings c. a form that is not poetry
   b. fancy words d. vivid pictures

6. Aesop's fables were told to illustrate ___?___. 6. ________
   a. common sayings c. slave life
   b. comparisons d. mysteries of nature

7. Because it brings light to the world, the sun is a(n) ___?___ of life itself. 7. ________
   a. representation b. picture c. explanation d. story

8. Legends might be considered an early form of ___?___. 8. ________
   a. writing about mysteries c. writing about the sun
   b. writing about people's lives d. writing about goddesses

9. In ancient times diaries and journals were the only forms of writing ___?___. 9. ________
   a. divided into line groups c. about one's own life
   b. with vivid pictures d. about someone else's life

10. Certain ___?___ are often repeated in literature. 10. ________
    a. words b. scenes c. main characters d. main ideas

Writing Assignment

You have entered a Library Week contest for which there is a prize. According to the rules of the contest, you must write a composition in which you tell which form of literature you like best and explain why. In your composition use five words from the lesson and underline each one.

Copyright © 1988 Houghton Mifflin Company. All rights reserved.

Name ______________________ Date ______________________

Reading Skills

READING SKILLS

The Suffixes *-ity* and *-hood*

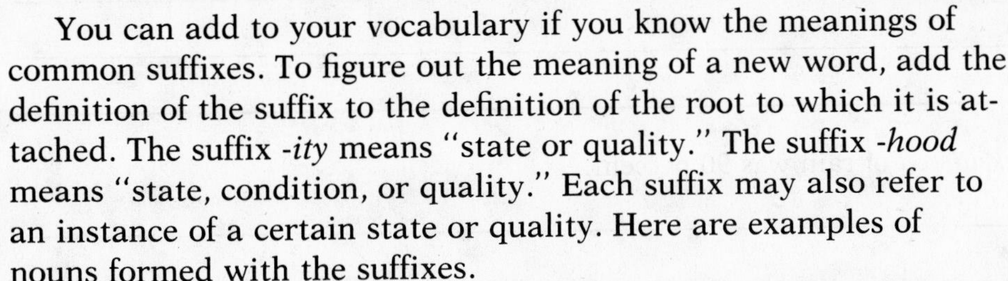

You can add to your vocabulary if you know the meanings of common suffixes. To figure out the meaning of a new word, add the definition of the suffix to the definition of the root to which it is attached. The suffix *-ity* means "state or quality." The suffix *-hood* means "state, condition, or quality." Each suffix may also refer to an instance of a certain state or quality. Here are examples of nouns formed with the suffixes.

SUFFIX/MEANING	WORD	DEFINITION
1. *-ity:* state or quality;	punctuality	the quality of being on time
instance of a quality	necessity	something that is needed
2. *-hood:* state, condition, quality;	childhood	the state or condition of being a child
instance of a quality	falsehood	something false

Necessity is formed from the Latin root word *necesse,* meaning "necessary," and the suffix *-ity.* The suffix makes the adjective *necessary* into a noun.

Exercise Using the Suffixes *-ity* and *-hood*

Step 1: Write your own definition of the italicized word in each of the following sentences. *Step 2:* In your own words, restate each sentence without using the italicized word. *Step 3:* Check your definition in a dictionary. Then write a sentence of your own in which you use the word correctly.

1. In 1959 *statehood* was granted to Alaska and Hawaii.

DEFINITION ______________________

RESTATEMENT ______________________

SENTENCE ______________________

2. The *acidity* of rain is an environmental problem.

DEFINITION ______________________

RESTATEMENT ______________________

SENTENCE ______________________

Please turn to the next page.

Copyright © 1988 Houghton Mifflin Company. All rights reserved.

3. The tale is about an African boy approaching *manhood.*

DEFINITION ______________________________

RESTATEMENT ______________________________

SENTENCE ______________________________

4. He had the *dexterity* to sew finely detailed patterns. (Clue: *-dexter-* is a Latin root meaning "skillful.")

DEFINITION ______________________________

RESTATEMENT ______________________________

SENTENCE ______________________________

5. The forecast said that the *likelihood* of rain was 90 percent.

DEFINITION ______________________________

RESTATEMENT ______________________________

SENTENCE ______________________________

6. Pam has an unusual *sensitivity* to others' feelings.

DEFINITION ______________________________

RESTATEMENT ______________________________

SENTENCE ______________________________

7. Is this bump an *abnormality* in the plant? (Clue: *ab-* is a Latin prefix meaning "away from.")

DEFINITION ______________________________

RESTATEMENT ______________________________

SENTENCE ______________________________

8. The review mentioned the *diversity* of talent in the show. (Clue: *diverse* is a root word meaning "distinct" or "different.")

DEFINITION ______________________________

RESTATEMENT ______________________________

SENTENCE ______________________________

Copyright © 1988 Houghton Mifflin Company. All rights reserved.

LESSON 1 antonym	LESSON 1 repetition	LESSON 2 badger	LESSON 2 mammoth	LESSON 3 awe	LESSON 3 fondness
LESSON 1 concept	LESSON 1 retain	LESSON 2 beastly	LESSON 2 parrot	LESSON 3 crave	LESSON 3 irk
LESSON 1 context	LESSON 1 specialize	LESSON 2 horseplay	LESSON 2 pigheaded	LESSON 3 detestable	LESSON 3 loathe
LESSON 1 define	LESSON 1 synonym	LESSON 2 hound	LESSON 2 scapegoat	LESSON 3 enchanting	LESSON 3 rave
LESSON 1 effective	LESSON 1 terminology	LESSON 2 lionize	LESSON 2 sheepish	LESSON 3 fascinate	LESSON 3 recoil

LESSON 3 **fondness** (fŏnd′nĭs) *n.* A loving or affectionate feeling. © 1988 HMCo	LESSON 3 **awe** (ô) *n.* A feeling of mixed wonder, fear, and deep respect. © 1988 HMCo	LESSON 2 **mammoth** (măm′əth) *adj.* Of enormous size; gigantic. © 1988 HMCo	LESSON 2 **badger** (băj′ər) *v.* To pester with constant questions or protests. © 1988 HMCo	LESSON 1 **repetition** (rĕp′ĭ-tĭsh′ən) *n.* The act or process of repeating. © 1988 HMCo	LESSON 1 **antonym** (ăn′tə-nĭm′) *n.* Word meaning the opposite of another word. © 1988 HMCo
LESSON 3 **irk** (ûrk) *v.* To annoy; irritate. © 1988 HMCo	LESSON 3 **crave** (krāv) *v.* To have a very strong desire or need for. © 1988 HMCo	LESSON 2 **parrot** (păr′ət) *v.* To repeat or imitate without understanding. © 1988 HMCo	LESSON 2 **beastly** (bēst′lē) *adj.* Disagreeable; nasty; bad. © 1988 HMCo	LESSON 1 **retain** (rĭ-tān′) *v.* To keep or hold in possession, use, or memory. © 1988 HMCo	LESSON 1 **concept** (kŏn′sĕpt′) *n.* A general idea or understanding; notion. © 1988 HMCo
LESSON 3 **loathe** (lōth) *v.* To dislike greatly; find repulsive. © 1988 HMCo	LESSON 3 **detestable** (dĭ-tĕs′tə-bəl) *adj.* Deserving strong dislike. © 1988 HMCo	LESSON 2 **pigheaded** (pĭg′hĕd′ĭd) *adj.* Stubborn, sometimes stupidly so. © 1988 HMCo	LESSON 2 **horseplay** (hôrs′plā′) *n.* Rowdy, rough play. © 1988 HMCo	LESSON 1 **specialize** (spĕsh′ə-līz′) *v.* To train or work in one special area. © 1988 HMCo	LESSON 1 **context** (kŏn′tĕkst′) *n.* The setting of a word or idea. © 1988 HMCo
LESSON 3 **rave** (rāv) *v.* To speak wildly or senselessly. © 1988 HMCo	LESSON 3 **enchanting** (ĕn-chăn′tĭng) *adj.* Very charming or attractive. © 1988 HMCo	LESSON 2 **scapegoat** (skāp′gōt′) *n.* Person or thing bearing blame for others. © 1988 HMCo	LESSON 2 **hound** (hound) *v.* To pursue without quitting; nag. © 1988 HMCo	LESSON 1 **synonym** (sĭn′ə-nĭm′) *n.* A word with a meaning like that of another word. © 1988 HMCo	LESSON 1 **define** (dĭ-fīn′) *v.* To state the meaning of; explain. © 1988 HMCo
LESSON 3 **recoil** (rĭ-koil′) *v.* To move or jerk back; shrink back in fear. © 1988 HMCo	LESSON 3 **fascinate** (făs′ə-nāt′) *v.* To capture and hold the interest of. © 1988 HMCo	LESSON 2 **sheepish** (shē′pĭsh) *adj.* Embarrassed, often in an apologetic way. © 1988 HMCo	LESSON 2 **lionize** (lī′ə-nīz′) *v.* To look upon or treat as a celebrity. © 1988 HMCo	LESSON 1 **terminology** (tûr′mə-nŏl′ə-jē) *n.* A particular set of technical terms. © 1988 HMCo	LESSON 1 **effective** (ĭ-fĕk′tĭv) *adj.* Producing a desired impression or result. © 1988 HMCo

LESSON 4 apparent	LESSON 4 genuine	LESSON 5 acute	LESSON 5 convalescence	LESSON 6 improvise	LESSON 6 visionary
LESSON 4 bluff	LESSON 4 impartial	LESSON 5 allergic	LESSON 5 endurance	LESSON 6 revision	LESSON 6 visor
LESSON 4 ethical	LESSON 4 integrity	LESSON 5 alleviate	LESSON 5 paralysis	LESSON 6 video	LESSON 6 vista
LESSON 4 fabricate	LESSON 4 obvious	LESSON 5 clinic	LESSON 5 soothe	LESSON 6 viewpoint	LESSON 6 visual
LESSON 4 frank	LESSON 4 reliable	LESSON 5 contagious	LESSON 5 thrive	LESSON 6 visible	LESSON 6 visualize

LESSON 6

visionary (vĭzh′ə-nĕr′ē) *adj.* Imaginary; seeing beyond the present.

© 1988 HMCo

LESSON 6

improvise (ĭm′prə-vīz′) *v.* To make up or perform on the spot.

© 1988 HMCo

LESSON 5

convalescence (kŏn′və-lĕs′əns) *n.* Time needed to return to health.

© 1988 HMCo

LESSON 5

acute (ə-kyo͞ot′) *adj.* Very sharp; severe; keen.

© 1988 HMCo

LESSON 4

genuine (jĕn′yo͞o-ĭn) *adj.* Actual; not copied or faked; sincere.

© 1988 HMCo

LESSON 4

apparent (ə-păr′ənt) *adj.* Easily understood or seen; clear.

© 1988 HMCo

LESSON 6

visor (vī′zər) *n.* Something that sticks out to protect the eyes.

© 1988 HMCo

LESSON 6

revision (rĭ-vĭzh′ən) *n.* A corrected or improved version.

© 1988 HMCo

LESSON 5

endurance (ĕn-do͝or′əns) *n.* Long-lasting strength.

© 1988 HMCo

LESSON 5

allergic (ə-lûr′jĭk) *adj.* Very sensitive to certain things.

© 1988 HMCo

LESSON 4

impartial (ĭm-pär′shəl) *adj.* Fair-minded; without prejudice.

© 1988 HMCo

LESSON 4

bluff (blŭf) *v.* To mislead or fool by boasting.

© 1988 HMCo

LESSON 6

vista (vĭs′tə) *n.* A distant or far-reaching view.

© 1988 HMCo

LESSON 6

video (vĭd′ē-ō′) *adj.* Relating to the picture part of television.

© 1988 HMCo

LESSON 5

paralysis (pə-răl′ĭ-sĭs) *n.* Loss of feeling or the ability to move.

© 1988 HMCo

LESSON 5

alleviate (ə-lē′vē-āt′) *v.* To relieve by making more bearable.

© 1988 HMCo

LESSON 4

integrity (ĭn-tĕg′rĭ-tē) *n.* Honesty in word and deed.

© 1988 HMCo

LESSON 4

ethical (ĕth′ĭ-kəl) *adj.* Right and proper; moral.

© 1988 HMCo

LESSON 6

visual (vĭzh′o͞o-əl) *adj.* Relating to the sense of sight.

© 1988 HMCo

LESSON 6

viewpoint (vyo͞o′point′) *n.* Particular way of looking at something.

© 1988 HMCo

LESSON 5

soothe (so͞o*th*) *v.* To relieve by calming or comforting.

© 1988 HMCo

LESSON 5

clinic (klĭn′ĭk) *n.* A specialized medical institution.

© 1988 HMCo

LESSON 4

obvious (ŏb′vē-əs) *adj.* Plain to see or understand; evident.

© 1988 HMCo

LESSON 4

fabricate (făb′rĭ-kāt′) *v.* To make up; lie; make or build.

© 1988 HMCo

LESSON 6

visualize (vĭzh′o͞o-ə-līz′) *v.* To form a mental picture of.

© 1988 HMCo

LESSON 6

visible (vĭz′ə-bəl) *adj.* Capable of being seen.

© 1988 HMCo

LESSON 5

thrive (thrīv) *v.* To grow or do well.

© 1988 HMCo

LESSON 5

contagious (kən-tā′jəs) *adj.* Spread by direct or indirect contact.

© 1988 HMCo

LESSON 4

reliable (rĭ-lī′ə-bəl) *adj.* Dependable; trustworthy.

© 1988 HMCo

LESSON 4

frank (frăngk) *adj.* Open and sincere; to the point.

© 1988 HMCo

LESSON 7 brisk	LESSON 7 perpetual	LESSON 8 blunt	LESSON 8 opaque	LESSON 9 bolero	LESSON 9 mesa
LESSON 7 fleet	LESSON 7 saunter	LESSON 8 coarse	LESSON 8 radiant	LESSON 9 escapade	LESSON 9 mustang
LESSON 7 linger	LESSON 7 scurry	LESSON 8 dense	LESSON 8 sheen	LESSON 9 fiesta	LESSON 9 poncho
LESSON 7 mingle	LESSON 7 stride	LESSON 8 dingy	LESSON 8 tinge	LESSON 9 guerrilla	LESSON 9 siesta
LESSON 7 nimble	LESSON 7 totter	LESSON 8 iridescent	LESSON 8 transparent	LESSON 9 lariat	LESSON 9 stampede

LESSON 9

mesa (mā′sə) *n.* A flat-topped hill with steep sides.

© 1988 HMCo

LESSON 9

bolero (bō-lâr′ō) *n.* A fast Spanish dance.

© 1988 HMCo

LESSON 8

opaque (ō-pāk′) *adj.* Not letting light through.

© 1988 HMCo

LESSON 8

blunt (blŭnt) *adj.* Not sharp or pointed; dull-edged.

© 1988 HMCo

LESSON 7

perpetual (pər-pĕch′o͞o-əl) *adj.* Continuing without interruption.

© 1988 HMCo

LESSON 7

brisk (brĭsk) *adj.* Lively; energetic.

© 1988 HMCo

LESSON 9

mustang (mŭs′tăng′) *n.* A wild horse of the North American plains.

© 1988 HMCo

LESSON 9

escapade (ĕs′kə-pād′) *n.* A reckless, sometimes illegal, adventure.

© 1988 HMCo

LESSON 8

radiant (rā′dē-ənt) *adj.* Giving out light or heat; filled with joy.

© 1988 HMCo

LESSON 8

coarse (kôrs) *adj.* Not fine in texture; rough.

© 1988 HMCo

LESSON 7

saunter (sôn′tər) *v.* To walk in a relaxed and carefree way.

© 1988 HMCo

LESSON 7

fleet (flēt) *adj.* Moving swiftly; rapidly.

© 1988 HMCo

LESSON 9

poncho (pŏn′chō) *n.* A blanketlike cloak with a center head hole.

© 1988 HMCo

LESSON 9

fiesta (fē-ĕs′tə) *n.* A festival or religious holiday.

© 1988 HMCo

LESSON 8

sheen (shēn) *n.* Shine; brightness.

© 1988 HMCo

LESSON 8

dense (dĕns) *adj.* Very thick; tightly packed together.

© 1988 HMCo

LESSON 7

scurry (skûr′ē) *v.* To run hurriedly; scamper.

© 1988 HMCo

LESSON 7

linger (lĭn′gər) *v.* To delay in leaving; remain alive.

© 1988 HMCo

LESSON 9

siesta (sē-ĕs′tə) *n.* An afternoon rest or nap.

© 1988 HMCo

LESSON 9

guerrilla (gə-rĭl′ə) *n.* A member of an unofficial military group.

© 1988 HMCo

LESSON 8

tinge (tĭnj) *n.* A tint; a trace of color.

© 1988 HMCo

LESSON 8

dingy (dĭn′jē) *adj.* Dirty; grimy.

© 1988 HMCo

LESSON 7

stride (strīd) *n.* A long step; a step forward.

© 1988 HMCo

LESSON 7

mingle (mĭng′gəl) *v.* To become mixed or blended.

© 1988 HMCo

LESSON 9

stampede (stăm-pēd′) *n.* A sudden racing of startled animals.

© 1988 HMCo

LESSON 9

lariat (lăr′ē-ət) *n.* A long rope with an adjustable loop at one end.

© 1988 HMCo

LESSON 8

transparent (trăns-pâr′ənt) *adj.* Letting light through; obvious.

© 1988 HMCo

LESSON 8

iridescent (ĭr′ĭ-dĕs′ənt) *adj.* Having shiny and rainbowlike colors.

© 1988 HMCo

LESSON 7

totter (tŏt′ər) *v.* To sway as if about to fall.

© 1988 HMCo

LESSON 7

nimble (nĭm′bəl) *adj.* Moving quickly and lightly.

© 1988 HMCo

LESSON 10 aloof	LESSON 10 recluse	LESSON 11 bankrupt	LESSON 11 larceny	LESSON 12 altimeter	LESSON 12 metric
LESSON 10 amiable	LESSON 10 responsive	LESSON 11 defendant	LESSON 11 lenient	LESSON 12 barometer	LESSON 12 metronome
LESSON 10 antisocial	LESSON 10 rival	LESSON 11 evident	LESSON 11 testimony	LESSON 12 diameter	LESSON 12 micrometer
LESSON 10 betray	LESSON 10 solitary	LESSON 11 fugitive	LESSON 11 verdict	LESSON 12 geometry	LESSON 12 odometer
LESSON 10 enmity	LESSON 10 treacherous	LESSON 11 just	LESSON 11 witness	LESSON 12 kilometer	LESSON 12 perimeter

LESSON 12

metric (mĕt′rĭk) *adj.* Referring to a system of measurement.

© 1988 HMCo

LESSON 12

altimeter (ăl-tĭm′ĭ-tər) *n.* An instrument to measure height.

© 1988 HMCo

LESSON 11

larceny (lär′sə-nē) *n.* The crime of keeping another's property; theft.

© 1988 HMCo

LESSON 11

bankrupt (băngk′rŭpt′) *adj.* Declared by law unable to pay one's debts.

© 1988 HMCo

LESSON 10

recluse (rĕk′lo͞os) *n.* A person who withdraws from society; hermit.

© 1988 HMCo

LESSON 10

aloof (ə-lo͞of′) *adj.* Reserved; distant.

© 1988 HMCo

LESSON 12

metronome (mĕt′rə-nōm′) *n.* Device marking time in steady beats.

© 1988 HMCo

LESSON 12

barometer (bə-rŏm′ĭ-tər) *n.* Instrument to measure air pressure.

© 1988 HMCo

LESSON 11

lenient (lē′nē-ənt) *adj.* Inclined to forgive; merciful.

© 1988 HMCo

LESSON 11

defendant (dĭ-fĕn′dənt) *n.* Person against whom legal action is taken.

© 1988 HMCo

LESSON 10

responsive (rĭ-spŏn′sĭv) *adj.* Reacting quickly to a suggestion.

© 1988 HMCo

LESSON 10

amiable (ā′mē-ə-bəl) *adj.* Good-natured; friendly; pleasant.

© 1988 HMCo

LESSON 12

micrometer (mī-krŏm′ĭ-tər) *n.* Device measuring small distances.

© 1988 HMCo

LESSON 12

diameter (dī-ăm′ĭ-tər) *n.* Straight line through a circle's center.

© 1988 HMCo

LESSON 11

testimony (tĕs′tə-mō′nē) *n.* A statement given under oath.

© 1988 HMCo

LESSON 11

evident (ĕv′i-dənt) *adj.* Easily seen or understood; obvious.

© 1988 HMCo

LESSON 10

rival (rī′vəl) *n.* A competitor.

© 1988 HMCo

LESSON 10

antisocial (ăn′tē-sō′shəl) *adj.* Avoiding the company of others.

© 1988 HMCo

LESSON 12

odometer (ō-dŏm′ĭ-tər) *n.* Device measuring distance traveled.

© 1988 HMCo

LESSON 12

geometry (jē-ŏm′ĭ-trē) *n.* A branch of mathematics.

© 1988 HMCo

LESSON 11

verdict (vûr′dĭkt) *n.* Decision reached by a jury at the end of a trial.

© 1988 HMCo

LESSON 11

fugitive (fyoo′jĭ-tĭv) *n.* A person who runs away or flees from the law.

© 1988 HMCo

LESSON 10

solitary (sŏl′ĭ-tĕr′ē) *adj.* Without the company of others.

© 1988 HMCo

LESSON 10

betray (bĭ-trā′) *v.* To commit treason against; be a traitor to.

© 1988 HMCo

LESSON 12

perimeter (pə-rĭm′ĭ-tər) *n.* Total length of any geometrical figure.

© 1988 HMCo

LESSON 12

kilometer (kĭl′ə-mē′tər) *n.* A unit of length equal to 1000 meters.

© 1988 HMCo

LESSON 11

witness (wĭt′nĭs) *n.* Someone who testifies in court.

© 1988 HMCo

LESSON 11

just (jŭst) *adj.* Honest; fair; suitable or proper.

© 1988 HMCo

LESSON 10

treacherous (trĕch′ər-əs) *adj.* Disloyal; traitorous.

© 1988 HMCo

LESSON 10

enmity (ĕn′mĭ-tē) *n.* Deep hatred, as between enemies or opponents.

© 1988 HMCo

LESSON 13 appease	LESSON 13 infuriate	LESSON 14 adjourn	LESSON 14 prolong	LESSON 15 ballad	LESSON 15 rhythm
LESSON 13 assuage	LESSON 13 reconcile	LESSON 14 cease	LESSON 14 repress	LESSON 15 choral	LESSON 15 serenade
LESSON 13 belligerent	LESSON 13 resent	LESSON 14 decisive	LESSON 14 shackle	LESSON 15 lyric	LESSON 15 shrill
LESSON 13 condone	LESSON 13 retaliate	LESSON 14 detain	LESSON 14 tarry	LESSON 15 opera	LESSON 15 symphony
LESSON 13 indignant	LESSON 13 wrath	LESSON 14 hinder	LESSON 14 undermine	LESSON 15 resonant	LESSON 15 tenor

LESSON 15

rhythm (rĭ*th*′əm) *n.* A repeated pattern of strong and weak beats.

© 1988 HMCo

LESSON 15

ballad (băl′əd) *n.* Poem, often intended to be sung, that tells a story.

© 1988 HMCo

LESSON 14

prolong (prə-lông′) *v.* To stretch out in time or extent; lengthen.

© 1988 HMCo

LESSON 14

adjourn (ə-jûrn′) *v.* To stop or put off until another time.

© 1988 HMCo

LESSON 13

infuriate (ĭn-fyo͝or′ē-āt′) *v.* To make furious; enrage.

© 1988 HMCo

LESSON 13

appease (ə-pēz′) *v.* To calm or soothe by giving in to demands.

© 1988 HMCo

LESSON 15

serenade (sĕr′ə-nād′) *n.* A musical piece that expresses honor or love.

© 1988 HMCo

LESSON 15

choral (kôr′əl) *adj.* Related to a chorus or choir.

© 1988 HMCo

LESSON 14

repress (rĭ-prĕs′) *v.* To control by holding back; restrain.

© 1988 HMCo

LESSON 14

cease (sēs) *v.* To put an end to; discontinue.

© 1988 HMCo

LESSON 13

reconcile (rĕk′ən-sīl′) *v.* To restore friendship between.

© 1988 HMCo

LESSON 13

assuage (ə-swāj′) *v.* To lessen the force or pain of.

© 1988 HMCo

LESSON 15

shrill (shrĭl) *adj.* High-pitched and piercing.

© 1988 HMCo

LESSON 15

lyric (lĭr′ĭk) *adj.* Of poetry directly expressing the poet's thoughts.

© 1988 HMCo

LESSON 14

shackle (shăk′əl) *v.* To keep from moving freely; restrict.

© 1988 HMCo

LESSON 14

decisive (dĭ-sī′sĭv) *adj.* Having the power to settle something.

© 1988 HMCo

LESSON 13

resent (rĭ-zĕnt′) *v.* To feel angry or bitter about.

© 1988 HMCo

LESSON 13

belligerent (bə-lĭj′ər-ənt) *adj.* Quick to fight or argue; hostile.

© 1988 HMCo

LESSON 15

symphony (sĭm′fə-nē) *n.* A long piece written for an orchestra.

© 1988 HMCo

LESSON 15

opera (ŏp′ər-ə) *n.* A dramatic play in which most of the words are sung.

© 1988 HMCo

LESSON 14

tarry (tăr′ē) *v.* To delay or be late in coming or going; linger.

© 1988 HMCo

LESSON 14

detain (dĭ-tān′) *v.* To delay by holding back; keep from proceeding.

© 1988 HMCo

LESSON 13

retaliate (rĭ-tăl′ē-āt′) *v.* To return like for like.

© 1988 HMCo

LESSON 13

condone (kən-dōn′) *v.* To forgive, overlook, or disregard without blame.

© 1988 HMCo

LESSON 15

tenor (tĕn′ər) *n.* The highest natural adult male voice.

© 1988 HMCo

LESSON 15

resonant (rĕz′ə-nənt) *adj.* Having a rich, full, pleasing sound.

© 1988 HMCo

LESSON 14

undermine (ŭn′dər-mīn′) *v.* To weaken bit by bit; drain.

© 1988 HMCo

LESSON 14

hinder (hĭn′dər) *v.* To get in the way of; hamper.

© 1988 HMCo

LESSON 13

wrath (răth) *n.* Violent, resentful anger; rage.

© 1988 HMCo

LESSON 13

indignant (ĭn-dĭg′nənt) *adj.* Feeling anger about something unjust.

© 1988 HMCo

LESSON 16 dormant	LESSON 16 restless	LESSON 17 conflict	LESSON 17 friction	LESSON 18 emancipate	LESSON 18 manual
LESSON 16 energetic	LESSON 16 sluggish	LESSON 17 consent	LESSON 17 negotiate	LESSON 18 impede	LESSON 18 manuscript
LESSON 16 industrious	LESSON 16 spry	LESSON 17 contrary	LESSON 17 pact	LESSON 18 manacle	LESSON 18 pedestal
LESSON 16 loiter	LESSON 16 strenuous	LESSON 17 cooperative	LESSON 17 rapport	LESSON 18 maneuver	LESSON 18 pedestrian
LESSON 16 lull	LESSON 16 vigor	LESSON 17 corroborate	LESSON 17 rift	LESSON 18 manipulate	LESSON 18 pedigree

LESSON 18 **manual** (măn′yo͞o-əl) *adj.* Operated or done by hand. © 1988 HMCo	LESSON 18 **emancipate** (ĭ-măn′sə-pāt′) *v.* To set free; liberate. © 1988 HMCo	LESSON 17 **friction** (frĭk′shən) *n.* A disagreement or clash. © 1988 HMCo	LESSON 17 **conflict** (kŏn′flĭkt′) *n.* A clash of opposing ideas or interests. © 1988 HMCo	LESSON 16 **restless** (rĕst′lĭs) *adj.* Unable to relax, rest, or be still. © 1988 HMCo	LESSON 16 **dormant** (dôr′mənt) *adj.* Temporarily inactive. © 1988 HMCo
LESSON 18 **manuscript** (măn′yə-skrĭpt′) *n.* A handwritten or type-written document. © 1988 HMCo	LESSON 18 **impede** (ĭm-pēd′) *v.* To slow down the progress of; block. © 1988 HMCo	LESSON 17 **negotiate** (nĭ-gō′shē-āt′) *v.* To discuss in order to reach agreement. © 1988 HMCo	LESSON 17 **consent** (kən-sĕnt′) *n.* Agreement; accep-tance; permission given. © 1988 HMCo	LESSON 16 **sluggish** (slŭg′ĭsh) *adj.* Showing little movement or activity. © 1988 HMCo	LESSON 16 **energetic** (ĕn′ər-jĕt′ĭk) *adj.* Full of energy; peppy; lively. © 1988 HMCo
LESSON 18 **pedestal** (pĕd′ĭ-stəl) *n.* A support or base for a column or statue. © 1988 HMCo	LESSON 18 **manacle** (măn′ə-kəl) *n.* A device for lock-ing or shackling the hands. © 1988 HMCo	LESSON 17 **pact** (păkt) *n.* A for-mal agreement; treaty. © 1988 HMCo	LESSON 17 **contrary** (kŏn′trĕr′ē) *adj.* Opposite in direction or purpose. © 1988 HMCo	LESSON 16 **spry** (sprī) *adj.* Active; nimble; lively; brisk. © 1988 HMCo	LESSON 16 **industrious** (ĭn-dŭs′trē-əs) *adj.* Hard-working. © 1988 HMCo
LESSON 18 **pedestrian** (pə-dĕs′trē-ən) *n.* A person traveling on foot. © 1988 HMCo	LESSON 18 **maneuver** (mə-no͞o′vər) *n.* A skillful action, move, or plan. © 1988 HMCo	LESSON 17 **rapport** (ră-pôr′) *n.* A relationship of shared trust and understanding. © 1988 HMCo	LESSON 17 **cooperative** (kō-ŏp′ər-ə-tĭv) *adj.* Working willingly with others. © 1988 HMCo	LESSON 16 **strenuous** (strĕn′yo͞o-əs) *adj.* Requiring great effort or energy. © 1988 HMCo	LESSON 16 **loiter** (loi′tər) *v.* To stand idly about; linger. © 1988 HMCo
LESSON 18 **pedigree** (pĕd′ĭ-grē′) *n.* A list of ances-tors; ancestry. © 1988 HMCo	LESSON 18 **manipulate** (mə-nĭp′yə-lāt′) *v.* To arrange or operate with the hands. © 1988 HMCo	LESSON 17 **rift** (rĭft) *n.* A break in friendly relations; split. © 1988 HMCo	LESSON 17 **corroborate** (kə-rŏb′ə-rāt′) *v.* To support by new facts. © 1988 HMCo	LESSON 16 **vigor** (vĭg′ər) *n.* Physical energy or strength. © 1988 HMCo	LESSON 16 **lull** (lŭl) *n.* A tem-porary lessening of activity or noise. © 1988 HMCo

LESSON 19	accumulate
LESSON 19	meager
LESSON 20	absurd
LESSON 20	habitual
LESSON 21	Congress
LESSON 21	judicial
LESSON 19	adequate
LESSON 19	partial
LESSON 20	authentic
LESSON 20	norm
LESSON 21	democratic
LESSON 21	legislation
LESSON 19	ample
LESSON 19	sparse
LESSON 20	bizarre
LESSON 20	novel
LESSON 21	economy
LESSON 21	monarchy
LESSON 19	colossal
LESSON 19	surpass
LESSON 20	exception
LESSON 20	superlative
LESSON 21	endorse
LESSON 21	municipal
LESSON 19	extensive
LESSON 19	trifle
LESSON 20	exotic
LESSON 20	universal
LESSON 21	forum
LESSON 21	veto

LESSON 21 **judicial** (jo͞o-dĭsh′əl) *adj.* Related to courts or judges. © 1988 HMCo	LESSON 21 **Congress** (kŏng′grĭs) *n.* The lawmaking body of the United States. © 1988 HMCo	LESSON 20 **habitual** (hə-bĭch′o͞o-əl) *adj.* Done by habit. © 1988 HMCo	LESSON 20 **absurd** (əb-sûrd′) *adj.* Against common sense or reason. © 1988 HMCo	LESSON 19 **meager** (mē′gər) *adj.* Lacking in quantity or quality; scanty. © 1988 HMCo	LESSON 19 **accumulate** (ə-kyo͞om′yə-lāt′) *v.* To pile up; collect. © 1988 HMCo
LESSON 21 **legislation** (lĕj′ĭ-slā′shən) *n.* The process of enacting laws. © 1988 HMCo	LESSON 21 **democratic** (dĕm′ə-krăt′ĭk) *adj.* Run by the people. © 1988 HMCo	LESSON 20 **norm** (nôrm) *n.* A typical pattern or standard for a specific group. © 1988 HMCo	LESSON 20 **authentic** (ô-thĕn′tĭk) *adj.* Genuine; not counterfeit or copied. © 1988 HMCo	LESSON 19 **partial** (pär′shəl) *adj.* Not total; incomplete. © 1988 HMCo	LESSON 19 **adequate** (ăd′ĭ-kwĭt) *adj.* Able to satisfy a requirement. © 1988 HMCo
LESSON 21 **monarchy** (mŏn′ər-kē) *n.* Government by a king or queen. © 1988 HMCo	LESSON 21 **economy** (ĭ-kŏn′ə-mē) *n.* The management of money or other resources. © 1988 HMCo	LESSON 20 **novel** (nŏv′əl) *adj.* Strikingly new, unusual, or different. © 1988 HMCo	LESSON 20 **bizarre** (bĭ-zär′) *adj.* Very unusual in manner, style, or appearance. © 1988 HMCo	LESSON 19 **sparse** (spärs) *adj.* Growing or settled far apart. © 1988 HMCo	LESSON 19 **ample** (ăm′pəl) *adj.* More than enough; plenty. © 1988 HMCo
LESSON 21 **municipal** (myo͞o-nĭs′ə-pəl) *adj.* Related to running a town or city. © 1988 HMCo	LESSON 21 **endorse** (ĕn-dôrs′) *v.* To approve; support. © 1988 HMCo	LESSON 20 **superlative** (so͞o-pûr′lə-tĭv) *adj.* Superior to all others; best. © 1988 HMCo	LESSON 20 **exception** (ĭk-sĕp′shən) *n.* Something that differs from the rule. © 1988 HMCo	LESSON 19 **surpass** (sər-păs′) *v.* To be better, greater, or stronger than. © 1988 HMCo	LESSON 19 **colossal** (kə-lŏs′əl) *adj.* Gigantic; enormous in size. © 1988 HMCo
LESSON 21 **veto** (vē′tō) *v.* To refuse to approve; prevent officially. © 1988 HMCo	LESSON 21 **forum** (fôr′əm) *n.* A place for public discussions. © 1988 HMCo	LESSON 20 **universal** (yo͞o′nə-vûr′səl) *adj.* Common to all persons, places, things. © 1988 HMCo	LESSON 20 **exotic** (ĭg-zŏt′ĭk) *adj.* Unusual because of being from another place. © 1988 HMCo	LESSON 19 **trifle** (trī′fəl) *n.* A small amount; bit. © 1988 HMCo	LESSON 19 **extensive** (ĭk-stĕn′sĭv) *adj.* Large or broad in area or range. © 1988 HMCo

LESSON 22 compress	LESSON 22 liberate	LESSON 23 accessory	LESSON 23 excess	LESSON 24 circumstance	LESSON 24 destitute
LESSON 22 concise	LESSON 22 propel	LESSON 23 appropriate	LESSON 23 frivolous	LESSON 24 consistent	LESSON 24 institution
LESSON 22 eject	LESSON 22 regulate	LESSON 23 auxiliary	LESSON 23 imperative	LESSON 24 constitution	LESSON 24 stately
LESSON 22 exclusion	LESSON 22 restrain	LESSON 23 entail	LESSON 23 pertinent	LESSON 24 destination	LESSON 24 stationary
LESSON 22 expulsion	LESSON 22 restriction	LESSON 23 essence	LESSON 23 significant	LESSON 24 destiny	LESSON 24 statistic

LESSON 24

destitute (dĕs′tĭ-to͞ot′) *adj.* Very poor; penniless.

© 1988 HMCo

LESSON 24

circumstance (sûr′kəm-stăns′) *n.* A condition affecting something.

© 1988 HMCo

LESSON 23

excess (ĭk-sĕs′) *n.* Something that is more than the normal amount.

© 1988 HMCo

LESSON 23

accessory (ăk-sĕs′ə-rē) *n.* An extra that goes with something.

© 1988 HMCo

LESSON 22

liberate (lĭb′ə-rāt′) *v.* To set free; release.

© 1988 HMCo

LESSON 22

compress (kəm-prĕs′) *v.* To force into a smaller space by pressing.

© 1988 HMCo

LESSON 24

institution (ĭn′stĭ-to͞o′shən) *n.* An established organization.

© 1988 HMCo

LESSON 24

consistent (kən-sĭs′tənt) *adj.* In agreement; not contradictory.

© 1988 HMCo

LESSON 23

frivolous (frĭv′ə-ləs) *adj.* Not significant or worth attention.

© 1988 HMCo

LESSON 23

appropriate (ə-prō′prē-ĭt) *adj.* Suitable for a particular situation.

© 1988 HMCo

LESSON 22

propel (prə-pĕl′) *v.* To cause to move or keep in motion.

© 1988 HMCo

LESSON 22

concise (kən-sīs′) *adj.* Clearly stated in a few words; brief.

© 1988 HMCo

LESSON 24

stately (stāt′lē) *adj.* Dignified; impressive; majestic.

© 1988 HMCo

LESSON 24

constitution (kŏn′stĭ-to͞o′shən) *n.* The basic laws of a nation.

© 1988 HMCo

LESSON 23

imperative (ĭm-pĕr′ə-tĭv) *adj.* Absolutely required; necessary.

© 1988 HMCo

LESSON 23

auxiliary (ŏg-zĭl′yə-rē) *adj.* Giving assistance or support.

© 1988 HMCo

LESSON 22

regulate (rĕg′yə-lāt′) *v.* To direct or control according to rules.

© 1988 HMCo

LESSON 22

eject (ĭ-jĕkt′) *v.* To throw out by force.

© 1988 HMCo

LESSON 24

stationary (stā′shə-nĕr′ē) *adj.* Not moving; fixed; at rest.

© 1988 HMCo

LESSON 24

destination (dĕs′tə-nā′shən) *n.* A place or point set out for.

© 1988 HMCo

LESSON 23

pertinent (pûr′tn-ənt) *adj.* Related in some specific way; relevant.

© 1988 HMCo

LESSON 23

entail (ĕn-tāl′) *v.* To have as a necessary part.

© 1988 HMCo

LESSON 22

restrain (rĭ-strān′) *v.* To check; control by holding back.

© 1988 HMCo

LESSON 22

exclusion (ĭk-skl o͞o′zhən) *n.* The act of keeping or shutting out.

© 1988 HMCo

LESSON 24

statistic (stə-tĭs′tĭk) *n.* A numerical item; datum.

© 1988 HMCo

LESSON 24

destiny (dĕs′tə-nē) *n.* Fate; fortune.

© 1988 HMCo

LESSON 23

significant (sĭg-nĭf′ĭ-kənt) *adj.* Having meaning; meaningful.

© 1988 HMCo

LESSON 23

essence (ĕs′əns) *n.* Basic nature; identifying quality.

© 1988 HMCo

LESSON 22

restriction (rĭ-strĭk′shən) *n.* The act or state of limiting.

© 1988 HMCo

LESSON 22

expulsion (ĭk-spŭl′shən) *n.* The act of forcing or driving out.

© 1988 HMCo

LESSON 25	LESSON 25	LESSON 26	LESSON 26	LESSON 27	LESSON 27
battalion	garrison	approximate	emphasize	anthropology	physiology
LESSON 25	LESSON 25	LESSON 26	LESSON 26	LESSON 27	LESSON 27
camouflage	infiltrate	assumption	essential	archaeology	psychology
LESSON 25	LESSON 25	LESSON 26	LESSON 26	LESSON 27	LESSON 27
casualty	parry	attentive	illusion	biology	sociology
LESSON 25	LESSON 25	LESSON 26	LESSON 26	LESSON 27	LESSON 27
corps	provoke	certify	probable	geology	technology
LESSON 25	LESSON 25	LESSON 26	LESSON 26	LESSON 27	LESSON 27
encampment	siege	distinguish	vague	mythology	theology

LESSON 27 **physiology** (fĭz′ē-ŏl′ə-jē) *n.* The study of life processes. © 1988 HMCo	LESSON 27 **anthropology** (ăn′thrə-pŏl′ə-jē) *n.* The study of human beings. © 1988 HMCo	LESSON 26 **emphasize** (ĕm′fə-sīz′) *v.* To state boldly or forcefully; stress. © 1988 HMCo	LESSON 26 **approximate** (ə-prŏk′sə-mĭt) *adj.* Close to in amount or number. © 1988 HMCo	LESSON 25 **garrison** (găr′ĭ-sən) *n.* A military post or the soldiers in that post. © 1988 HMCo	LESSON 25 **battalion** (bə-tăl′yən) *n.* A large unit of soldiers. © 1988 HMCo
LESSON 27 **psychology** (sī-kŏl′ə-jē) *n.* Study of the mind and resulting behavior. © 1988 HMCo	LESSON 27 **archaeology** (är′kē-ŏl′ə-jē) *n.* Study of remains of past civilizations. © 1988 HMCo	LESSON 26 **essential** (ĭ-sĕn′shəl) *adj.* Basic; necessary. © 1988 HMCo	LESSON 26 **assumption** (ə-sŭmp′shən) *n.* An idea or fact that is taken for granted. © 1988 HMCo	LESSON 25 **infiltrate** (ĭn-fĭl′trāt′) *v.* To enter gradually or secretly. © 1988 HMCo	LESSON 25 **camouflage** (kăm′ə-fläzh′) *n.* The use of coloring and patterns to hide. © 1988 HMCo
LESSON 27 **sociology** (sō′sē-ŏl′ə-jē) *n.* The study of human social behavior. © 1988 HMCo	LESSON 27 **biology** (bī-ŏl′ə-jē) *n.* The study of plant and animal life. © 1988 HMCo	LESSON 26 **illusion** (ĭ-lo͞o′zhən) *n.* A misleading or mistaken impression or idea. © 1988 HMCo	LESSON 26 **attentive** (ə-tĕn′tĭv) *adj.* Paying attention; listening; observant. © 1988 HMCo	LESSON 25 **parry** (păr′ē) *v.* To turn aside, as in self-defense. © 1988 HMCo	LESSON 25 **casualty** (kăzh′o͞o-əl-tē) *n.* Someone injured, killed, or captured. © 1988 HMCo
LESSON 27 **technology** (tĕk-nŏl′ə-jē) *n.* The application of scientific knowledge. © 1988 HMCo	LESSON 27 **geology** (jē-ŏl′ə-jē) *n.* Study of history and structure of the earth. © 1988 HMCo	LESSON 26 **probable** (prŏb′ə-bəl) *adj.* Likely to happen or be true. © 1988 HMCo	LESSON 26 **certify** (sûr′tə-fī′) *v.* To declare to be true or genuine. © 1988 HMCo	LESSON 25 **provoke** (prə-vōk′) *v.* To cause an action or an emotion by stirring up. © 1988 HMCo	LESSON 25 **corps** (kôr) *n.* A branch of the armed forces with a certain job. © 1988 HMCo
LESSON 27 **theology** (thē-ŏl′ə-jē) *n.* The study of God and religious truths. © 1988 HMCo	LESSON 27 **mythology** (mĭ-thŏl′ə-jē) *n.* The study of old-time stories. © 1988 HMCo	LESSON 26 **vague** (vāg) *adj.* Not clearly expressed or thought out; unclear. © 1988 HMCo	LESSON 26 **distinguish** (dĭ-stĭng′gwĭsh) *v.* To see or hear clearly. © 1988 HMCo	LESSON 25 **siege** (sēj) *n.* The act of trying to capture a place by surrounding it. © 1988 HMCo	LESSON 25 **encampment** (ĕn-kămp′mənt) *n.* A camp or camping place. © 1988 HMCo

LESSON 28 ancestor	LESSON 28 hereditary	LESSON 29 admit	LESSON 29 permissible	LESSON 30 autobiography	LESSON 30 prose
LESSON 28 clan	LESSON 28 kin	LESSON 29 compromise	LESSON 29 premise	LESSON 30 biography	LESSON 30 proverb
LESSON 28 compatible	LESSON 28 matrimony	LESSON 29 emit	LESSON 29 remit	LESSON 30 folklore	LESSON 30 stanza
LESSON 28 domestic	LESSON 28 spouse	LESSON 29 mission	LESSON 29 submit	LESSON 30 metaphor	LESSON 30 symbol
LESSON 28 filial	LESSON 28 tradition	LESSON 29 omit	LESSON 29 transmit	LESSON 30 narrate	LESSON 30 theme

LESSON 30

prose (prōz) *n.* Speech or writing that is not poetry.

© 1988 HMCo

LESSON 30

autobiography (ô′tō-bī-ŏg′rə-fē) *n.* A person's story of his or her own life.

© 1988 HMCo

LESSON 29

permissible (pər-mĭs′ə-bəl) *adj.* Allowable; permitted.

© 1988 HMCo

LESSON 29

admit (ăd-mĭt′) *v.* To allow to enter; let in.

© 1988 HMCo

LESSON 28

hereditary (hə-rĕd′ĭ-tĕr′ē) *adj.* Passed down biologically.

© 1988 HMCo

LESSON 28

ancestor (ăn′sĕs′tər) *n.* A person from whom someone is descended.

© 1988 HMCo

LESSON 30

proverb (prŏv′ûrb′) *n.* A short, common saying that expresses a truth.

© 1988 HMCo

LESSON 30

biography (bī-ŏg′rə-fē) *n.* A person's life story written by another.

© 1988 HMCo

LESSON 29

premise (prĕm′ĭs) *n.* A statement that is the basis of a conclusion.

© 1988 HMCo

LESSON 29

compromise (kŏm′prə-mīz′) *v.* To settle differences by giving in.

© 1988 HMCo

LESSON 28

kin (kĭn) *n.* One's blood relatives.

© 1988 HMCo

LESSON 28

clan (klăn) *n.* A tribal group descended from the same person.

© 1988 HMCo

LESSON 30

stanza (stăn′zə) *n.* Two or more lines in a poem functioning as a unit.

© 1988 HMCo

LESSON 30

folklore (fōk′lôr′) *n.* Traditional customs and legends of a people.

© 1988 HMCo

LESSON 29

remit (rĭ-mĭt) *v.* To send money.

© 1988 HMCo

LESSON 29

emit (ĭ-mĭt′) *v.* To give off or send out.

© 1988 HMCo

LESSON 28

matrimony (măt′rə-mō′nē) *n.* The state of being married; marriage.

© 1988 HMCo

LESSON 28

compatible (kəm-păt′ə-bəl) *adj.* Getting along well together.

© 1988 HMCo

LESSON 30

symbol (sĭm′bəl) *n.* An object that stands for something greater.

© 1988 HMCo

LESSON 30

metaphor (mĕt′ə-fôr) *n.* A comparison between two dissimilar things.

© 1988 HMCo

LESSON 29

submit (səb-mĭt′) *v.* To offer for consideration or review.

© 1988 HMCo

LESSON 29

mission (mĭsh′ən) *n.* Special duty or task that a person is sent to do.

© 1988 HMCo

LESSON 28

spouse (spous) *n.* A marriage partner; a wife or husband.

© 1988 HMCo

LESSON 28

domestic (də-mĕs′tĭk) *adj.* Relating to the family or household.

© 1988 HMCo

LESSON 30

theme (thēm) *n.* The main thought of a literary work or speech.

© 1988 HMCo

LESSON 30

narrate (năr′āt′) *v.* To tell a story orally or in writing.

© 1988 HMCo

LESSON 29

transmit (trănz-mĭt′) *v.* To send from one person or place to another.

© 1988 HMCo

LESSON 29

omit (ō-mĭt′) *v.* To remove; not include.

© 1988 HMCo

LESSON 28

tradition (trə-dĭsh′ən) *n.* The passing down of customs and beliefs.

© 1988 HMCo

LESSON 28

filial (fĭl′ē-əl) *adj.* Appropriate to or describing a son or daughter.

© 1988 HMCo